Industrial Britain

THE STEEL INDUSTRY IN POST WAR BRITAIN

David W. Heal

David & Charles
Newton Abbot   London
North Pomfret (VT)   Vancouver

ISBN 0 7153 6565 7

Library of Congress Catalog Card Number 74–80501

© David W. Heal 1974

For Pamela

Set in 11 on 13 point Times
and printed in Great Britain
by Clarke Doble & Brendon Limited Plymouth
for David & Charles (Holdings) Limited
South Devon House Newton Abbot Devon

Published in the United States of America
by David & Charles Inc North Pomfret
Vermont 05053 USA

Published in Canada by Douglas David &
Charles Limited 3645 McKechnie Drive
West Vancouver BC

Contents

List of Illustrations

Plates

Reproduced by courtesy of the British Steel Corporation

Figures in Text

Preface

THE INDUSTRIAL GEOGRAPHER'S primary interest is in the understanding of locational patterns of industrial activity. Yet I must confess that although I work as a geographer, an interest in the locational pattern of the steel industry became my primary interest only after several years during which I had been more interested in its financial and technical performance. It is probable that this shift in my interests from technology to finance to location reflects the order of priorities of concern in the industry itself. That is to say, the industry is consciously more involved with, and is therefore better equipped to solve, financial and technical problems than it is to solve locational problems. Certainly, the post-war years witnessed dramatic changes in the industry's technology, but until the early 1970s the rate of locational change seemed incommensurate with the rate of technological change. It therefore seemed worthwhile to enquire whether this placing of new processes in old locations had resulted from deliberate choice, or whether relocation was never considered desirable, or whether a desire to relocate had been thwarted by outside pressures.

In essaying an answer to these questions I attempted to view the situation as it might have appeared from within the industry rather than from a remote outside pinnacle. My view could not be the same as the industry's because I have had the undoubted benefit of hindsight, and the result, I feel, might be described as a 'spatial biography' of the industry. With an emphasis upon spatial factors the details of steel production have been, perforce, largely ignored. But these manufacturing processes demand teamwork—which I was privileged to experience for a month as a supernumerary member of an open-hearth team in Rotherham—and produce a sense of community, the force of which explains why many of the decisions of the period were taken as they were. The selectivity of this study determined, among other things, the choice of photographs, all of which illustrate specific points in the text.

Dramatic process-shots which recall the atmosphere of the industry had to be excluded. My working hypothesis is that if new technologies require new skills and new forms of organisation they also require new locational arrangements for their complete utilisation. The alternative is to say that location is irrelevant to industrial efficiency, but if that is true it makes nonsense of a large part of social and industrial planning in post-war Britain.

Aberaeron, Cardiganshire   D.W.H.

1

Industry and Location

THE BRITISH STEEL INDUSTRY in 1945, seen from the vantage point of the 1970s, was dominated by two principal features: a low level of output and a fragmented pattern of control and production. The combined output of 11·8 million tons of ingots and castings was shared by no fewer than 140 companies. Many of these were engineering concerns, but there were about 50 companies that included the production of steel among their foremost interests. The majority of these were small-scale producers of special steels, but in modern terms even the larger producers of common steels operated small concerns, and no single company had an ascendancy over the industry at large. In figurative terms, the 'profile' of the industry resembled a low, broad-based pyramid.

The dimensions of that pyramid are given more precise expression in Table 1, which lists those companies whose annual capacity exceeded 0·1 million ingot tons: together these represented 95 per cent of the volume of the pyramid—11·26 million tons. The low median level of output of these twenty-three companies, 0·22 million tons, gives added emphasis to the small scale of operations which were traditional to the industry. Five companies each produced more than one million tons, but the largest company, The United Steel Companies Limited, controlled only 13 per cent of the national output.

Behind this company structure, which was the operative framework within which investment decisions were made, were the works at which the steel was produced. These served, as it were, to tie the industry's organisational structure to the ground. The works were, in turn, the constituent elements of a second pyramid, similar to the first, but with an even broader base and with more gently sloping sides (see Table 2 p 24). Although there were at least 180 ingot-producing works, the bulk

Table 1
ESTIMATED OUTPUT OF THE MAJOR BRITISH STEEL COMPANIES, 1945

Company	Estimated output (million ingot tons)
MULTI-WORKS COMPANIES	
1 Colvilles Ltd	1·30
2 Dorman, Long & Co Ltd	1·20
3 English Steel Corporation Ltd	0·40
4 Guest Keen & Baldwins Iron & Steel Co*	1·20
5 John Summers & Sons Ltd	0·60
6 Richard Thomas & Baldwins Ltd	1·30
7 South Durham Steel & Iron Co Ltd	0·50
8 Stewarts & Lloyds Ltd	0·78
9 The United Steel Cos Ltd	1·55
SINGLE-WORKS COMPANIES	
10 Bairds & Scottish Co Ltd	0·10
11 Wm Beardmore & Co Ltd	0·10
12 Briton Ferry Steel Co Ltd	0·20
13 Bynea Steelworks Ltd	0·12
14 Consett Iron Co Ltd	0·38
15 T. Firth & J. Brown Ltd	0·13
16 Hadfields Ltd	0·12
17 Lancashire Steel Corp Ltd	0·33
18 Llanelly Steel Co (1907) Ltd	0·13
19 Park Gate Iron & Steel Co Ltd	0·22
20 Partridge Jones & Paton Ltd	0·13
21 Patent Shaft & Axletree Co Ltd	0·12
22 Round Oak Steelworks Ltd	0·15
23 Skinningrove Iron Co Ltd	0·20

Source: Industry and Company records
* Includes Port Talbot

of this second pyramid was composed of the fifty-two works located in Fig 1. These were the works operated by the companies in Table 1. The largest works, producing 5·5 per cent of the national total, was United Steel's Appleby-Frodingham works at Scunthorpe, which had an annual capacity of 0·70 million ingot tons. There were eight other works with a capacity of more than 0·5 million ingot tons, and a further twelve with a capacity exceeding 0·25 million tons. The median capacity level was 0·18 million ingot tons, but ten of these fifty-two works produced less than 0·1 million tons. The production base of the industry, therefore, was composed of numerous small units, many of which failed to allow efficient scales of production even for the technologies available at the time.

By 1965, the year of record output under private ownership, total production had increased by 129 per cent to 27·1 million ingot tons, but the fragmented pattern of ownership and production persisted with only minor modifications. The twenty-three companies listed in Table 1

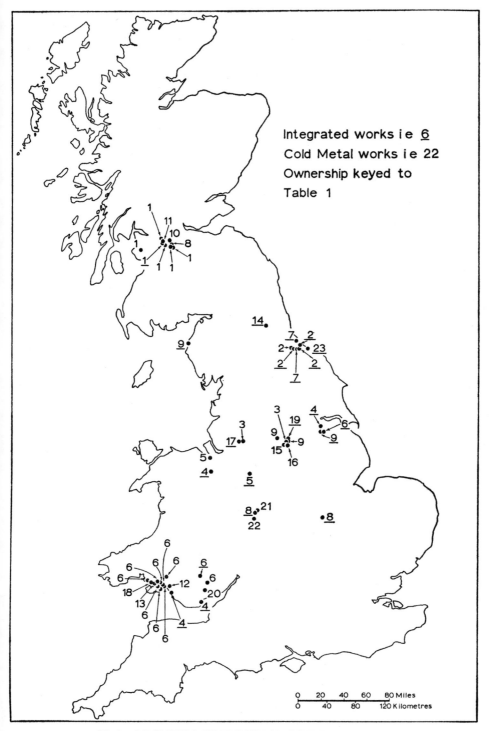

Integrated works i e <u>6</u>
Cold Metal works i e 22
Ownership keyed to
Table 1

Fig 1. LOCATION OF PRINCIPAL STEELWORKS, 1945

had been reduced to nineteen, but their median level of production had been multiplied five times to 1·0 million tons. The output of the largest company had been doubled to reach 3·3 million tons. In this twenty-year period thirteen of the fifty-two works in Fig 1 had been closed and two new works had been built, leaving forty-one works in operation. Their median level of output was more than double the 1945 level, but the output of the largest works—Port Talbot—was more than four times greater than at Appleby-Frodingham in 1945. At both company and works levels the pyramidal profile observed in 1945 persisted: the pyramids were now taller, but no single company or works was able to dominate the industry.

In July 1967 those companies whose output had exceeded 0·475 million ingot tons in the year ending June 1964 were nationalised, and their assets were vested in the British Steel Corporation. Although there were still about 140 companies making steel in Britain, the Corporation, whose output in 1970 (the record year to date) equalled 90 per cent of the total 27·8 million tons, was clearly in a dominant position: the organisational pyramid no longer existed. The precise effects of this legislation on the pyramid composed of the steelworks cannot yet be known, but they are likely to be equally dramatic. It is probable that by 1980 a single works on Tees-side will produce more steel than the entire industry produced in 1945, and that that works will provide approximately 30 per cent of the new total of 38 million tons. Elsewhere it is anticipated that there will be two works with a capacity of 6·0 million tons, two of 3·0 million tons, and one of 2·0 million tons. The remainder will all produce less than 1·0 million tons, and the majority will produce less than half that amount. Although the exact number of works that will be in operation in 1980 cannot be known it is certain that the old production pyramid will also have been replaced. In figurative terms the emerging 'profile' of the industry has a closer resemblance to the podium-with-tower of twentieth century architecture than to the more earth-bound edifices of earlier ages.

The profiles described above are the ultimate expression of the industry for any given time. Changes in the profile between one time and another are factual, impartial summaries of the changes which have taken place within the industry—changes in markets, raw materials, technology, employment and capital. To these should be added changes in location, the examination of which is the principal concern of this study. Each of these internal sources of change which mould the profile of the industry is linked to all the others, and each is essential to the others—an isolated blast furnace without raw materials, workers and markets is conceivable only as an historical relic or as a philosophical conundrum—and the choice of location as the focus of inquiry is therefore partial and subjective. But the act of choosing one sector for special emphasis creates its own perspective, and the relevance of technological developments, for example, is therefore determined by the way in which those developments impinge upon the locational issue. Location is sometimes a cause and sometimes an effect, and therefore the locational pattern which is sometimes seen as a constraint upon the activities of the industry is at other times seen to be constrained by the industry's technological or capital structure. In this study the first question is not how was the steel produced but *where* was it produced? The second, but more intriguing question is what is the exact relationship between industry and location? At this point the question must be regarded as an open one and the provision of even tentative answers is inappropriate.

Location

Location is composed of two components: situation and site. The elements of *situation* include the traditional areas of concern of the locational theorist, namely the relative position and availability of raw materials, labour, capital and markets. To these should be added company affiliation, and, in the case of oligopolistic industries, industry associations and federations. These elements of situation can be viewed as existing in a horizontal plane defined by the flow of materials, energy and information. The elements of *site* are the size, shape and slope of the operational area required and will vary from industry to industry. These site elements can be viewed as existing in a vertical plane and are related to fixed investment. In the same way as it is possible to indicate an optimum situation for an industry according to any chosen set of criteria—least cost, maximum profit, maximum employment, minimum environmental disturbance, etc—so too is it possible to describe an optimum site. In neither case is it implied that an industry cannot operate away from this optimum, but when doing so its aims will be compromised. Both aspects of location are relevant to the aims of an industrial enterprise, but once a set of locations has been established the conditions within those locations—the site conditions—are under closer managerial control than are the conditions in the situation at large. There is, in consequence, a tendency to ignore or to tolerate the conditions in the situation and to focus all improvement policies upon the sites.

Locational Change

The choice of a given location presupposes that that location can satisfy, either in whole or in part, the industry's requirements expressed in terms of both situation and site. Any subsequent developments will serve to enhance or to erode either or both elements of the location, but there is no *a priori* reason for supposing that such developments will affect these elements equally. It is possible, for example, that trading factors will enhance the value of a particular situation at the same time as technological factors are rendering the sites within that situation obsolete. Presumably if both situation and site become obsolete the location will be abandoned. Conversely, if both these elements are enhanced the industry will develop further at that location. In between these extremes there exists the difficult position when reference to one set of factors suggests development at the same time as reference to the other set suggests abandoning the location.

There exist, therefore, two sources of demand for locational change, and this variety of source helps to explain the diverse range of such changes which appear. Locational change can take three basic forms. The first form, *absolute change*, is the most simple, but is the least likely to occur. Its negative aspect is expressed in the closing of an existing works, resulting from a variable combination of obsolescence of situation and site. The positive aspect of absolute locational change, the creation of a new works, presupposes favourable, but not necessarily perfect, situational and site factors at that location.

The second form of locational change is *comparative change*, and involves different rates of growth or decline across the range of locations, without the complete cessation of activities at any one location, or the creation of new centres of production. It is a less extreme form of change and is therefore more common than absolute change, and presupposes that the minimum situation and site requirements are still being met. This form of change also has its negative and positive aspects, which are measured by comparing one location with another, or by measuring against the production trend of the industry as a whole. In a growth industry it is possible for output to increase at all locations, but an above-average rate of growth at a few locations indicates that the industry is becoming more geographically concentrated. Such changes indicate fresh evaluation of the existing set of situations and sites. The locations of above-average growth are the clearest examples of positive comparative change. Locations of slow growth or of decline display

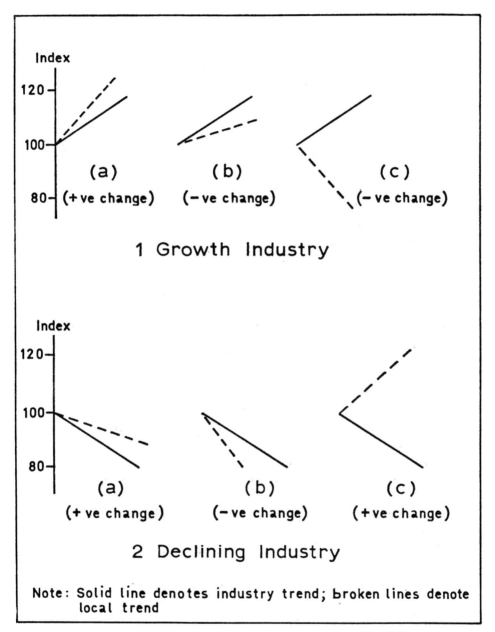

Fig 2. FORMS OF COMPARATIVE LOCATIONAL CHANGE

negative comparative change. Comparative change will also be displayed in declining industries. Hypothetical examples of positive and negative comparative change are given in Fig 2.

The third form of locational change is *relative change*, and is concerned more with the relationship of a particular works with its sources of raw materials, or its market, or its competitors, than with its level of output or the levels of output of its competitors. In view of the large number of items involved, such changes are the most common of all, but are mainly the result of decisions taken outside the industry concerned. In Fig 3 three hypothetical examples of relative change are presented diagrammatically. This type of locational change emphasises more clearly than the others that the significance of any location is measured only by its relationships with the other objects in the same economic system.

The occupation of any given location is as much the result of human decisions and initiatives as is the choice of a given technology. These decisions result from human appraisal of the existing set of conditions, and are influenced by the aspirations and ambitions of the people involved. Although the current pattern is the result of decisions taken in the past, any positive changes, locational or technological, which occur will be the result of conscious assessments of the present and the future. Negative change has an additional source of origin, namely accident. Most decisions are routine and automatic, and follow upon an earlier decision to enter upon a particular enterprise. Furnaces must be kept hot, wages must be paid, and the chosen locations must be serviced, and routines are therefore established to serve those needs. Even in periods of rapid change the volume of routine decisions will be dominant.

In all manufacturing processes, however, there is a time allotted for repair and maintenance, and such times provide opportunities to modify the current procedures. Such modifications are installed consciously and deliberately, and the cumulative effect over a prolonged period can be the construction of an extensively altered plant. In technology, therefore, there is present an in-built process of modernisation. The results of this modernising process are either an improved product or higher levels of output. To the extent that modernisation of plant is not uniformly spread across a particular industry it will result in comparative locational change. An important consequence of this process is that over a period of time comparative locational change should be the expectation rather than the exception.

The history of industrial technology shows that in all processes there

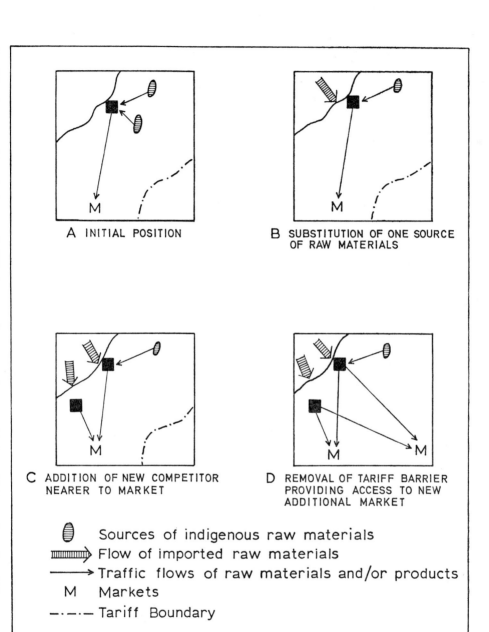

A INITIAL POSITION

B SUBSTITUTION OF ONE SOURCE OF RAW MATERIALS

C ADDITION OF NEW COMPETITOR NEARER TO MARKET

D REMOVAL OF TARIFF BARRIER PROVIDING ACCESS TO NEW ADDITIONAL MARKET

Sources of indigenous raw materials
Flow of imported raw materials
Traffic flows of raw materials and/or products
M Markets
—.—.— Tariff Boundary

Fig 3. THREE EXAMPLES OF RELATIVE LOCATIONAL CHANGE

is a limit to what can be achieved by modernisation and piecemeal adaptation. When this limit is reached further progress can be made only by adopting a new process. During these critical periods there is frequently uncertainty as to which of the available alternative processes has the greatest long-term potential. The choice of the best process could prove to be critical, and is certainly subject to an element of chance. The same considerations apply, *a fortiori*, to the choice of a new location, for the history of location shows a higher degree of conservatism than does the history of technology. Furthermore, it is unusual for all sectors in a multi-process industry to reach this critical phase simultaneously, so an unwise choice in one process may not vitiate the entire enterprise. In the choosing of location, however, although the cost of the site itself may not loom large in the total budget, the construction costs of the entire complex are frequently sufficient to ensure that relocation is no longer a practical alternative. It should, however, again be emphasised that locational costs are, in their essence, comparative, and although a best location, or a set of best locations can, in theory, be found, operationally all that is required is the best competitive location. Modern efficient plant should not be placed in obsolete, inefficient locations. Conversely, obsolete plant in the best locations will not produce the highest possible return.

In this chapter parallels between technology and location have been deliberately emphasised. Locational costs are only one of the sets of costs which enter into the total cost figure. Similarly, locational decisions are only one set of decisions which have to be taken by management. In all organisations the first responsibility is to maintain the health of the present concern, but gradual cumulative changes lead to better furnaces, perhaps, and to comparative locational change: the two phenomena are closely associated. At infrequent intervals, however, technology and location need to be basically reappraised. Such reappraisals produce new processes, and can produce new locations. In multi-purpose industries, however, a new process in one sector is not in itself likely to demand a new location, so, once again, comparative change may be all that is required: new processes in old locations. Finally, inasmuch as no industry is in control of its environment its relative location can be transformed, favourably or unfavourably, by decisions made outside the industry. The result is that relative locational changes are taking place continuously; comparative locational changes are common; absolute locational changes are rare even in a society such as ours in which change appears to be the positive value and the distinguishing characteristic.

2

A Varied Inheritance

Situation

THE SPATIAL PATTERN of the fifty-two works which composed the bulk of the British steel industry in 1945 showed a clear tendency towards clustering (Fig 1). So marked was the clustering that the mean straight-line distance from one works to its nearest neighbour was as low as seven miles. The modal distance was one mile or less (eighteen out of fifty-two works) and in only seven cases was a works more than ten miles from its nearest neighbour. The most isolated works operated by the major companies was Workington Iron & Steel, which was seventy-two straight-line miles from Consett Iron.[1] The second most isolated works was Corby which was fifty-eight straight-line miles from Patent Shaft. As Corby is among the most central locations in industrial Britain this represents but the first manifestation of the peripheral geographical position adopted by this industry whose position in the economy is so central.

This spatial pattern was the reflection of human responses to the changing location factors that had influenced the iron industry, and then the steel industry over the previous two centuries.[2] But the important questions in 1945 were not with origins, but with the ways in which that pattern could be adapted, modified and extended to meet the requirements of the post-war era. The fulfilment of those requirements depended primarily upon the imagination and creativity of management, but those forces were, and are, subject to many physical and human constraints, the most immediate of which, at any given point in time, is the pattern of ownership. Advantages could be gained at industry and company levels both from the wide scatter of the clusters and from the close proximity of works within the clusters, but full advantage of the short distance between neighbouring works could

21

be taken only if the works were owned by one company. The nearest approaches to this position being realised for complete clusters were in Scotland and the North East Coast. In Scotland six of the nine works were owned by Colvilles whose five Lanarkshire works were on average only six straight-line miles from each other. On the North East Coast, Dorman Long operated four of the five works on the south bank of the river Tees. Within these two clusters there had developed a limited degree of integration of operations between works of common ownership; Dorman Long, in particular, were actively working in that direction.

In contrast to those two companies operating within the limits of one cluster, the interests of United Steel, Stewarts & Lloyds and Richard Thomas & Baldwins were widely dispersed. The average distance between United Steel's three works in Yorkshire and Lincolnshire was twenty-seven straight-line miles and Workington was a further 122 miles from Rotherham. Nevertheless, these four works were more fully integrated the one with the other than were Appleby-Frodingham and Redbourn at Scunthorpe which belonged to different companies. The only direct link between those two Scunthorpe works was a coke oven gas-main, whereas Appleby-Frodingham was the sole supplier of basic pig iron for the cold metal open-hearth furnaces at Steel, Peech & Tozer and Samuel Fox. Similarly, Workington Iron & Steel supplied the Yorkshire works with spiegeleisen and with hematite pig iron. There was a similar flow of materials between the Bilston and Corby works of Stewarts & Lloyds and the Redbourn and Ebbw Vale works of Richard Thomas & Baldwins.

The development of these multi-works companies had been mainly a gradual process. The first to develop its approximately modern form was the United Steel Companies, which had its origin in the nucleus of an association between Steel, Peech & Tozer and Samuel Fox in 1917.[3] These two cold metal steel producers in Rotherham and Stocksbridge acquired the Scunthorpe works of the Frodingham Iron & Steel Company in order to secure a supply of basic pig iron. The Frodingham company itself was already a joint owner of the neighbouring Appleby Iron Company, and, in 1918, when the United Steel Companies was formed, the holding of the Steel Company of Scotland in Appleby Iron was also acquired. United Steel also acquired the Workington Iron & Steel Company and the Rother Vale Collieries to guarantee supplies of hematite pig iron to the Sheffield area works, and coking coal for Appleby-Frodingham.

There was considerable overlap of production between these separate members of the new company, so the merger took on a mixture of horizontal and vertical industrial integration characteristics. In the 1930s, but not before then, a policy of rationalisation of production was carried through resulting in the continued production of plates and heavy sections at Appleby-Frodingham, railway materials and billets and bars at Steel, Peech & Tozer, and light products such as rods and wire at Samuel Fox, which also became the centre of alloy steel production. The manufacture of railway lines and associated materials was concentrated at Workington, which also remained in the hematite and blast furnace ferro-alloys trades. The group of companies emerged from World War II with this policy completed (see Table 2).

The Colvilles group also had its nucleus in cold metal operations in the Dalzell works at Motherwell. The company purchased Clydebridge and the integrated works at Glengarnock in 1916 (the seven blast furnaces were closed in 1930), the James Dunlop Clyde Iron works, located directly across the river from Clydebridge, in 1930, and the works of the Lanarkshire Steel Company adjacent to Dalzell at Motherwell, in 1936. In 1940, the control of the Steel Company of Scotland, which operated works at Hallside and Blochairn, was finalised and formalised. A policy of total rationalisation was implemented, but by 1945 little had been achieved other than the linking of Clydebridge and Clyde Iron by a bridge across the river. This made it possible to operate one of the Clydebridge melting shops on a hot metal basis. Although the Colvilles development had a more compact geographical expression, it lacked the powers of diversity found in the United Steel Companies, not only in terms of location but in product and steel-making technology (see Table 2).

The Dorman Long group, the formation of which was completed in 1929 with the amalgamation of Dorman Long and Bolckow Vaughan, also had a compact geographical expression. By 1945 the Clarence works on the north bank of the Tees had been closed, and the company operated a cold metal plant at Britannia and hot metal plants at Acklam, Cleveland and Redcar. It also owned the undeveloped Lackenby site between Cleveland and Redcar. A policy of rationalisation had concentrated the production of plates at Redcar, of semis and sleepers at Acklam, and of rails, billets, slabs and joists at Cleveland, while both Cleveland and Britannia continued to produce a wide range of sections (see Table 2). Further rationalisation had been impeded by the war, and the three integrated plants still operated individual ore wharves. At the same time, for a company which produced no more than 0·7 million tons of pig iron and 1·2 million ingot tons on adjacent

Table 2

MAJOR STEELWORKS 1945—OUTPUT, TECHNOLOGY AND PRODUCTS

Class size (000 tons)	Works	Technology	Principal products
600–700	Appleby-Frodingham	Integrated	Plates and sections
	SPT	Cold metal	Multiple product
500–600	Corby	Integrated	Tubes
400–500	Cardiff	Integrated	Billets, rails, sections
	Cleveland	Integrated	Sections, rails
	Ebbw Vale	Integrated	Sheets, tinplate
	Dalzell	Cold metal	Plates
	Port Talbot	Integrated	Plates, rails
300–400	Consett	Integrated	Plates and billets
	Shotton	Cold metal	Sheets
	Clydebridge/Clyde Iron	Integrated	Plates
	Irlam	Integrated	Billets, rods
	Redbourn	Integrated	Slabs
	Redcar	Integrated	Plates
	Glengarnock	Cold metal	Rails, sections
	Lysaghts	Integrated	Billets and slabs
200–300	Cargo Fleet	Integrated	Sections, rails
	W. Hartlepool	Integrated	Plates
	Eng. Steel	Cold metal	Forge and castings
	Lanarkshire	Cold metal	Sections
	Shelton	Integrated	Sections
	Park Gate	Integrated	Bars and sections
	Bilston	Integrated	Tube billets
	Skinningrove	Integrated	Angles, rails
	Acklam	Integrated	Billets
	Briton Ferry	Cold metal	Bars and billets
100–200	Britannia	Cold metal	Sections
	Stocksbridge	Cold metal	Alloy and stainless
	Round Oak*	Cold metal	Bars and sections
	Firth Brown	Cold metal	Alloy and stainless
	Workington	Integrated	Railway materials
	Taylor Bros	Cold metal	Railway materials
	Brymbo	Integrated	Slabs and billets
	Llanelly	Cold metal	Sheet bars and billets
	Bynea	Cold metal	Tinplate
	Hallside	Cold metal	Plates and sections
	Heccla/E. Heccla	Cold metal	Foundry and special
	Clydesdale	Cold metal	Tubes
	Patent Shaft	Cold metal	Plates
	Coatbridge*	Cold metal	Sections and bars
	Parkhead	Cold metal	Foundry and press
	Pontymister	Cold metal	Tinplate
Less than 100	Works operated by the above companies on cold metal practice: Blochairn (plates); Panteg; Gowerton; Gorseinon; Cwmfelin; Pontardawe; Llanelly; Dyffryn; Elba; Landore (tinplate).		

Source: Industry and company records
* The site contained blast furnaces but the steel furnaces operated on a cold metal basis.

sites, it possessed a bewildering variety of blast furnaces (twenty) and steel furnaces (thirty-three).[4]

Much had been achieved, but there was still great potential for further rationalisation and development within the Dorman Long group.

These examples, which could be augmented by the records of other companies, suffice to demonstrate the manner in which the 1945 pattern of ownership had developed. Although there had been local reverses, notably the breakdown of merger talks between Dorman Long and South Durham in 1933, the trend appeared to be towards further consolidation of ownership and control. From the point of view of the industry as a whole there were potential gains to be won from further consolidation within the clusters, but the examples also show that there were forces working at the company level for operating works in more than one cluster. The strength of United Steel, for example, lay in its ability to integrate parts of the Scunthorpe and Sheffield clusters in one organisation. But the freedom to integrate operations both locally and nationally depended either on the formation of larger companies or on closer co-operation between the existing companies. In either case, the pattern of ownership, and the presence or absence of co-operation between the companies, were the most important aspects of the industry's geographical situation in 1945.

The second group of items in the analysis of situation relate to raw materials, in particular to iron ore and coal. Among the works using home ore the lowest cost situation was at Corby, which used the local ore exclusively. In view of the added cost of transport on ores from the South Lincolnshire and 'Northants' fields, the Scunthorpe works were not so well situated, although the costs of their local ores were as low as those at Corby. In contrast the smaller integrated plants of the West Midlands, West Riding, and South Lancashire had to absorb freight charges on all their ores brought over distances ranging up to 130 miles. Of the major works using foreign ore, eight could receive ore directly over a wharf, and seven were linked to their wharves by rail over distances ranging up to twenty-five miles. All the South Wales integrated plants used a mixture of foreign and home ore, the latter being obtained from the Oxfordshire and 'Northants' fields. On Teesside, Dorman Long used foreign ore and the local Cleveland ores, but South Durham was dependent upon the 170-mile haul from the 'Northants' field. There can be no doubt that the situation *vis-à-vis* ore supplies for the industry as a whole was sub-optimal in respect of aggregate costs.

The industry was better situated with regard to coal, but because of the lower tonnages involved the financial gain was not commensurate with the debits involved in access to ore. Even so, the picture was not as simple as it appeared. At Workington, for example, local coal had to be supplemented with coal from Durham. The main apparent centre of weakness in the system was that the potential growth areas of steel production at Scunthorpe and Corby, which produced 1·5 million tons of pig iron in 1945, were the least favourably situated. Costs were partly reduced by transporting some of the coal required for the blast furnaces in the form of coke, but this had the associated disadvantages of raising the proportion of coke breeze and deprived the works of coke oven gas. Furthermore, these comparatively new coking areas were using the cheaper coals from South Yorkshire and the East Midlands, and although war-time official policies had sought to equalise the cost of coal from all sources, an overall advantage was probably still held at the home ore locations. These two aspects of ore supply and coal supply have been extensively reviewed by geographers and economists.[5]

The third major raw material, scrap metal, occupies a special position, because of the manner in which it originates as an incidental product of metal forming and fabrication. In a mature industrial economy, the production of steel scrap is approximately 40 per cent of the ingot tonnage produced in any one year. This scrap arises, firstly, in the steel rolling mills themselves, the amount depending upon the type of product being rolled, and secondly, in the steel-consuming industries. The location of scrap arising is therefore divided between the centre of steel production and that of steel consumption, with a marginally higher tonnage being derived in the British case from the latter source. The third source of scrap is provided when capital equipment has become obsolete. In the pre-war years the demand for scrap in the United Kingdom exceeded supply and was satisfied with imported scrap. In 1945 the Federation was operating a scheme which sought to equalise the price of purchased scrap to all consumers and also to compensate the steelmakers who used an above-average proportion of higher-priced pig iron in their operations.[6]

The final element in the industry's geographical situation relates to the position of the markets. The intention of the industry in the years following 1945 was to export approximately 20 per cent of its output expressed in terms of ingots, but the importance of export markets varied from sector to sector. In 1938, for example, 52 per cent of tin plate production was exported, but only 10 per cent of steel plates was

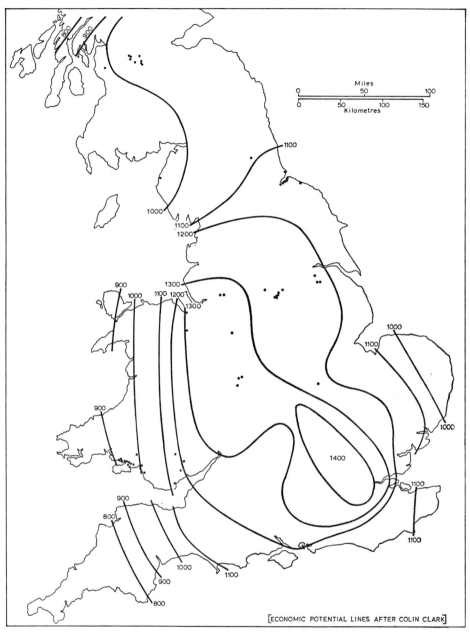

Fig 4. SITUATION OF PRINCIPAL STEELWORKS IN RELATION TO THE
GENERALISED MARKET

directly exported.[7] Although these variations in emphasis have locational effects on individual works, the overall orientation of the British industry was towards the domestic market.

A generalised view of the location of the British market for all goods and services can be obtained by use of the concept of economic potential, a concept derived by analogy from that of electrical potential in physics. The index of economic potential at any point is defined by the sum of incomes for all the points within the field, with each income value divided by a figure held to represent the cost of reaching it.[8] The isolines of equal economic potential calculated by Colin Clark for Britain in the early 1960s are included in Fig 4, together with the fifty-two principal works.[9] Areas of high potential provide suitable conditions for industrial development, but it is immediately apparent from Fig 4 that none of the principal steelworks was situated within the area of maximum potential. Furthermore, only 14 per cent of the total output (1·7 million tons) was produced within the area of 1,300–1,400 units.[10] The eccentric situation of the steel industry to the total British market for goods and services is obvious.

It is possible that the effects of this peripheral position were minimised by a closer association between the industry and its principal customers, and between individual producers and their neighbouring conurbations. Indeed, it is traditional to assume that the purpose of the Scottish steel industry is to satisfy the local market and the market in Northern Ireland. Certainly the Tyneside and Tees-side conurbations were the single most important destination for ten out of eleven types of rolled steel produced by one North East Coast producer, but even if this was the pattern for most companies there still remained a clear deficit of steel supply in the axial belt of England.[11] A supposed merit claimed for the Park Gate Company in Rotherham was that it sold 70 per cent of its output within a radius of fifty miles from the works, and 98 per cent within the larger radius of 100 miles.[12] Similar patterns can be hypothesised for the other companies situated within the English manufacturing belt. A complete measure of the adequacy of the industry's marketing arrangements could be obtained only by relating each works to its actual and potential customers. Such information is, regrettably, not publicly available.

Site

Knowledge of the peculiar advantages and disadvantages of any location is derived from acquaintance with the conditions of site as well as with the local lets and hindrances to the flows of material. This knowledge plays an important part in development policies, but these are also influenced by the view that is taken of imminent technological and trading conditions. During the first part of the twentieth century technological development in the steel industry had taken an evolutionary path, which had called for, and allowed, constant small-scale modifications to existing plant. In 1945 there were no recognisable indications that this evolutionary progress was about to be interrupted. Even the implications of the continuous strip mill had not been fully recognised, and in the ironworks, for example, the ironmakers were only tentatively exploring the advantages to be gained from the use of sinter: the main preoccupation was still with the blast furnaces themselves. Furthermore, it was thought that an increase in steel output of no more than 25 per cent would be adequate for the peace-time economy of the 1950s. The approach to the future was instinctively conservative and cautious, which is not to say that that was the approach which was required.

Interpretations of the site conditions of the industry should be made in the light of, firstly, the division between integrated and cold metal operations, secondly, the level of output, and thirdly, the type of finished steel produced at each works (Table 2). In view of the diversity of the industry displayed in that table, a similarly disparate range of site conditions should be expected (Table 3). The most important characteristic of site is size, and this characteristic, measured for the fifty-two major works, ranged from 1,700 acres at Appleby-Frodingham to about 20 acres at Cwmfelin in Swansea. No fewer than nineteen individual works occupied less than 100 acres, whereas only five occupied sites of more than 500 acres.[13]

The information in Tables 2 and 3 shows that marked variations in the size of the steelworks sites persisted even after allowance is made for scale of output and type of technology. The information suggests an apparent freedom on the part of the industry to choose almost indiscriminately from, and to adapt to, a bewilderingly heterogeneous display of conditions, but allowance must be made for the industry's historical legacy, as well as for the recognition that there is an important distinction between that which is ideal and that which is tolerable. The outstanding anomaly was the case of the East Moors, Cardiff, works of Guest Keen & Baldwins. On that uninterrupted site of no more than 140 acres the company had built an integrated plant with a capacity of 0·45 million ingot tons, that is, 3,215 ingot tons per annum from each acre. This intensity of output was matched by no

Table 3

IRON AND STEELWORKS 1945—SITE

Area (acres)	Works	Process	Shape	Slope (ft)	Interruptions to site — River	Rail	Road	Canal	Slag	Road	Encroachments on site — Rail	Canal	Docks	Housing	Industry	Physical features
1500–2000	Appleby-Frodingham*	Hot	Irregular	25		x	x		x	x	x				x	
	Redcar	Hot	Rectangle			x	x		x	x	x		x	x	x	Estuary
	Port Talbot	Hot	Irregular		x	x	x		x	x	x		x	x		
1000–1500	Cleveland	Hot	Triangle			x	x		x	x	x				x	River
	Shotton†	Cold	Triangle				x			x	x				x	River
500–1000	Consett	Hot	Irregular	200		x	x		x	x	x					Hillside
	Moss Bay	Hot	Rectangle	50	x		x		x	x	x			x		Shore
300–400	C.I./Clydebridge	Hot	Irregular		x	x	x		x	x	x					
	Park Gate	Hot	Irregular			x	x		x	x	x				x	
250–300	Corby*	Hot	Irregular		x		x			x	x			x		
	Normanby Park	Hot	Irregular			x	x		x	x	x					
	Shelton	Hot	Irregular	50		x	x		x	x	x			x	x	Hillside
	Stocksbridge	Cold	Rectangle			x	x		x	x				x		
200–250	Ebbw Vale	Hot	Rectangle	200		x	x			x	x			x		Hillside
	Glengarnock‡	Cold	Rectangle	100		x	x	x	x	x	x					Loch
	Irlam	Hot	Rectangle		x	x				x	x					
	S. Peech & Tozer	Cold	Rectangle			x	x		x	x	x			x	x	
150–200	Britannia	Cold	Rectangle			x	x		x	x	x			x	x	River
	Cargo Fleet	Hot	Irregular			x			x	x	x			x	x	River
	Dalzell	Cold	Rectangle	50					x	x	x			x		
	Skinningrove	Hot	Irregular				x		x	x	x			x	x	Shore
100–150	Acklam	Hot	Irregular							x	x				x	River
	Bilston	Hot	Irregular						x	x	x	x		x	x	Shore
	Briton Ferry	Cold	Rectangle	75					x	x	x		x			
	Clydesdale	Cold	Rectangle						x	x	x		x		x	
	East Moors	Hot	Rectangle						x	x	x			x		
	Hallside	Cold	Irregular							x	x				x	
	Heccla/E, Heccla	Cold	Rectangle		x		x			x	x			x		
	Lanarkshire	Cold	Irregular						x	x	x				x	
	Llanelly	Cold	Irregular				x			x	x					
	Redbourn	Hot	Irregular	50		x	x		x	x	x			x	x	
	Round Oak	Cold	Rectangle		x	x	x	x	x	x	x			x	x	
	West Hartlepool	Hot	Rectangle						x	x	x			x	x	
50–100	Atlas	Cold	Rectangle	100		x	x		x	x	x			x	x	Hillside
	Brymbo	Hot	Irregular						x	x	x			x		
	Bynea	Cold	Irregular						x	x	x			x	x	
	Gorseinon	Cold	Rectangle							x	x					
	Coatbridge	Cold	Irregular					x		x	x	x				
	Patent Shaft	Cold	Rectangle				x			x	x					
	Parkhead	Cold	Irregular		x					x	x	x				River
	Pontardawe	Cold	Irregular		x		x		x	x	x			x	x	
	River Don	Cold	Irregular				x			x	x			x	x	
	Taylor Bros	Cold	Rectangle							x	x			x	x	
<50	Blochairn	Cold	Irregular			x				x	x				x	
	Cwmfelin	Cold	Irregular							x	x					
	Dyffryn	Cold	Rectangle						x	x	x			x	x	River
	Elba	Cold	Irregular						x	x	x				x	River
	Gowerton	Cold	Rectangle							x	x					
	Landore	Cold	Irregular		x				x	x	x			x	x	
	Llanelly	Cold	Irregular							x	x				x	Shore
	Panteg	Cold	Rectangle				x			x	x			x	x	
	Pontymister	Cold	Irregular							x	x					River

other integrated works in Britain, and was only approached, among the cold metal operators, at Steel, Peech & Tozer where 2,650 annual ingot tons were produced for each acre.

There was, however, a generalised relationship between site, level of output and steelmaking technology. Of the nineteen works which individually covered less than 100 acres, only Brymbo was an integrated operation. Conversely, only three works which individually covered more than 250 acres operated the cold metal process. If the industry was static, then these site size differences could possibly be regarded with equanimity, but if changes in output or in technology were anticipated the limitations imposed upon individual development projects by the size of the area available could be intolerable. The size of a site is not a strictly deterministic factor, because it can be modified by the other elements of site, but it is one important control on development, and in many cases of equal importance to situation.

The first factor capable of modifying the effects of site size was the shape of the works perimeter. The preferred shape was a rectangle with a ratio of short axis to long axis of about 1 : 1·5, whereas the realised shapes in the British industry were almost always irregular.[14] In a very large works in theory the plant could be arranged to maximum advantage regardless of the shape of the perimeter, but in a small works the outer shape influenced profoundly the distribution of the items of plant.

A second modifying factor to the size element was whether the site was interrupted or continuous. Unfortunately, in the British case interruptions to the site by railways, roads, other industrial properties, and even canals, were the rule rather than the exception. The extreme example was at Park Gate, where the 310 acres were distributed over seven unequal parcels of land, divided the one from the other by roads and main-line railways. At no more than fifteen sites were such disturbances absent. Access to road, rail or canal is, of course, essential, but in an ideal case public lines of communication would not cross the works and interrupt its interior layout.

Similarly, encroachment upon the works by public lines of communication, and other forms of industrial activity, should also be kept to a minimum. Where these parallel and define a major boundary they act as obstacles to those developments which demand more space. In the instance of adjacent housing what was seen as an advantage in the nineteenth century was now seen as a disadvantage not only from the social point of view but from the operational. Because most British steelworks were creations of the nineteenth century most of them were ringed about with houses. Proximity to metal-using industries is usually ranked as an asset, the clearest example in the British case being East Moors which was almost adjacent to its major consumer, the Castle Works of the parent company, Guest Keen & Nettlefolds. Of the natural phenomena which encroach upon a works, rivers have positive and negative effects, but steep slopes outside the property impose limitations of varying magnitude as at Consett, Ebbw Vale and Stocksbridge. At Skinningrove, on the other hand, slag was tipped down the adjacent slope on to the foreshore. At times of expansion, steep slopes, estuaries and rivers can clearly be major obstacles.

The combined effects of interruptions to, and encroachments upon, a site can well be illustrated by reference to three works of Dorman Long and to the Sheffield area works of United Steel. The Acklam and Britannia works occupied together a cramped site of about 300 acres in the old ironmasters district in Middlesbrough, which was contained within a tight loop of the river Tees. The fourth side of the quarter was defined by an LNER shunting yard and main-line railway, beyond which was the nineteenth-century town. Both works contained obsolete equipment, and it had already been determined that they should be closed when modern capacity had been installed on the Lackenby site, purchased in 1943. This would be a clear case of development at a new location preceding the implementation of a decision to close an unsatisfactory plant in the accomplishing of absolute locational change. The situation of these two nineteenth-century works within Middlesbrough was no longer attractive to a company which had an alternative and superior site available.

The Cleveland works, which was the hub of the whole Dorman Long operation, had a site of approximately 1,000 acres, which was crossed by a branch line and a main line of the LNER (see page 66). These interruptions, together with a large area used for slag disposal and ore stocking, confined the manufacturing activities to an area of under 200 acres and complicated the flow of materials between the coke ovens, the three sets of blast furnaces, two melting shops and two groups of mills which were being operated. There was additional encroachment upon the works from housing (ie, Bessemer Street, and Bolckow Terrace), schools and other public buildings, and industrial sites. As long as the area was to maintain these diverse functions, it would be impossible for the works to expand unless some space-saving technology were developed. (The illustration of the Cleveland Works was taken in 1966, by which time some of the housing that had encroached upon the works had been demolished in accordance with twentieth-century views of land-use planning.) The scale of operations at Cleveland in 1945 seemed to be fixed by the complicated nature of its layout and the congestion of its site.

Page 83 shows views of the fourteen-furnace Templeborough melting shop and the seven-furnace Rotherham melting shop at the Steel, Peech & Tozer works of the United Steel Companies at Rotherham. Together they produced a larger tonnage (0·61 million ingot tons) than any other British works with the exception of Appleby-Frodingham (0·66 million ingot tons). The congestion of the melting shops and their adjustment to the conditions of site is, however, readily apparent. The older Rotherham shop was girdled by railways and the river Don and physical expansion was impossible even if it was needed. The Templeborough shop, built in 1916, was fitted closely into a long, narrow extension of the works at the Sheffield end defined by the main road and a marshalling yard. It was the longest such shop in Europe. Both pictures, taken in 1959, show the intimate relationship between place of work and place of rest acceptable at the time that the works were built. By 1965 the houses had been demolished, part of the liberated area was incorporated into the works, and only a few of the old service functions of the area were retained.

The Stocksbridge works (Samuel Fox) of the United Steel Companies, whose areal extent was similar to that of Steel, Peech & Tozer, was similarly encroached upon, and had the additional complications associated with its position on the floor of a narrow steep-sided valley. The picture of the Stocksbridge Works on page 84, taken in the early 1950s, shows the original five-storey stone-built nucleus of the works, which still contained the small spring and umbrella departments, and, at ground level, the hand rod mill. The melting shops and billet mill were beyond this nucleus with the scrap yard at the top end of the works. The limitations of space and the operational problems of this elongated site are most evident in the frequent crossing of road and rail within the works, and in the terraces excavated on the hillside to make room for the developments in the stainless steel departments. These latter were served only by road.

The output of the works in 1945 was about 0·2 million tons, but the deliberate emphasis was upon quality rather than quantity, with the result that neither of these objectively adverse site characteristics would vitiate the life of the works. Nevertheless, the demolition of the coke ovens provided the space for the continuous rod and bar mill built at the far end of the works in the late 1950s. This was in keeping with the tradition of a works in which, at earlier times, a redundant reservoir

c

had been drained to provide the site for the billet mill, and an old open-hearth and Bessemer melting shop had been replaced with the beginnings of electric steelmaking. There can be no doubt that the site of the works fell short of the ideal, but the continuous irritation of its existing compromises was preferable to the upheaval of relocation in both social and financial terms.

Most British steelworks had been built upon sites which were approximately level, the major exceptions being at Consett, Ebbw Vale and Stocksbridge. In an industry which handles large tonnages of material, some operational benefits could be obtained if the major movements were down-slope. That position almost applied at Consett Iron, situated at an average elevation of about 750 feet, where the ore trains from the wharves on the rivers Tyne and Wear unloaded at an elevation of about 800 feet. Thereafter the raw material flow-lines within the works were predominantly down-grade, and slag and other waste products were tipped along the western edge of the works at its lowest elevation.

The position at Ebbw Vale was almost the exact opposite (see page 84). The works sloped upwards from 750 feet at the main entrance at the south end of the works to 950 feet at the north end. The blast furnaces, which were the only items of plant inherited from the Ebbw Vale Steel Iron & Coal Company, were located near the south-east corner of the site but fifty feet above the valley bottom, so that incoming ore was hauled to the top end of the works whence it was returned to the south end along the western flank of the valley—a total journey within this long and narrow works of almost five miles. The direct distance between the ironworks and the melting shop was 300 yards, but because of differences in elevation the hot metal was taken on a journey of almost a mile which included two uphill sections and a downhill section.[15] Similarly, the ingots from the melting shop followed a down-valley and up-valley movement to the soakers at the south end of the mill. It was a situation which the Grand Old Duke of York would have fully appreciated. Only coal and limestone movements, entering from the north end, derived maximum benefit from the aid of gravity.

These local problems, the situational inadequacies of the location, and the special circumstances which surrounded the origins of this works, explain why in an integrated plant the three major units of ironworks, steelworks, and rolling mills should be out of balance. In the early post-war years 0·2 million tons per annum of ingots and slabs had to be obtained from outside (mainly from Scunthorpe) to feed the mill. This was not the only example of such imbalance in the industry or in South Wales, but it was the most extreme case, and nothing could be done quickly to rectify the position.[16] A third blast furnace was built in 1945, but only two could be operated at any one time. In contrast to Stocksbridge, the shape and size of the Ebbw Vale site presented major operational difficulties which would also inevitably affect the profitability of further developments should these be contemplated. Sooner, rather than later, the conditions of site would impose a limit upon expansion.

Site conditions interact with the available technology, and with the historical legacy, to produce the actual layout of the departments within the works. At Redcar, for example, a predominantly foreign ore using integrated plant with its own wharf, the ironworks, which had originally operated as a separate concern belonging to Walker, Maynard & Co, was located at the furthest point from the wharf, and on the far side of the LNER main line which bisected the works. The melting shop and plate mills had been added by Dorman Long in the years following 1916. Although the materials flow was along predominantly straight and level lines, the works had been, in the intervening years, 'upside down'. After 1945, this was rectified when the ore supply for the entire Dorman Long group was centralised on the South Bank Wharf and ore-receiving area at the Cleveland Works.

A notable feature of works development in the industry as a whole was the reluctance or inability of management to change existing usages of areas within the works. The main effect of this policy was to sacrifice long-term efficiency for short-term aims, but the policy had its roots in the extreme financial difficulties of every company at one time or another in the 1920s and 1930s. It illustrates the point that only a financially healthy industry can afford to produce a structure which can satisfy its own long-term optimal operational requirements. Present capital shortages, or the expectation of low profits, lead to situations in which present and future levels of revenue are adversely affected. It is a self-perpetuating problem.

When the East Moors works was rehabilitated in the 1930s the lines of the blast furnaces and melting shop in the pre-existing works, which had otherwise been razed, were retained and extended without any apparent reduction in efficiency. A similar conclusion can be drawn from the development at Consett, where the new blast furnaces were being built on the line established in the nineteenth century. It has already been shown that an identical policy was followed at Ebbw Vale, where there was possibly no alternative. It is, however, surprising to discover that at Corby, which is usually considered to be the only green-field development of the inter-war era, the blast furnaces which had been operated by the Lloyds Ironstone Company on that site were modernised and were made the starting-point of that new integrated works. The adoption of this policy explains the position of the ironworks in the south-west corner of this extensive site, and added minor complications to the materials flow of the works, but in this perfectly situated works such idiosyncrasies of design would not seriously affect the success of the operation. Similar examples were to be found influencing the precise position of melting shops and rolling mills within the different works, but with more serious consequences.

Occasionally, however, a clear break from the past is made within or adjacent to an existing works. This happened at Appleby-Frodingham in 1932. In 1945 the works was divided into four areas (Fig 5), each of which related to an earlier stage in its history. The focus of attention in 1945 was the South Works where a coke-oven plant, ore preparation and sinter plant, and the nation's two largest blast furnaces (22-foot-diameter hearths) had been opened in 1939. It was intended to build more blast furnaces and a new melting shop here to replace that in the Frodingham works.

The South Works had been the site of the North Lincolnshire Iron Company, and had belonged briefly to Stewarts & Lloyds. When that company decided to build its new works at Corby the Scunthorpe site was offered first to Richard Thomas, who owned the adjacent Redbourn works, and then to the United Steel Companies, which bought it in 1932.[17] This purchase gave the company space, and it was space which was essential if the best use was to be made of the local ironstones.

The ore being used was drawn from fifteen different quarries in the local Frodingham and the distant South Lincolnshire and 'Northants' fields, and varied in its moisture, sulphur, lime and iron content. The average iron content of the self-fluxing Frodingham ores was only 22 per cent, whereas the 'Northants' ore usually contained more than 26 per cent and commonly 33 per cent.[18] In addition, each ore consisted of lenses of different hardness, so that the blasting operations to break the hard beds also pulverised the softer beds. The result was a high proportion of ore fines in the untreated burden. The hard ore still required crushing, and although this was a straightforward operation with the Frodingham ores, the sticky 'Northants' ores needed to be dried. 'Northants' ores were, however, needed to offset the superabundance of lime in the Frodingham ores.

South Ironworks had been built to overcome all these problems. The inclusion of a bedding plant in which the whole range of ores, excluding

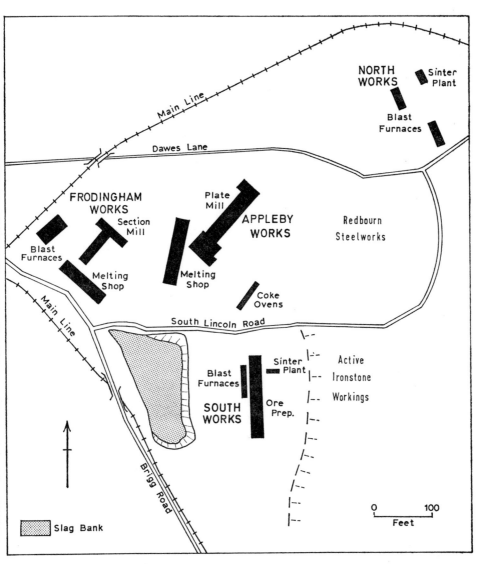

Fig 5.   APPLEBY-FRODINGHAM, 1945

the ore fines, could be mixed was an innovation within the British industry, but with each pile being fifty yards long it was a space-consuming process. The ore fines were sintered in a new continuous plant which gave operational advantages over the batch process used at the North Ironworks. In view of subsequent developments it is important to note that it was thought at the time that there was a technical limitation on the use of sinter at about 39 per cent of the furnace charge, but that that limit might be overcome with the use of even larger blast furnaces; the economic limit was thought to be 34 per cent. The total area of the developed part of the South Works was sixty-six acres, which in itself was larger than the area of fifteen of the works in Table 3 and was half the area of the neighbouring Redbourn integrated works.

One unavoidable disadvantage accruing to this development on the periphery of a pre-existing works was that it extended the lines of internal communication. After the development had been completed some of the ores travelled as much as three miles within the works. The coal for the coke ovens, the first to be built at Appleby-Frodingham, had a similar internal journey, and, in some instances, the hot metal travelled almost one mile between blast furnaces and melting shops. The costs of the ore and coal movements in 1953 were about twopence per ton mile,[19] and although the works layout had been simplified between 1945 and 1953 the average load within the works travelled 1·28 miles.[20] In 1945 the cost was lower but the distances were greater. With an output of 0·65 million ingot tons the works railways were carrying a minimum of eight million tons of materials each year. It could almost be said that the site of Appleby-Frodingham was so large as to impair efficiency, but if this was so it was because the evolved nature of the works had placed the units of plant mainly on the periphery of the works. Certainly, it could not be argued that the 1,700 acres were being used to maximum technical efficiency in the production of 0·65 million ingot tons, but economic efficiency is measured in terms of capital charges in addition to operating charges.

Technology

The course of development in the post-war years, which was influenced so profoundly by the variety in the locational heritage, was also fashioned by the equally diversified technological legacy. One expression of this diversity is found in Table 2, where the major products of each of the fifty-two works together with the method of steel melting are listed. Apart from the uniformity of the alloy, stainless and heavy forging trades which used a cold metal process, there was a variety of compositions of products and technology. In the sheet steel trade, for example, one continuous hot strip mill, Ebbw Vale, was part of an integrated works using the basic Bessemer process, whereas the other, at Shotton, was backed by two cold metal open-hearth melting shops. By contrast, in the plate trade there was regional variety. In England the large plate mills were in integrated works, whereas in Scotland the largest plate works, Dalzell, was a cold metal operation.

The variations in these, and in the other trades, suggest three possible areas of explanation. Firstly, that the large categories used in this classification of products conceal important differences in the qualities, sizes, and usages of the product. Secondly, that the industry had defined an optimum technology for each product, and was steadily working towards that end. In such a case, variations would be explained by the fact that each works occupied a different position on the various development schedules. Thirdly, it was possible that a variegated industry provided the best total reaction to the industry's trading environment as a whole. All three explanations are partially true.

The category of plates, for example, could be divided, on the basis of thickness alone, into heavy and medium plates, with the latter merging into steel sheets. Within each category there are further divisions based upon width, length and final usage. In contrast, the sheet steel industry was undergoing a technological revolution which had been interrupted by the war, and the general assumption seems to have been that blast furnaces would be provided at Shotton in due course. The contemporary evidence, however, is equivocal, but some observers of the industry expressed surprise when the blast furnace development at that location was announced.[21] Finally, in an economy which could choose between home and foreign ores, and in which there was a large volume of low-priced scrap metal, it was perhaps inevitable that there should be not only a variety of location but a variety of technology. It is possible that the seeming uncertainty of purpose displayed in the subject-matter of Table 2 is an expression of strength rather than of weakness: the ability to respond to all the changes which were likely to appear. Such a possibility was a part of the truth, but not the whole truth.

In 1945 there were three major steelmaking methods in use in Britain, the open-hearth, the Bessemer converter, and the electric arc and induction furnaces, contributing respectively 86 per cent, 9 per cent, and 5 per cent of the total ingot output. The acid Bessemer process was a technological relict feature to be found only at Workington,[22] while the basic Bessemer process had witnessed a revival at Corby and Ebbw Vale in the 1930s for the conversion of home ores to pipes and tin-plates. Both Bessemer processes required liquid pig iron and were found only in integrated works. The electric arc and induction furnaces were cold metal processes used in the production of high carbon, and alloy steels. The backbone of the industry, the open-hearth, was present in both its acid and basic forms. The acid process was entirely cold metal with a maximum melting capacity, in Britain, of 100 tons per melt. There were 114 of these furnaces, 60 per cent of which were to be found in Sheffield and South Wales. The basic open-hearth could be operated according to either the cold metal or hot metal process, and was found in the form of fixed furnaces or tilting furnaces, which were particularly valuable in the processing of the high phosphorus ores of the Frodingham field. A generalised view of the regional variations in the importance of these processes is displayed in Fig 6 from which it appears that some regional specialisation of steelmaking process had developed.

The open-hearth furnace varied in relative importance from one dis-trict to another, with an extreme range of 100 per cent at Scunthorpe to virtually nothing in District 1, but in the districts which made use of this process there were important underlying variations. The most significant contrast was between Scotland and the North East Coast. In Scotland, the ratio of liquid pig iron to cold pig iron charged to the steel furnaces was 1:7·5, which compared with 1:0·6 for the British industry as a whole; and the ratio of hot metal to total cold metal was 1:24·0, which compared with the national ratio of 1:2·6. On the North East Coast, where the product range was similar but not so extensive, the hot metal to total cold metal ratio was 1:1·2. Such wide variations in steelmaking practice were not to be explained on the basis of deliberate regional specialisation. Rather, a major problem of the Scottish industry was its inability to use the limited tonnage of pig iron which was available to it in the most efficient manner. At Clydebridge, the sole integrated plant, over 60 per cent of the material charged to the furnaces was cold metal. There were locational reasons to adequately explain the small tonnage of pig iron produced in Scotland, but the inefficient use of the material that was available was the result of the fragmented development of the Scottish industry. This was a problem which would be difficult to solve within the existing Scottish locational pattern.

The British steel industry in 1945 was dominated by a single

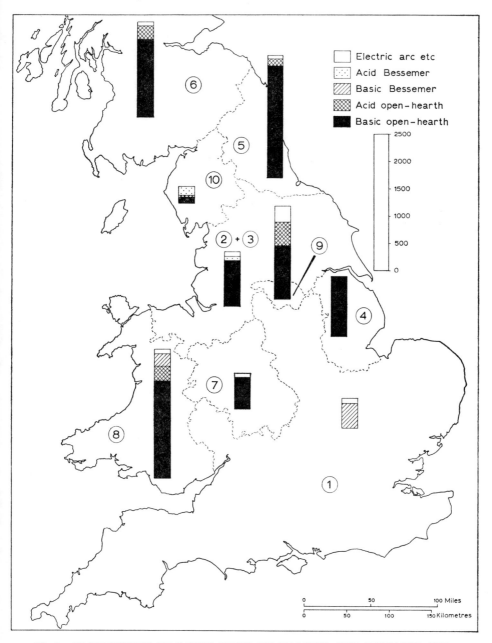

Legend:
- Electric arc etc
- Acid Bessemer
- Basic Bessemer
- Acid open-hearth
- Basic open-hearth

Fig 6.   PRODUCTION OF INGOT STEEL BY PROCESS AND DISTRICT, 1945

theme—variety: variety of situation, variety of site, variety of technology and variety in the level of modernisation already achieved. With careful forethought and wise planning this factor could be developed into a positive strength. For example, if the cost trends favoured home ores a nucleus of works already existed to use them. Equally, if foreign ores were cheaper, there was a profusion of coastal works which needed only improved docking facilities to make use of them. By linking the integrated and cold metal works the full benefit of the cost differential between the hot and cold metal practices could also be gained. Again, if the trend was to be towards large works there were already sites available for development. Nevertheless, without foresight this potential source of strength could become a major handicap. All that was needed was confidence, but the experiences of the previous two decades had bred caution.

3

Sufficient unto the Day

IN DECEMBER 1945 the industry presented to the Government a Report outlining its post-war development proposals. This was made public in May 1946.[1] It foretold an expenditure of £168 million on all sectors of the industry. Output would be raised 37 per cent by 1952 to 16·0 million ingot tons, of which 3·0 million ingot tons would be exported. Steelmaking would be based on a scrap metal:pig iron ratio of 55:53. This would require the annual importing of 250,000 tons of scrap, and a basic and hematite blast furnace capacity of 9·0 million tons. As in the pre-war years, 0·5 million tons of hematite iron would be exported. These levels of output would require 20 million tons of coal, of which rather more than half would be coking coal, 12·5 million tons of home ore, and 7·5 million tons of imported ore. It presented, as Burn wrote, 'a prospect that could not fail, at first sight, to dazzle'.[2]

In subsequent years the Report has been subjected to extensive critical review, and it is necessary to emphasise only two points here.[3] Firstly, it was stated that all foreign-ore-based developments would be concentrated on coastal sites. Unfortunately, it was a misleading promise to the extent that the envisaged coastal zone was wide enough to contain all the works in South Wales and on the North East Coast, and probably all the works in Scotland. It certainly included Consett and Ebbw Vale, twenty-five miles inland and 800 feet above sea-level, which seems to be stretching the term coastal beyond breaking point. The reasoning appears to have been that all integrated works using predominantly foreign ore were by definition, and tautologically, coastal. Twenty years later Scunthorpe was to become a 'coastal' works.[4]

The second point was that the authors of the Report confused wish with fulfilment. The desired future pattern for the industry, they wrote, was to be gained by the closing of small, obsolete works, the rationalisation of finished steels, and the construction of three new major integrated works. The first was illustrated by reference to the North East Coast and the second by reference to the rail trade. Promises were given that similar 'concentration' and 'rationalisation' in the other districts and trades would be obtained.[5] This illustration of likely works closure was scorned by the chief company concerned the day after publication, which was something unlikely to create confidence.[6]

The three major proposals for new works consisted of a Clydeside works to which the name of no company was attached; a home-ore works in Northamptonshire to which Stewarts & Lloyds and United Steel were supposed to be giving their attention; and a redevelopment of the Port Talbot works under the aegis of Richard Thomas & Baldwins. Colvilles took three years to prove their lack of interest in the first, Stewarts & Lloyds and United Steel allowed the second to be forgotten, but the third was built and gave rise to a new creation, the Steel Company of Wales.

The main fault of the Report was in implying that the consensus of opinion within the industry, namely that modernisation was required, extended down to the detailed implementation of that policy; that there was agreement over strategy and tactics. In reality the companies adopted a policy of sacrificing long-term industry-wide aims for short-term individual gains. Over the short term this policy was successful in meeting the unexpectedly high and prolonged level of demand because it left the companies free to concentrate upon boosting output from existing capacity. All previous production records were broken, and the level of output proposed in the Report was exceeded. It was, nevertheless, a policy dominated by expediency.

Outside commentators were divided as to whether the plan would mould the future form of the industry for one or two generations.[7] The Economist concluded that 'all future plans for steel would certainly proceed by way of modification of this one', but the modifications were already under way.[8] If future plans were to be more influential they would have to be compiled in a different context. In 1946 there was the appearance of a co-ordinated and agreed Report, but the reality was no more than a congeries of plans.

The Level of Demand

A minority of dissentients thought that the 1946 Report's estimate of future demand was too conservative. Notable among these was G. D. H. Cole who proposed that capacity should be raised to 26·0 million ingot tons by 1955.[9] The consensus view, both inside and outside the industry, was that the Federation's estimate was a truly likely one, and that it could be reached within the existing structure of the industry. This last point was important, because apart from the argument about nationalisation there were no moves made to reorganise the corporate structure of the industry outside South Wales. The aim was to be producing 16·0 million ingot tons a year by 1952, and thereafter it was assumed that with a static and ageing population the level of demand would stabilise.[10] The method was for each company to pursue its own ends subject only to the informal discussions within the Federation and the loose control exerted by the Iron & Steel Board.

The war-time policy of steel rationing supervised by government departments was continued into the post-war quinquennium, so it is impossible to produce anything other than a generalised record of demand by sector. Although the output of steel did not pass the pre-war peak until 1948, domestic demand for steel reached the 1937 level of 11·6 million tons in 1946. In the three years that followed the end of hostilities domestic consumption increased by an average rate of 1 million tons a year, so that the 1952 estimated requirements were reached in 1947–8, and by 1949 were exceeded at 14·5 million tons. Individual producers were reporting full order books, and in some sections were anticipating 'a high level of demand for a number of years'.[11] The trade literature was replete with expressions indicating 'the utmost need for every ton', 'extraordinarily strong or unrelaxed demand', or an 'industry inundated with orders'.

The hard-pressed consumers were not so happy, even though the government compelled some producers to restrict their level of exports to well below the pre-war levels.[12] The government, on the other hand, anticipated 'no serious gap between the supplies available in 1947 and the major steel-consuming industries' because it proposed to discourage the expansion of those industries, and was already restricting exports.[13] This policy was implemented more successfully than some others. The home demand for motor cars was strictly curtailed, and the shipbuilders had their steel allocation cut by half.[14]

In 1948 the steelmakers argued that they had the capacity to produce 15 million tons but had lost 1 million tons through shortages of foreign ore and German scrap upon which they had relied to meet sudden increases in demand. Furthermore, it was difficult to dispatch the steel that they had made because of the inadequacy of the railways.[15] The railways, in turn, were suffering from a shortage of steel plates for wagons. Blame was laid on the steelmakers for following restrictive policies in the inter-war period, and the industry blamed the current uncertainty imposed upon it by the threat of nationalisation.[16] In such a situation all were blamed, and all held themselves blameless.

By 1948 the industry recognised that the trading pattern in the 1950s was unlikely to repeat that of the 1920s, and revised its production target to 18 million ingot tons.[17] Nevertheless, it claimed that with the retention of some capacity that had been intended for scrapping, and with the higher-than-anticipated output of some of the new capacity, no new major developments would be required. It did not say what the effect of this old, high-cost marginal capacity would be on the industry as a whole, nor whether it was happy with these higher outputs from locations chosen with lower targets in mind. Perhaps it was true that development upon a variable base permitted this flexible response.

In 1949 there was a temporary lull in demand and mention was made of a possible European steel surplus of 8 million tons by 1953.[18] The shipbuilders' needs were temporarily satisfied. The motor industry received a higher, but still not satisfactory allocation. The export of tubes was increased. Sir John James of Lancashire Steel spoke of a buyers' market, and Chetwynd Talbot of South Durham predicted hard times.[19] At least one minor company, Arthur Balfour, curtailed its development programme. It began to appear as though the traditional caution of the industry would be vindicated, and that it had been wrong to revise its target.

Such vindication was denied, however, by the onset of rearmament and the Korean War, but with the benefit of hindsight the lull in demand would appear to have been only temporary even without these additional causes. By October 1950 the shipbuilders had received more than twice as many firm orders as in the whole of the preceding year, and the 'clamour for steel of all descriptions' was to be heard echoing through the land again.[20] The controlled distribution of steel under a rationing scheme, which had been abolished in the middle of 1950, was reimposed early in 1951.

The effect of this period of unsatisfied demand which persisted through 1952 was to make it possible to sell all the steel which was produced regardless of the technical and locational inefficiencies of the industry. The industry had largely equalised the situational costs accruing from raw material supplies by means of the scrap levy and the ingot levy. This 'complex and hidden' system, as it was called by *The Economist*, had the effect of causing the home ore consumers to subsidise the foreign ore consumers, and the scrap users the pig iron users. Although the system was capable of revision its retention in part or in whole was felt to be to the general benefit of the total assembly if not to some of its constituent parts.[21] During the period of the 1946 Report differences in raw material costs between the companies were kept to a minimum, and developments were determined by the sector of the market to which the works were related and by the variable nature of the sites.

The Fate of the Major Proposals

Major developments had been listed in the 1946 Report for Clydeside, Northamptonshire, and Port Talbot. Each of these schemes had its particular purpose, merits, and proponents, but whereas the first two were in some senses optional schemes about which the industry still had time to think, the third required immediate action. Although the full implications of the continuous hot strip mill for the production of sheet for tinplate had not yet been fully assimilated it had been apparent to some in 1940 that a revision of the industry's organisation, technology and location was imperative. The prolonged discussions between the tinplate companies themselves, and between the industry and the official governmental overseeing bodies, were not about reform but about the thoroughness of that reform.

The Choice of Port Talbot

The high period of these discussions lasted from early in 1943 until December 1947. It was characterised by a growing volume of proposals and counter-proposals, by changes of emphasis, by disagreement between experts, and finally by compromise. After this long period of gestation the industry was delivered of a 72in continuous hot strip mill and cold reduction mill added to the expanded integrated works at Port Talbot, and an associated tinplate works at Trostre, Llanelly. The Port Talbot works had been owned by Guest Keen & Baldwins, but the new and revitalised operations were vested in the new Steel Company of Wales, which was incorporated on 1 May 1947.

In his detailed analysis of these discussions and of the merits and demerits of their outcome Warren has demonstrated that even when there is a common realisation that change is necessary the practical formulation of that change is fraught with difficulties.[22] These are composed of an amalgam of a diversity of goals, of uncertainty about the capabilities of new equipment, of uncertainties about the future, and of the apparent need to reconcile new developments with the legacy of the old. Warren also emphasised firstly that the origin of the scheme lay in the need to rationalise and to improve the production of tinplate rather than uncoated cold reduced sheets, and secondly that the size of the envisaged development was repeatedly revised upwards from 0·3 million tons to 1·2 million tons.

It is clear, therefore, that Port Talbot was chosen not as the basis of a new sheet steel industry, but as the second pivot of the reorganised but old tinplate industry. In that context the rationale of a West Wales location was superior to that of Ebbw Vale in the 1930s. But, although tinplate has remained a major product of the Port Talbot works and its associated mills at Trostre and Velindre, the impetus for continued growth has come from the uncoated sheet steel market. The location of the works relative to its markets has therefore changed in time, and the merit of the original location decision has been unavoidably devalued. Port Talbot represents a prime example of a location which was chosen in the context of one trade, but which has been required to serve another.

There were three determining factors in the initial choice of Port Talbot as opposed to the many other suggested sites west of Bridgend. Firstly, GKB had progressively modernised the primary departments of the works and had rebuilt the three blast furnaces during the period 1943–6. Secondly, the works was truly coastal with the ore stockyard immediately behind the wharf. Thirdly, there were 1,700 acres of undeveloped land available immediately to the south of the works. This factor of unlimited space was entirely beneficial, whereas the first two factors presented some irritation even in 1947. Such discomfiture is inevitable in all instances when the new is grafted on to the old, and in this case with the passage of time it was to create operational difficulties, which were publicly recognised by the men at Port Talbot themselves.[23]

The Port Talbot development was dominated by the twin themes of the availability of the land on the new Abbey site and the practicability of grafting this new technology on to the existing Margam and Port Talbot sites (see page 149). A third melting shop, Margam II, with a capacity of 1·0 million ingot tons obtained from eight 200-ton tilting open-hearth furnaces, was added to the two shops already in operation. The new building had room for twelve such furnaces, and it was intended that in due course the additional four would replace the 0·5 million tons obtained from Margam I and Port Talbot. Such a replacement would simplify the traffic flows in the works, and liberate space behind the ironworks.

Later the capacity of the initial eight furnaces was raised to 1·25 million tons by conversion to oil-firing, and the extra four furnaces were built, but the old melting shops were still kept in operation until the early 1960s. By 1950 the company was also contemplating basic Bessemer furnaces, and, following trials in the United States, the use of oxygen in the open-hearth furnaces. It thereby demonstrated a greater willingness than the industry at large to consider alternatives to the open-hearth, but some of its later innovations were not entirely success-ful. The attractions of the Bessemer and the oxygen-assisted processes were in the speed of operations rather than in the cost of their steel. It was already becoming apparent that the appetite of the hot strip mill was almost insatiable, and output was more important than cost.

The construction of the mills, and of the Trostre works, approved as late as June 1947, proceeded along a comparatively smooth and uninterrupted course in marked contrast to the years of indecision which had gone before.[24] Minor civil engineering difficulties were encountered with old coal workings abandoned as long ago as 1906, but the contrast with the problems which had been experienced at Ebbw Vale in the 1930s could scarcely be more stark. The scheme was in operation by mid-1951 at a total cost of £73 million. Typical levels of consumption and output when the works was in full operation were as listed in Table 4. The most important deviation between the actual and the planned was an 8 per cent shortfall in the amount of foreign

Table 4
EARLY OPERATING EXPERIENCE AT PORT TALBOT
(000 tons week)

Coal to coke ovens	19·8	Pig iron produced	15·8
Coke produced	14·4	Ingots produced	23·8
Own coke used	14·6	Slab mill rolled (ingots)	27·2
Purchased coke used	2·5	Hot strip	17·7
Home ore used	10·0	Sheets and plates	2·8
Foreign ore used	24·2	Cold reduction mill	4·7

Source: Iron and Coal Trades Review 'Steel Company of Wales' (special issue)

ore used. This had resulted from the higher-than-anticipated cost of foreign ore boosted by the freight rates which followed the outbreak of the Korean War, and the continued shortage of coal in Europe.[25] They were compounded in this case by the inadequacy of the ore dock which, being restricted to carriers of 6,500 tons, limited the range of foreign ore fields which could be tapped. Proposals to increase the size of ship which could be handled to 12,000 tons were already being mooted in 1951, but these were not even firm plans. Accordingly, the

D

consumption of the lower-grade home ores was a third higher than anticipated. These were brought from Oxfordshire, which dramatised one situational defect of the location—the lack of local ore.

An immediate effect of this high tonnage of home ore was to increase the demand for coke. This in turn complicated the operations at the coke ovens, as the company was compelled to extend its range of coal sources to at least fifty. A final change from the plan was a lower level of output in the Port Talbot melting shop. This was caused by the difficulties of obtaining sufficient scrap in that scrap-deficit region but also by the fact that the yield of better-quality steels from the oil-fired furnaces in the Margam shops was higher than expected: a combination of trading and technical factors. Nevertheless, for the most part the plan had been put into operation, but in November 1952 a second plan was announced as the full potential of this combination of site and technology was uncovered, and as the level of demand for sheets continued to grow: two factors which were not foreseen in 1945 or in 1947.

The decision to locate this integrated tinplate complex at Port Talbot and Trostre rather than elsewhere in Britain illustrates clearly the nature of major investment decisions in a mature industrial economy. The primary need was to solve the presently existing set of problems, for these were sufficient in themselves. It was hoped that this solution would not put the industry in a locational strait-jacket which could not be adjusted to meet different needs in the future. But, in the final analysis, the future—because it is unknown—must be left to take care of itself. In the solution of this particular set of locational problems an important assumption was that the manufacture of tinplate should be in South Wales, and on that basis alone locations in England and Scotland were excluded on principle. Also, for employment reasons the investment had to be located west of Bridgend. There can be no doubt that these two needs were satisfied by the decision which was taken.

The need to locate in that comparatively remote scrap-deficit area was almost sufficient to ensure that an integrated works was required. The alternatives would have been to rely upon imported scrap, or to build two or more semi-continuous cold metal works with lower individual outputs. Some of these would need to be located closer to the areas of scrap supply. The first solution was excluded on the ground of the high cost of imported scrap, and the second would have failed to satisfy the labour requirements of West Wales. The choice of an integrated operation on a greenfield site would have extended the period of construction and increased the capital costs. These obstacles could be overcome through the selection of an existing works which had adequate primary departments, and which was capable of receiving the new space-consuming mills. The only location in Britain which could approach the satisfaction of all these requirements was Port Talbot.

It is clear that no one of these factors in isolation was *sufficient* to decide the issue, but taken together they represented a powerful combination of *necessary* conditions. However, Port Talbot was only the best compromise solution for the existing set of problems. There is no evidence which would suggest that it was considered an ideal solution, even at that time, but neither was there any pretence that anything other than a possible solution was being sought. All decisions which involve a conflict of interests, and which are taken by agreement, result in compromise, and the locational decision in general and the Port Talbot decision in particular were no exception. The alternative is to raise one of the conflicting elements to a position of primacy and to impose a solution on that basis. Even so, there is potential conflict between long-term and short-term interests, and in a changing world what starts out as an ideal solution is quickly compromised. The selection of maximum profitability as the sole measure of merit is an arbitrary selection, and is certainly inappropriate as a measure of deviations from the ideal in locational decisions in post-war industrial Britain.[26]

Clydeside rejected

The response of the Scottish industry to the revised Clydeside proposals was to ignore them. In this respect management and unions acted in common accord. The view of the Iron & Steel Trades Confederation was that it was doubtful whether 'such a diversion of labour and materials and the social upheaval could be contemplated' in the existing state of the country, and suggested that blast furnaces should be built again at Glengarnock and *de novo* at Motherwell.[27] The social argument had been used to keep the hot strip mill and the tinplate mills in West Wales; in Scotland it was also used to keep things as they were.

Some people still hoped for change. Mr William Stewart, a former secretary and director of Colvilles, in an address to the Glasgow Fabian Society expressed the view that the private industry's policy of sticking to old locations 'must eventually result in the decline of the industry through its inability to meet the competition of modern, well-sited, highly integrated plants in other districts'.[28] He wanted a nationalised industry to build five blast furnaces, coke ovens, melting shop and mills at Erskine to produce 1·0 million tons of foundry and pig iron and 0·4 million tons of rolled steel. In 1948, Mr G. Strauss affirmed that the issue was still under 'active consideration' and that the Government expected a final recommendation before the end of the year.[29]

The final recommendation issued by Colvilles was that 'on economic grounds the scheme could not be justified', and in practice the company was already attacking its many problems within its own formalised strategy of limited locational change.[30] To the outsider the Clydeside scheme had, and still has, great appeal in terms of grandeur and neatness, but it is clear that none of the people directly involved were anxious to face the upheaval that it would have created. Such absolute locational change as did occur took the form of the closure of the Blochairn works in 1952, by which time extra capacity had been installed elsewhere. This closure had been foretold in the 1946 Report.

Elsewhere, the company increased the capacity of the ore dock at Rothesay, and built a third blast furnace at Clyde Iron. Larger steel furnaces of up to 350 tons were installed at Clydebridge and some at Lanarkshire Steel were enlarged to 150 tons. A £2 million melting shop was built at Dalzell and oil-firing was introduced both there and at Glengarnock. Finally, as a harbinger of future developments, 300 acres of land were bought adjoining the Dalzell and Lanarkshire Steel works. In this variety of ways output was raised to 1·9 million tons by 1949, which was approximately 20 per cent more than in 1939.

The heavy dependence of the company upon scrap metal operations was amply demonstrated in 1951 and 1952 when, with the sudden removal of German scrap from the international market, output fell below 1·7 million tons as the No 1 melting shop at Clydebridge and four of the Dalzell furnaces were temporarily closed. The obvious solution was to increase even further the output of pig iron at Clyde Iron. Iron had been made on that site since 1786, but although the area had been extended over the years to more than 150 acres, the Fullerton Road separated the coke ovens from the ironworks and the works was encroached upon by railways, other roads, and the river Clyde. It would have been possible to squeeze in a fourth blast furnace in line with the existing three (but at the cost of increased congestion), or possibly to enlarge the existing furnaces. Instead, the company resorted to the use of 'high top' pressure, which was a new departure for the British industry. Such technical adaptations had been made in the United States and had resulted in higher levels of output, but the Colvilles management approached the development with only cautious optimism, and after two years of operation was prepared to say only that there was no evidence to suggest that the experiment had failed.[31]

Nevertheless, the experiment is of interest in that it exhibits the imprecise way in which development takes place in this industry; there is only an approximation to the ideal of a controlled experiment. The similarities between this type of experiment and locational experiments are so apparent as not to need emphasis. In both cases the area of uncertainty would appear to be of comparable magnitude. From Colville's point of view it was of considerable importance that the new technology could be installed quickly and cheaply. By 1950 the output of pig iron had been raised by 20 per cent to 0·6 million tons, which was three times the level of output in 1939.

The major aim of the 1946 Report was not accomplished, but the subsidiary aims of works closure, plant specialisation, fuel saving, and greater use of hot metal, had been observed and partly realised. There had been a far-reaching transformation in the operations of the company between 1939 and 1949, but by that latter year the operational limits imposed by the existing framework of the works were being reached.[32] The only further addition was that of sixty-eight new coke ovens at Clyde Iron, which came on stream in 1953 and increased the output of coke by over a third.

Northamptonshire superseded

The major distinction between the proposed works at Port Talbot and on Clydeside and that which was proposed for Northamptonshire was that the first two would be more than matched by works closures elsewhere, whereas the third works was to be a net addition. A reduction in the total number of works was an important theme in the 1946 Report, and it is consequently surprising that the alternative policy of rapid expansion at existing works on the East Midlands ore fields was not preferred. The one which was proposed was an improvement on the two which were called for by *The Economist*, but in retrospect the failure of the industry to implement this part of the Report was one of its happier accomplishments.[33]

If the new works was to be built it was reputedly to have been a joint venture of the United Steel Companies and Stewarts & Lloyds. Both companies had proved their ability to operate a number of widely separated works, and there was a tradition of co-operation between them, but that had never extended to the joint operation of a single works. Such a venture would have been a new departure for the British industry, but could not be entirely discounted on that basis alone. Other important factors which diminished the likelihood of this works being built were that the value of the finished product, billets, was low and neither company was heavily committed to that sector of the steel trade. Furthermore, the results of the operation of the Industry Fund were such as to minimise the financial inducements to undertake new and expensive ventures on the home ore fields.

The most important obstacle to the creation of the new works was none of these factors but the fact that both companies were fully committed to improving the operations which they already owned. Not only was this policy a low-cost policy, but it could be implemented quickly. The explanation for the failure of the Northamptonshire works to materialise is therefore not to be sought in an assessment of the intrinsic merits of the scheme but in the fact that in any set of alternative possible actions some will be omitted on comparative grounds alone.

In his last annual address to shareholders (1945) Sir Alan Macdiarmid revealed that Stewarts & Lloyds had already received approval for six development projects. These included an open-hearth shop and additional tube mill at both Corby and Clydesdale, alterations to the Bilston steelworks, and minor adjustments to the Newport tube works and Scottish tube mills. Along with proposals for additional capacity at Stanton for iron pipes, nothing was omitted. This in itself was significant in that Sir Alan had in the 1920s proved himself capable of breaking out of a constricting situation, but was now following a policy of universal betterment and repair, which was supposedly antithetical to the ethos of the Report. By 1947 the company had agreed with an air of reluctance tinged with altruism to make provision to roll 0·4 million tons of billets, at Corby, 'as a contribution to the national shortage of semi-finished steel'.[34] This was not what the 1946 Report had promised, but it was a more tidy arrangement, and inasmuch as it was cheaper was to be welcomed.

The actions of Stewarts & Lloyds raised the output of steel at Clydesdale, brought the operations at Bilston near to their long-planned capacity of 0·17 million ingot tons, and increased the output at Corby by 60 per cent to 0·8 million ingot tons. This last achievement, which was in general agreement with the background thinking of the 1946 Report, was partly accomplished by the opening of an open-hearth melting shop in 1950. The output of pig iron for the Bessemer shop was increased by the addition of a second sinter strand. The open-hearth shop provided an outlet for the scrap arising in the works and for the enlarged volume of coke-oven gas now available. The extension of the

Corby coke-ovens was an attempt to circumvent the effects of the variations in the quality of purchased coke, but in so doing the number of coals used was increased, as it had been at Port Talbot. In 1939 coal had been obtained from thirty-four collieries on the Silkstone seam and in South Wales roughly in the proportion of three to one. In the late 1940s the proportions were the same but the number of collieries had been increased to sixty-five.[35]

The failure of the United Steel Companies to interest themselves in the proposed Northamptonshire works can be similarly explained in terms of their preoccupation with a necessary policy of modernisation and betterment at their existing works. The enacting of this policy clearly illustrates the consequential increase in output as well as reduction in unit costs, and to the extent that the industry was looking for an overall increase in output of only 37 per cent it is a further indication of why there was little inducement to build a greenfield works. If the closure of some other works could be guaranteed, the inducement would have been greater, but no such guarantee could be given.

The main steelmaking need at Appleby-Frodingham was to find an alternative source of ingots to the obsolete four-furnace Frodingham melting shop, whose function had been to supply the section mills of the same name. During the war a seventh furnace had been built in the Appleby shop in order to make rimming steels for Steel, Peech & Tozer.[36] It was possible that that furnace would revert to the Scunthorpe works, in which case an eighth furnace would suffice for existing needs. Such a scheme, however, would fail to provide any basis for future expansion. The site of the Frodingham melting shop was needed for an extension to the Frodingham mill building, so the pre-war intention to build a new melting shop in South Works, parallel to the blast furnaces, was reactivated and completed in November 1947. The cost was £1·3 million, and included two 300-ton furnaces, and the foundation of two more: a clear indication of future expansion.

In comparison the expenditure of £2·3 million on the modifications to the section mill seems high. It was again, however, an indication of how much a totally new works would have cost, because the decision to rebuild the mill *in situ* seems to have been taken in the realisation of the high cost of relocating the extensive finishing banks installed in 1936–7.[37] The scheme is also a further illustration of the gradual, piecemeal way in which development and modernisation take place in this industry.

In the ironworks the key to future progress was in the rapid developments in sintering. An extension of the sinter plant was essential if the effects of deteriorating local ores, marked by an increase in their sulphur content, and the effects of higher sulphur coke were to be avoided. A major breakthrough was obtained when it was realised that if the ore fines *and* the sinter fines were screened, and returned to the sinter plant, it would be possible to reduce the coke rate by 8 per cent and to increase the output of the existing blast furnaces by 20 per cent. Consequently, in 1949, the planned addition of two extra blast furnaces at South Works was deferred.

It should again be stressed that these developments consisted of pioneering work, and that it was still not known how far the use of sinter could be extended. In practice, with the additional aid of an extra battery of coke ovens, the level of desulphurising was raised from 50 per cent to 80 per cent. This improved furnace burden required a smaller slag volume, which in turn reduced the coke consumption, which again reduced the sulphur level and resulted in higher output. In 1951 the original intention to extend blast furnace capacity at South Works was reactivated together with an extension of ore preparation and sintering. In June 1952 the first 100 per cent sinter burden was used with success, and the sinter plant, rather than being considered an adjunct, was now being considered 'as equally important as the blast furnace itself'.[38]

Writing of these developments in 1955, Mr G. D. Elliot, the iron-works manager, emphasised the stimulus effects of the indifferent raw materials, and the gradual manner in which 'false theories and many cherished illusions' had had to be set aside.[39] By 1953 the works was producing more than 1 million tons of pig iron and steel, and it was clear that the pig iron would soon be obtainable from four blast furnaces only. Developments such as these could not have been foreseen in 1945, but when extended on a national scale they explain why it was possible for the output of pig iron to increase at the same time as the number of blast furnaces was declining: the clearest example of diverging trends in the geography of products and the geography of fixed investment.

The board of the United Steel Companies was also preoccupied with modernisation at its other three major branches. By 1953 the output at Steel, Peech & Tozer had been raised to 0·8 million tons and that at both Stocksbridge and Workington to almost 0·3 million tons without any major changes being made to the furnaces. At Templeborough, for example, the tapping capacity of the furnaces was raised from sixty to ninety tons, but limitations of crane capacity limited them to eighty tons. On the other hand, important changes in all the mills were undertaken.

At Steel, Peech & Tozer the new primary mill had an initial capacity of 0·7 million tons and most developments at the works were designed either to realise that potential or, especially in the railway products mills at the Ickles end of the works, to raise the quality and quantity of products. By 1949 the old primary mill had been installed at Workington where it could handle the smaller throughput and the lighter ingots. In this way a niche in the total industry structure was obtained for both works. The company intended also to build a Sendzimir stainless sheet mill at Stocksbridge, but the application to the Ministry of Supply to obtain such a mill from the United States coincided with a similar application from Firth-Vickers Stainless. In view of the size of the market and the restrictions upon dollar spendings, in which field Port Talbot had been given priorities, the two companies agreed to share facilities at Shepcote Lane at Tinsley in Sheffield on a 33:66 basis (Fox: Firth-Vickers). Fox's share would be provided with steel from Stocksbridge whither the sheet in the form of coil would be returned for finishing. This arrangement involved a round trip of about eighteen miles, which was by no means prohibitive in view of the value of the product. At Stocksbridge itself the capacity of the primary mill was increased by 50,000 tons per annum, but the desire to install a continuous rod and bar mill was deferred, partly through lack of space.

In ways such as these the Northamptonshire project, like the Clydeside project, was forgotten. It was not that the companies lacked vision, but that their separate views of what should be done did not coincide with those of the compilers of the 1946 Report. In due course the desirability of keeping Corby and Scunthorpe was to be questioned, but the Clydeside proposals were to be resurrected in an even larger form and then reinterred. Meanwhile, the industry laboured to satisfy by any means the high level of demand: strategy was overwhelmed by tactics.

Dorman Long and Consett Iron: a Contrast in Opportunities

In 1945 Dorman Long produced 1·20 million ingot tons from its four works situated at sea-level on the south bank of the river Tees. Consett Iron produced less than 0·4 million ingot tons from its single works situated approximately 750 feet above sea-level, twenty-two miles south of the river Tyne. In spite of the fact that both companies were 'heavy steel' producers it would be hard to imagine a greater contrast in the total decision environment of the two boards of directors.

Dorman Long

The major itemised proposals for Dorman Long in the 1946 Report included a new open-hearth melting shop and the nation's first universal beam mill. Both were to be built on the undeveloped Lackenby site situated between the Cleveland and Redcar works. In due course both were built, but neither scheme was completed within the seven-year period to which the Report referred. The reasons for the delay were associated with a shortage of dollars for the mill equipment, and with the company's first concern to revitalise its ore supply and ironmaking facilities.

When seen from the outside the sequence of the post-war developments at Dorman Long appears more logical than at any other company. It started with the reorganisation of the ore supplies and progressed through ore preparation, blast furnaces, steel furnaces, and eventually the rolling mills. Such a straight-line progress is appealing in its simplicity, but it should be remembered that when modernising an integrated industry the logical place to start is either at the point of tightest operational constriction, or at the place of quickest return. In the case of Dorman Long the reorganisation of the ore arrangements would relieve a bottleneck and could be quickly completed.

The South Bank wharf at the Cleveland works was developed to receive 15,000-ton ore carriers. Ore preparation and storage facilities to handle up to 1·5 million tons of foreign ore and 0·5 million tons of Cleveland ore were set out in the extensive area behind the wharf. From this central point the existing blast furnaces at Cleveland works could be supplied by conveyor, and the ironworks at Acklam and Redcar could be reached using the mixed assortment of wagons used in bringing ore from the mines in the Cleveland field. All the ores were crushed and the screened ore fines were sent to the 8,000-tons-per-week sinter plant. These arrangements were in accordance with the best practice of the time, and were aimed at reducing the coke rate and at raising the output of the ironworks already operating at the three integrated works.

The beneficial effects of the use of a 40 per cent sinter charge on the Redcar and Bessemer (Cleveland works) blast furnaces were immediately apparent. The evidence is that it boosted production on Bessemer No 5 by up to 37 per cent and on Redcar No 1 by 14 per cent. The coke rate was reduced by 17 per cent and 9 per cent respectively.[40] In the light of this evidence it is not surprising that the second stage of the development programme, announced in 1949, included a second sinter strand to double the installed capacity. In 1947 it had been decided to resurrect the Clay Lane ironworks, the first stage of which was to be two 27-foot-diameter furnaces at an *estimated* cost of £4,640,782. On that 48-acre part of the Cleveland works it was said that there was room for five or six such furnaces, but the subsequent improvements in blast furnace technology were such that only three were built. These three eventually replaced all the old furnaces at the same time as the company increased its pig iron output by 75 per cent (1945–65).

Meanwhile, minor modifications, principally the use of oil-firing, were made to the existing steel furnaces, until the time when the Lackenby shop should be built. The firm plans for the shop, which started production in September 1953, appeared in 1949 and represented the theoretical best at this critical stage in post-war developments. It could not be known at the time that they also represented the culminating point in the long development of the conventional hot metal open-hearth process, not only for Tees-side, but for Britain as a whole.

The plan included six 360-ton tilting furnaces in a shop to be built diagonally across the virgin 680-acre Lackenby site. This alignment was necessary because of the great length of this building and of the proposed beam mill which was to be built alongside on a parallel axis. The whole scheme was designed to facilitate traffic movement by rail. This was not quite the last major development to be built round a rail network, but it again represented the culminating point in the design of such schemes. There were four sets of reception sidings with a total capacity of 2,000 wagons, which were situated separately from the 700-wagon-capacity sorting sidings. These were divided into individual sections for scrap, ore, and furnace materials. The sidings for assembling the hot ingots for Cleveland and Redcar and the cold ingots for the Acklam and Britannia works were again separate. The whole arrangement was in marked contrast to the evolved layout at the adjacent Cleveland works, and demonstrated the operational advantages which could be derived from new developments on large and unencumbered sites. The major weakness was in the comparatively remote situation of this shop from the burgeoning Clay Lane ironworks, from which it obtained its metal.

By mid-1954 five furnaces were operating on a total hot metal:cold metal ratio of 3:1 and were each producing 18,500 ingot tons per month. The Britannia works melting shop had been closed in 1953 along with some furnaces at the Cleveland works, but the output of the company had been raised to 1·85 million ingot tons. The completion of

Stage II therefore marked a major step in the rationalisation of the company's operations. It was in full accordance with the philosophy of the 1946 Report in that it concentrated production in large units, increased the use of hot metal, and reduced the consumption of fuel. As a foreign-ore user it was admirably located at a truly coastal location. Nevertheless, nine years after the appearance of the Report, and at least eleven years from the first publication of the company's intentions, the awaited beam mill was still only at the construction stage; Lackenby was not built in a day.

Consett Iron

The last attempt to dislodge Consett Iron from its hill-top location and to develop on the banks of the river Tyne failed in 1934.[41] The company opened a rolling mill at Jarrow in 1940, but was otherwise free to focus its talents and energies upon the works at Consett. Outsiders were unanimous in their expression of horror at the Consett site conditions, but the post-war developments were characterised by internal contempt for these views and an almost heroic dismissal of the material obstacles which threatened to hinder their progress.

The elevated terrace site, honeycombed with abandoned and flooded nineteenth-century coal workings, contained two blast furnaces, coke ovens, an open-hearth melting shop, a plate mill, and a bloom and billet mill (see Fig 7). It was crossed by one major and one minor public road and by the Consett branch of the LNER. There can be little doubt that had the compilers of the 1946 Report been given an entirely free hand they would have recommended no more than a short-term holding operation at the works. As it was, they suggested only that the production of billets would cease in accordance with a policy of co-operation and co-ordination with South Durham and Dorman Long, the aim of which was to build a new centre for billet production, probably at Cargo Fleet. Consett Iron was to concentrate on plate production, and the intention to raise output to 0·6 million ingot tons, plus 0·5 million tons of pig iron, was accepted.

One of the blast furnaces (No 2) had been built in 1943, and it was the intention to scrap the other (No 8) after a second new furnace had been built along the same line and between the new and the old. This second furnace was completed with great difficulty by October 1947, and by the spring of the following year was vying with the new Margam furnace for British and European output records. By 1950, however, the company had decided to rebuild rather than to scrap No 8 furnace,

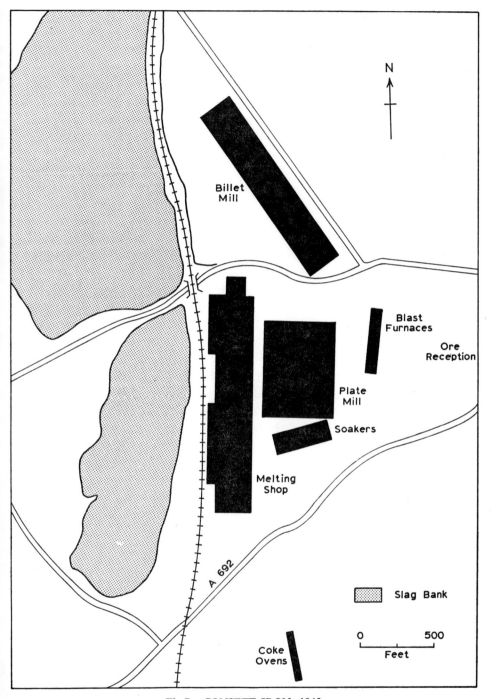

Fig 7. CONSETT IRON, 1945

intending it to act, firstly, as an immediate stand-by for the two new furnaces and, secondly, as *the basis for future expansion* to 0·725 million tons per annum. This was a clear modification of the 1946 Report.

Elsewhere in the works a power station and a second battery of coke ovens were built, and the ten open-hearth furnaces were upgraded from 70 tons to 150 tons tapping capacity. With improved firing and a higher percentage of hot metal, steelmaking capacity was raised to the target level of 0·6 million tons by 1950.

Impressive as this was, the major difficulties were associated with the newly proposed slab, bloom and billet mill to replace units of fifty and twenty-five years' usage. The approval of this scheme was one of the last acts of the Iron & Steel Board before it was disbanded in October 1948. It represented a major amendment to the 1946 Report and was a tacit admission that the looked-for inter-company co-operation would not be forthcoming.

In spite of the size of the Consett site (650 acres) space was at a premium because of the earlier decision to rebuild the blast furnaces in the middle of the works on the line established in 1870. The area to the east of that line was occupied by stock yards and services, and the area to the west by the other production departments and offices. The company decided that 'the only reasonable site for the mill, in so difficult a hilly district, was on the filled-in area to the west'.[42]

This 'reasonable' site was the slag bank which had been built over the previous eighty years, and which lay on the west side of the railway line, which at that time still carried passenger trains as well as freight. The line had been built on an embankment, but the long history of tipping had converted its course into a 'cutting'. The slag bank was a mixture of broken brick, flue dust, and slag which varied in size from crushed material to slag balls of seven-foot diameter. In some areas molten slag had been tipped to form an almost solid rock with cleavage planes inclined at about 40 degrees. The fill varied in depth from 3 to 180 feet.

It was decided to build the 1,350-foot-long building on an east–west axis crossing over the railway. To do this the line, which had to be kept in operation, was placed 'underground' and the floor level of the mill raised above train level. In consequence, the foundations of the supporting stanchions had to be taken down to a level of thirty-five feet below the level of the line, or eighty feet below the level of the mill floor. There were local difficulties in the form of underground fires in previously dumped combustible material, but the project was completed in 1952. Compared with the ease of construction at other works, the programme was exceedingly complex, and suggests that at Consett there is a special meaning to the word 'reasonable' (see page 167).

Once the company had initiated and largely completed its internal development programme it turned its attention to the iron ore supply. It was decided to concentrate all ore imports at the Tyne Dock, twenty-two miles away, where facilities were provided to receive carriers of 33,000 tons. In this way a works with an indifferent total situation was provided with the most efficient ore dock in the country. The annual capacity of this dock was at least 1·2 million tons, which was more than double the amount which had been brought from the old facilities on the Tyne and Wear combined. Once it had been decided to modernise these arrangements it was difficult to install a smaller capacity, with the result that the transformation of this initial bottleneck into a wide-open door set up reverberations through the whole system. In the future there would be a temptation to use this capacity to a maximum, which implied an increase in pig iron production, which in turn implied, in the isolated situation of the works, an increase in steel output.

The guiding principle of the scheme was to provide the quickest turn-around for the ships, but because the dock worked on two shifts and the railways on three, and because the trains had to be fitted in with local railway traffic, a buffer stock of up to 120,000 tons capacity was provided behind the quay. Thirty special 56-ton wagons with vacuum brakes and power-operated side-discharge doors were provided to replace the 600 hopper wagons which had previously been in use. Each train of nine wagons would move 500 tons at a time.[43] There were three trains in all, each headed by two diesel locomotives capable of moving the train from rest on the gradients of up to 1:35 which were met on the route to Consett. With a journey based on 1 hour 45 minutes to Consett, 15 minutes at Consett, and 1 hour 15 minutes back to the Tyne Dock the aim was to move fourteen trains each day.

The whole of the Consett Iron saga illustrates the importance of perspective as a formative factor in locational development. It also shows, when compared with the Port Talbot scheme, that physical problems of site, even in this extreme case, were more tractable than the problems of company co-operation. Permission to build the billet mill was not sought until 1948, by which time South Durham and Dorman Long were already fully committed to their own developments, and the mill was operational in less than four years. Once the decision had been taken to stay at Consett the range of policies was restricted to stagnation or growth. A policy of minimal modernisation would have produced some growth, but this was compounded in this case by a refusal to accept the outside view that the company should leave the billet trade, and the individual developments had a cumulative effect. The local situational defects of iron ore supply were minimised but could not be entirely eliminated. In general terms, as the only English works using exclusively foreign ore, the operation benefited from the cost-distorting effects of the Industry Fund. The total cost of the development up to 1952 was about £16 million, of which £9 million was spent in the last two years. In 1952 the profits of the company, after depreciation, were £1·4 million, which compared with £5·3 million for Dorman Long.

John Summers: an Example of Backwards-Integration

Experience in Britain and elsewhere shows that the starting-point for any individual development programme can be at any position in the chain of integrated stages between the processing of raw materials at one end and the final rolling and cutting of finished steel at the other. The post-war developments at Dorman Long, it has been shown, started at the raw material end and worked forwards. In contrast, John Summers at Shotton followed their traditional course of starting with mills and integrating backwards to the ingot and pig iron stages.

Britain's second hot strip mill had been grafted on to the cold metal operations at Shotton in 1937–9. The original development scheme had included the provision of a new melting shop to replace the two which had been built in 1904 and 1917, and permission to build this shop, sought in 1945, was granted in May 1946. The 1946 Report, published in the same month, indicated that the company intended also to build an ironworks. This announcement was greeted with surprise, and subsequent criticism,[44] but the internal evidence for any such decision having been firmly taken is slight. Furthermore, the Report itself suggested that a higher-than-average proportion of scrap metal would be used at the works. Certainly, the original 1936 scheme had envisaged a cold metal operation, with the necessary supplementary supply of cold pig iron being brought from Shelton. Summers had purchased that small West Midlands works in 1920 in order to obtain some control over that material supply, but pig iron was still brought by sea from Workington as well.

The problem at Shotton was that the capacity of the individual departments no longer balanced each other. The melting shops had a maximum capacity of 0.4 million ingot tons and the new shop was designed to produce a net addition of 0·15 million ingot tons. The

Page 65: *Spencer Works, Llanwern: the only new integrated works in fifty years of radical industrial change*

Page 66: *Morphological contrast: Cleveland Works* (above) *and Lackenby Works* (below)

capacity of the slab mill was 0·6 million tons, but experience with the total mill since 1939 had indicated that the finishing stands could handle up to 1·0 million tons. In consequence there was considerable inducement to uprate the slab mill, and to a lesser extent the output of the melting shop. The alternative was to obtain a guaranteed supply of slabs and ingots from elsewhere. Indeed, in the years up to 1950 the company was given priority use of imported American slabs and ingots.

It has already been seen that the mills at Ebbw Vale and East Moors were partly fed with Lincolnshire slabs, but there were two obstacles in the way of such a policy being used at Shotton. Firstly, a higher proportion of the output of the Shotton mill was sold in an uncoated form, and steel quality was therefore a more important consideration than elsewhere. Attempts had been made, apparently without success, to produce slabs for the Shotton mills at Appleby-Frodingham, but these had been discontinued. Perhaps a firmer commitment by United Steel would have solved the problem, but, as it was, that company restricted its involvement to an injection of cash into the Shotton scheme by means of extending its ordinary share holding in the smaller company. The second obstacle was, of course, that whereas common ownership tied the Lincolnshire works of Richard Thomas and Guest Keen to their South Wales operations, Summers lacked that particular strength through diversity. It would seem, therefore, that the conclusion of the debate at Shotton was that the maximum benefit of the finishing mill could be obtained only by the construction of an ironworks on the works. This would enable the new melting shop to operate the hot metal process, and in this way the capacity of the works would be raised to 1·0 million tons. Permission to build the ironworks was sought and granted in the year 1947–8.

Any internal anxieties that there might have been about the scheme, and all external criticism, centred on the issue of situation, because, in terms of site, conditions at Shotton works came closer to the ideal than at any other in Britain. The area available for development was virtually unlimited and entirely free of interruptions. The new ironworks eventually covered 280 acres. Even in terms of situation Shotton was well placed with regard to the markets when compared with most British works, so the criticisms related to raw material assembly costs. The question of scrap availability was not greatly altered by the proposed change in technology, because a 25 per cent scrap charge would still be required for the new shop, and scrap and cold pig iron would be used in the 1917 shop. Even so, the works was better situated than Port

E

Talbot. The main problems were quite clearly those of coal for the coke ovens and, more especially, ore for the blast furnaces.

The first authorisation was for one blast furnace and one battery of coke ovens, which came into operation in 1952. By that date, however, a second furnace and set of coke ovens were already under construction. This doubling-up of facilities was probably intended from the start, because once the decision had been taken to use hot metal on such a large scale it would have been hazardous to operate with only one furnace.[45] Had it been possible to charge the single furnace, the largest yet built outside the United States, exclusively with foreign ore, an annual output of 0·37 million tons would have been feasible. As it was, a minimum proportion of 25 per cent of the charge was Oxfordshire ore, and this kept the output below 0·3 million tons.

In order to supply this new ironworks a rail haul from the Bidston dock at Birkenhead employing 120 company-owned 50-ton-capacity wagons was introduced, because Shotton was yet another example of a works situated on tidal water which could not be provided with adjacent docking facilities. The major operational problem of the new scheme was that the slow-moving ore trains had to cross the commuter lines on the Wirral, resulting in a twice-daily interruption to the ore traffic. The similarities with the Consett scheme were pronounced, but at Shotton both the journey times and unloading period (an amazing six minutes) were shorter. Compared with Ebbw Vale where the round trip to Newport took thirty-six hours, twenty-six of which were spent in the works itself, the scheme was admirable. Arguably, comparisons should be made with Dorman Long and Port Talbot rather than with Consett Iron and Ebbw Vale.

The total Shotton development demonstrates the momentum which is built up once a works has come into being. As at Port Talbot, no pretence was ever made that the end result represented a theoretically ideal solution. Nevertheless, there was the conviction that, given the pattern of ownership in the industry and the persistent high level of demand, and given the size of capital already invested at Shotton and the level of current expenditure possible, the Shotton response was the best practical solution. The provision of something better would have required a major restructuring of the industry. This development, like the others, took place at the time of political debate over ownership of the industry, but the protagonists of nationalisation had themselves thought no further than the act itself. No one argued that the Shotton scheme should be delayed until that larger argument had been settled. In such ways tomorrow's problems are created by the solution of today's.

The New Structure: an Evolved Form of the Old

The preceding case studies, which relate to the activities of the largest companies, demonstrate four interacting principal points. Firstly, the traumatic 1920s had established an ingrained habit of caution within the industry which the brief years of prosperity in the 1930s had been unable to dispel. So it was that when the companies came to assess the future course of demand they chose conservative estimates, which they matched with low-cost development policies of individual betterment and repair. If errors were to be made they would be errors of omission rather than of commission; it was a fail-safe policy designed to minimise the visible cost penalties. Reporting financial losses produces a maximum of discontent among shareholders and feelings of insecurity among management, but any level of profits will satisfy some shareholders and assuage the self-doubt of some managers. When profits are increasing only the hyper-critical will ask whether they might not be even higher.

Secondly, within this general atmosphere of caution the industry followed a set of policies which were designed to keep all those who wished in business. This ensured that any radical restructuring of the industry could be achieved only on a voluntary basis. The limited likelihood of such co-operation being realised had been demonstrated in the years which led up to the rebuilding of Ebbw Vale, and even with men of greater willingness to compromise than Sir William Firth the birth of the Steel Company of Wales had been a long and protracted affair. Sir William had been obliged to prepare his own way by buying obsolete capacity to ensure its closure, and even his conciliatory successor, Sir Ernest Lever, was driven to threatening the remaining tinplate makers with unilateral action if needs be. The tinplate companies had all been small compared with the steel companies which emerged from World War II, and many had been making operational losses, and a policy of take-over followed by closure would have been an expensive undertaking in the prosperous years of the late 1940s.

Thirdly, the large companies were all convinced that the important thing was to improve the profitability of their existing domains, and they restricted their co-operation to not interfering with each other. For example, the chairman of South Durham, whose West Hartlepool works was to be scheduled for closure in the Report, wrote encouragingly of the benefits to the steel-consuming industries at home and abroad which would follow careful planning and joint operation or amalgamation of

works. In the same document, however, he revealed that the directors
had already sanctioned 'considerable capital expenditure for modernisation of plant . . . All these schemes' he added 'are already well in hand'.[46]
Such sanctions and actions were hardly conducive to co-operation on a
large scale.

Each citadel of decision-making granted its own distinctive view of
the total environment. The leaders of the industry were prepared to
rationalise, but only within their own boundaries. Thus it was that the
only melting shops to be closed, Blochairn, Bryngwyn, Landore and
Britannia, belonged to multi-works companies. In each case the closure
followed after the same companies had provided alternative capacity
within their other works. The limited rationalisation of finished steel
which took place was characterised either by consolidation upon other
mills within each group or by the elimination of products which were
not important to that particular company. Similarly, United Steel,
aware of Dorman Long's intentions, deferred its plans to build a wide
beam mill, but did not consider leaving the section trade altogether.
In this case, as in all other cases, there were good and sufficient local
and company reasons for doing as they did, but the impression persists
that the hope was that the greatest benefit to all could be obtained by
each looking after his own. There can be little doubt, for example, that
had the decision-makers for Consett Iron been located on Tees-side
they would not willingly have undertaken the post-war development
scheme at that works. The geography of the industry would have been
poorer but the industry may have been more affluent.

Occasionally the belief that there were certain underlying deterministic reasons perpetuating the existing structure of the industry came to
the surface. In a paper given at Middlesbrough, Sir Andrew McCance,
comparing the British with the American industry, assembled evidence
to support the theory that the small size of British steelworks resulted
from the small size of the total industry.[47] In each country the largest
works produced about 5 per cent of the total output and represented the
peak of a pyramid of works with a very wide base. To break this size
relationship between the works in each system, and between the largest
works and the total output figure, would be to 'court failure'. If this
theory was widely accepted the implication was that in an industry
which was aiming to produce 16·0 million tons the largest works should
not exceed 1·0 million tons. Furthermore, the theory provided justification for not closing the small works, because they were needed to
maintain the wide base of the pyramid.[48]

The fourth point to emerge from the preceding case studies was the important one that with the exception of the strip mills technological progress was also a cautious and slow movement. In this respect there was no discordance between the commercial, organisational and production functions of the industry. There was no major break between the technology of 1939 and that of 1945, so the programmes which had been interrupted by the war could now be completed. The individual works, gradually evolving to a state of improved efficiency and marginally higher output, would each contain ironworks, melting shops and rolling mills which were similarly no more than modified and larger versions of their pre-war counterparts.

These four points applied *a fortiori* to the small companies whose range of strategies did not include the possibility of rationalisation by absorption of smaller companies. Their strategic choice was limited to growth, stagnation or death. Almost without exception they chose limited growth. Within that strategy, however, there was some rationalisation of products, which was best exemplified by the decision at Park Gate to leave the plate trade (foretold in the 1946 Report and accomplished in 1948) and by the decision of the Briton Ferry Steel Company to withdraw from the Port Talbot scheme in 1947 and to develop as an independent billet maker. The fact that the large billet mills included in the 1946 Report were not being built facilitated this latter change, but West Wales was not the best situation for manufacturing billets for the Midlands using a scrap-based technology.

By 1950 William Beardmore was claiming to be the first of the 'major' companies to have completed its post-war development programme, and at Skinningrove a £2 million development scheme, designed to raise output to 0·3 million ingot tons, was well under way.[49] According to the 1946 Report, Skinningrove was destined for no more than a medium-term future life, but the scheme included a new large blast furnace and steel furnace and modifications to the mill.

At Round Oak £3·2 million was borrowed from the Finance Corporation for Industry to raise the capacity from 0·16 million tons to 0·25 million ingot tons and to build an improved bar mill. This scheme has been criticised on the grounds that the rebuilt works could not obtain the maximum benefits of scale, and that its continued existence would deprive other producers of the benefits of maximum loading of plant.[50] The criticisms were based on the realisation that on that congested and divided site a large development would be impossible with the technology which existed at the time. As it was, the company was obliged to install a cross-country mill because the almost four-square site could not contain a longer building with an operationally simpler interior layout.

Nevertheless, as one of the few scrap-metal-based producers in the large scrap-surplus West Midlands, the works had considerable situational advantages in terms of raw material assembly costs and in its proximity to its customers.

Two important developments played into the hands of the large and small producers alike. Firstly, in April 1947 the steel unions accepted the principle of the continuous working week, which resulted in an estimated 10 per cent increase in output for the industry as a whole. Secondly, the use of oil-firing on the open-hearth furnaces resulted in a 25 per cent increase in output for the industry as a whole.[51]

The two developments were partly integrated. On the gas-fired furnaces the weekends had been used for cleaning the flues which quickly became blocked. The cleaner oil-fired furnaces had no need of this recurring period of prolonged down-time, and the furnace lining could be maintained in a red-hot condition. With the old system the prospective gains of the continuous working week would have been largely dissipated.

Oil-firing was introduced at Irlam, Dalzell, Clydebridge, Glengarnock, Templeborough, Normanby Park, Briton Ferry and Cardiff, to name but eight from many, and the higher cost of the oil, measured on a therm-by-therm basis, was offset by higher output from the melting shops and mills as a whole. In many cases similar increases in output could have been obtained by building extra furnaces within the existing shops or, taking the industry as a whole, by building new works. On occasion, as at Park Gate, the choice was limited to a new melting shop or a modification of the existing furnaces.

The new Roundwood mill at Park Gate required higher output from the congested, circumscribed primary departments, but considerable operational difficulties had already been encountered in the reconstruction of the ironworks. An extension to the melting shop was impossible, and the higher output was needed quickly. The oil conversion programme was carried out between July 1947 and March 1948, and resulted in an increased output ranging between 16 per cent and 22 per cent when compared with the older operations. This was marginally lower than the gain for the industry as a whole, but it illustrates the way in which the technological developments of the time freed some operations from the tight constraints of their sites and enabled expansion to take place in what might be considered the third dimension—the technological rather than the spatial frontier.

Repeated across the industry, the adoption of oil-firing shows how it was that although the target for the industry was raised in 1948 to 18 million ingot tons it was still not necessary to build any new works. The Port Talbot scheme had been designed to raise output by 0·5 million tons only. Oil-firing procured, on a conservative estimate, an extra 3·0 million tons for the industry as a whole.

During the years up to 1953, £310 million was spent on development compared with the £168 million estimate of the 1946 Report. The divergence is to be explained in terms of escalating costs, and also by the continuous addition of individually small but collectively large new proposals. These served to more than offset the costs which would have been incurred on Clydeside or in Northamptonshire. The overall achievement was an increase of 48 per cent in ingot production.

All districts shared in this growth, but not in equal proportions (see Fig 8). Two districts, South Wales and Lincolnshire, recorded 70 per cent increases, with most of the extra output coming in the last two years. Major schemes such as those at Port Talbot and Appleby-Frodingham take time, and time was not available in the immediate post-war years. The extra output of the small schemes was invaluable, but served also to compromise the future. On a district basis the smallest proportional gains were in Scotland (32 per cent) and on the North West Coast (23 per cent).

Similarly, at the works level there were important variations in growth rates, with a tendency for the large works to grow the more quickly in absolute and relative terms. Output at Port Talbot was more than doubled, and at Shotton, the eighth largest producer in 1945, a 70 per cent increase was obtained. Elsewhere, the 60 per cent gain at Appleby-Frodingham ensured that it would be the first British works to exceed 1·0 million tons per annum, and Lackenby was clearly a great gain over Britannia. Even if a common growth rate had obtained, the largest absolute gains would have been found at the big works. What was missing was the elimination of the small works such as Skinningrove, Brymbo, Shelton and Bilston.

With the exception of the four works which were closed, locational change was expressed only in comparative and relative terms. The realisation that as much capacity was added in eight years as had been added in the first twenty years of the century is enough to indicate that the relationship between production and location is an elastic one indeed. But that elasticity was matched also in the realm of technology. The industry was not only using the same locations, it was also using the same technology. Of equal significance, it was also operating within the same organisational framework as in the 1930s. In all three cases change

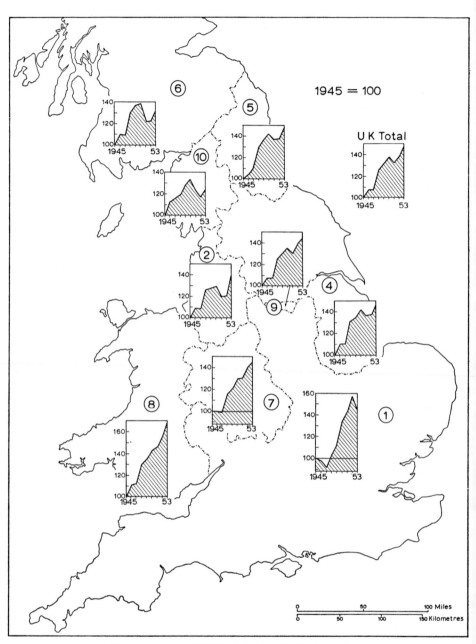

Fig 8. INGOT OUTPUT BY DISTRICT, 1945–53

had been gradual and evolutionary. That had been the desired pattern, which is not to say that it was the needed pattern, even when need is expressed in terms of satisfaction rather than of maximum efficiency. The years 1945–52 were years of evolutionary rather than revolutionary change, the presence of the 1946 Report notwithstanding.

4

The Prosperous Years

IN FEBRUARY 1951 the British iron and steel industry was nationalised. By consolidating control of development into one body this act provided a unique opportunity to carry through a radical reconstruction of the industry's corporate structure, if not of its location, and thereby to break with one of the traditions of the past. In the following October, however, when a general election returned the Conservative party to Westminster, the infant Iron & Steel Corporation of Great Britain was smothered, and procedures for returning the industry to private ownership were put in hand. The opportunity to reconstruct the industry was subsequently lost, not through the decision to denationalise, but through the manner in which the process was carried out. The Denationalisation Bill created a new Iron & Steel Board (ISB) with supervisory powers over development and prices, and a Holdings & Realisation Agency (ISHRA) whose task was to supervise the return to ownership by the private sector as quickly as possible.

The disposal of the industry by ISHRA took the form of public and private sales. Through the offer of the ordinary capital to the public, the largest companies such as United Steel, Summers, Consett and Dorman Long reappeared in their exact pre-nationalisation form, the only important exception being the complete separation of the Steel Company of Wales from Richard Thomas & Baldwins. Through private sales GKN repossessed their works at Cardiff, Scunthorpe and Wrexham, but new initiative came from other engineering companies. Tube Investments took a direct interest in steel production for the first time through the purchase of Round Oak (1954) and Park Gate (1955). Inasmuch as both works were small, and Park Gate was in need of a major capital injection as an alternative to closure, there must have been doubts about the long-term value of the investment, but the persistently high level of demand for steel made the possession of a captive source desirable in the short term. Similarly, the Duport Group purchased two billet making works at Briton Ferry (1956) and Llanelly (1960). Richard Thomas & Baldwins bought the Pontymister works of John Paton & Partridge Jones and the Elba works of Bynea, both independent tinplate producers, and eventually closed them. In this way control of the tinplate industry was finally rationalised into two groups. By March 1957 the process was largely completed and ISHRA was left in possession, firstly, until 1963, of a collection of small concerns such as Bairds & Scottish and Skinningrove which were sold to a consortium of ten companies and, secondly, of Richard Thomas & Baldwins. Although it was the intention to sell this company, the right combination of stock-market conditions, trading conditions and profitability never materialised. The company remained as a state-owned business, but in all other ways was indistinguishable from the other large companies.

There were two alternative methods of denationalisation which might have been taken. Had the Agency been given powers to rationalise the industry prior to denationalisation it could either have retained the small works and ultimately closed them, or, following the practice of the salerooms, have included a small works in the same lot number as a choice item. As it was, the choice items were quickly denationalised. The major obstacle which prevented these alternatives from being given serious consideration was the continued existence of the original boards of directors. These remained in office through both changes of owner-ship, and the evidence is that they were adamantly opposed to such changes. Some small works were offered to the major companies, but they could not be considered tempting morsels. It would appear that Park Gate was offered to United Steel on the pretext that the blast furnaces could be used to supply Steel, Peech & Tozer with pig iron. The furnaces were, however, too small to support hot metal operations on the scale that would have been required if the idea was worthwhile, and the company already had a more efficient larger source of cold pig iron at Scunthorpe. It was the steelmaking capacity and not the ironworks which attracted Tube Investments to Park Gate, and as output was further increased the company was obliged to purchase the Renishaw ironworks in north Derbyshire from the Agency not only to increase its ironmaking capacity but to improve the quality of the pig iron. There was no reason why United Steel should voluntarily add Park Gate to its problems.

It is also said that United Steel was offered the Redbourn Hill works

at Scunthorpe to merge with Appleby-Frodingham, but the temptation
to secure the coke ovens was resisted in view of the condition of the
remainder of the works. On the other hand, United Steel had already
decided that all future growth would be internally generated, and that
growth itself would be a secondary consideration after increased
efficiency and limited further vertical integration.[1] More surprisingly,
no serious attempt was made to merge the producers on the North East
Coast. Perhaps it was realised that the opportunity had already passed
with the revitalisation of West Hartlepool and Consett. Among the
other companies there were no obvious candidates for merger although
United Steel once again took up its shareholding in John Summers
when that company was denationalised in October 1954.

In these ways the brief period of nationalisation passed across the
face of the industry without erasing any of the older scars of time. The
act of denationalisation which could have rejuvenated the industry
served only to restore the *status quo ante*. Nevertheless, without anyone
noticing it, the depressing influence of the inter-war years had been left
behind. All the pre-1945 plans of the companies had been completed,
with the exception of Lackenby, and the leaders of the industry no
longer assumed that demand was about to stabilise at a low level. They
were, in part, prepared to expand their capacity to an undetermined
level, albeit at a steady rate and with caution. In 1952 the Federation
estimated that demand in 1957–8 would reach 21·0 million tons. In
1956 it fixed an estimate for 1962 at 28·0 million, which was marginally
higher than Professor Cole's estimate made in 1947. The estimate was
revised upwards once again in 1957 to 29·0 million ingot tons for 1962.
Individual estimates varied while being in general agreement with those
of the Federation, but these were all superseded by an Iron & Steel
Board estimate in 1959 of 35·0 million tons for 1965.

The change in attitude was, however, gradual. The importance of
this cannot be stressed too heavily. At no point had any single group of
directors been prepared to make a 'quantum jump' in their estimates of
the level of the path that they should take. At all times tomorrow was
seen as a marginally larger version of today. As each year of higher
output was closed, industry spokesmen, full of praise for what had been
accomplished, expressed anxiety for what was about to be. It was as
though the industry had not, even by 1955, come to believe fully in its
own good fortune. By 1956, however, optimism was the dominant
theme and mention was being made of the need to build at least one new
greenfield works. The Federation came to agree with the Board that the
industry should now plan to satisfy peak demands instead of only

trend demands, although the two authorities continued to disagree on the size of the margin. Ironically, this new optimism materialised about the time when the storm clouds began to gather once again around the industry.

The 1958–9 Recession

The 1958–9 recession, which was caused more by customer de-stocking than by a decline in final demand, was a harbinger of things to come. It was felt most strongly in the heavy section trade where demand in the third quarter of 1958 was 33 per cent lower than in the same period of the previous year. At the other extreme, the demand for sheets declined by only 2 per cent which masked a 29 per cent decline in the deliveries from the hand sheet mills and a 5 per cent increase in supply from the continuous mills. Demand for steels generated by the railways and by coal mining declined by 30 per cent, whereas general engineering and the consumer durable industries reduced their total demand by no more than 5–8 per cent. It was clear that the general advance of demand covered a situation in which there would be variations in the rate of advance between growth sectors, coinciding with some sectors which were in absolute decline. The recession simply emphasised the trends which were already apparent.

The impact varied at individual works, company or district level, according to the degree of special dependence on the depressed sectors of demand. During the recession Richard Thomas & Baldwins, for example, finally closed the Cwmfelin, Llanelly and Grovesend sheet works and started to convert the Panteg works to the production of alloy steels. Colvilles closed Dixon's Ironworks, which they had revived in 1954. At Lackenby the long-awaited beam mill came into operation but averaged no more than six shifts each week during its first production year. It seemed an inadequate reward for the company's foresight, but by 1960, when this sector had improved, the heavy section mills at Appleby-Frodingham, Cargo Fleet, and Lanarkshire were being modified to roll these wide-flange beams. This imitation confirmed the need for the original mill, but it did little to help its loading. Among the sheet steel producers the Steel Company of Wales continued to advance from the 2·0 million tons it produced at Port Talbot in 1957, and at Shotton, Summers advanced from the 1·0 million tons it had produced in the same year. Even at Ebbw Vale output continued to rise as the production for the group as a whole declined. In contrast, Dorman Long and Colvilles registered a 25 per cent decline in output

between 1957 and 1959, but South Durham, heavily committed to the
international steel pipe trade, suffered only a minor setback.

The regional impact of the recession was most marked in Scotland
where in August 1958 the industry produced less than 60 per cent of the
output of August 1957 (see Fig 9). The national figure was 80 per cent.
In Sheffield it was as high as 95 per cent. Moreover, the recession lasted
longer in Scotland than in the other districts, in most of which only one
of the two years 1958–9 was below the 1957 levels. In Scotland both years
were not only below the 1957 level but below the 1950–1 average. The
other district in which production in 1958 and 1959 was markedly
below the 1957 level was the North East Coast, where, again, there was
a concentration on heavy steels. Whereas the North East Coast and
South Wales had each contributed 20 per cent of the British output in
1945, by 1959 the South Wales share had grown to 25 per cent, and all
the additions in the other district had been sufficient to do no more than
retain the original 20 per cent share. Inasmuch as technological and
locational change are facilitated by rapid growth which allows
experimentation, the heavy steel producers of northern Britain were
seriously disadvantaged by their allegiance to the slow-growth demand
sectors.

Works Size

The recession passed, and the years 1959–60 witnessed a rash of
development proposals the estimated cost of which was a record
£423 million.[2] Characteristically, the proposals related to almost every
works in the country with the major absentees being accounted for by
those who had recently completed a development programme. But
even the new-found optimism (the Federation estimate for 1965 was
30 million tons compared with the 24 million produced in 1960)
was not sufficient to encourage a break with the locations of the
past.

It has already been noted that the output at Port Talbot had been
pushed beyond 2·0 million ingot tons by 1958, and in 1960 it exceeded
2·8 million, or 12 per cent of the British total. The validity of the earlier
views of Sir Andrew McCance had not been substantiated in this particular instance. In 1960 there were a further five works whose individual capacity exceeded 1·0 million ignot tons. Four of the five were
integrated: the fifth was the cold metal works of Steel, Peech & Tozer.[3]
Nevertheless, the basic broad-based pyramidal structure endured, and
the industry was still opposed to a policy of selecting a few points for

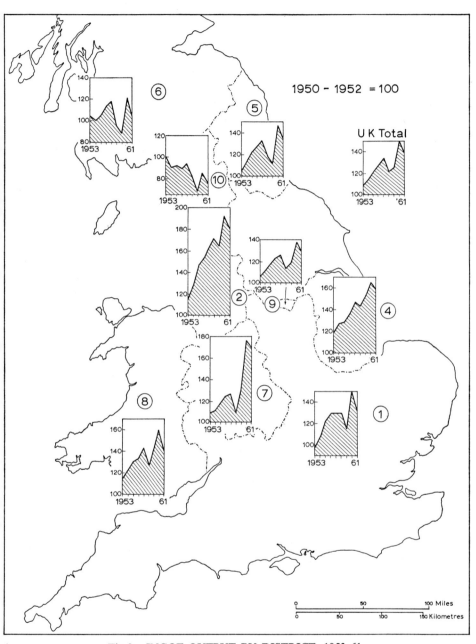

Fig 9. INGOT OUTPUT BY DISTRICT, 1953–61

rapid growth.[4] In view of its fragmented directorial control, such opposition was to be expected.

The issue of an ideal capacity for a works had been a major component of the 1946 Report, and it was reactivated in the *Productivity Report* issued in 1952.[5] The recommendations of the Anglo-American team, under the leadership of Sir Charles Goodeve, were that the optimum size for an integrated works in Britain should be between 0·75 and 1·0 million ingot tons, and that cold metal operations should be between 0·5 and 0·85 million ingot tons.[6] On the other hand, even the authors of this new report were none too sanguine about the chances of achieving these new objectives, for they recognised that Britain was 'a land of old traditions' possessed of a 'passion for equity and compromise' which resulted in a thin spread of resources over a diffuse field.[7] The leading trade journal observed in the context of the integrated works that it would come as 'a surprise to many to learn that there are at present no more than three works in this country of this "ideal" capacity'.[8] If that was so, the many would also be surprised at how recently those three had attained to that happy state. By the end of the decade, *eight* years after the publication of the report, there were seven integrated works producing more than 0·7 million tons, and Normanby Park was approaching that level. Among the cold metal works Samuel Fox and Round Oak were approaching 0·5 million tons, Dalzell continued to hover on the border, but only Steel, Peech & Tozer had exceeded the level (1·1 million). By 1960, however, the optimum size for an integrated works had been raised yet again.

The response of the industry was expressed in what was done, and in what was written and said. The developments at Normanby Park are one case in point. The post-1948 plan for that works was to raise output to 0·5 million ingot tons, but by 1955 the works was already producing around 0·6 million. At an Institute discussion on Lincolnshire developments Sir Charles Goodeve, the Director of BISRA and the leader of the Productivity Team, asked whether it would be possible to produce an extra 0·5 million tons when this was required 'without radical alterations'.[9] The reply of the managing director, Mr James, contained three important points. Firstly, he admitted that the works was 'very circumscribed' but said that there was room for such development on the other side of the boundary road. Secondly, the cost of such development would be 'very heavy indeed'. Thirdly, all developments should be achieved at minimum prices, 'so that when the easy days have gone our industry will be able successfully to withstand the challenge of competition'.[10]

Page 83: *Steel, Peech & Tozer: Templeborough* (above) *and Rotherham Melting Shops* (below)

Page 84: *Valley constraint: Stocksbridge* (above) *and Ebbw Vale Works* (below)

It is important to recognise the area of common ground in this inter-change. Firstly, both sides were agreed that expansion should be obtained at minimum cost. Secondly, neither side challenged the assumption that expansion at Normanby Park, as a separate unit from the other Scunthorpe works, was desirable. Thirdly, both sides could see that the seller's market, which had already persisted longer than most people had thought possible, would in due course disappear, and that only the low-cost producers would be able to flourish in a buyer's market. On the other hand, neither side appeared to consider seriously the possibility that the achievement of short-term minimum costs might jeopardise long-term cost savings and thereby the total industry's competitive position. It could be argued that this was not Mr James's task, but it should have been the task of the leader of the Productivity Team. Such interchanges lead one to believe that there was a happy agreement that the tradition of 'equity and compromise' should be allowed to continue. Only time would tell whether it had already been allowed to continue too far.

Further insight into the industry's state of mind in the context of the optimum works size for Britain can be obtained from reactions to the possible uses of continuous casting. At the time of the drafting of the *Productivity Report* the major arbiter of works size was considered to be the primary rolling mill. Such a mill could be expected to roll up to 1 million ingot tons of blooms or slabs, depending upon the amount of finishing that it was required to engage in. The continuous casting process promised a way round this expensive plant item. It was widely suggested that a combination of 80-ton arc furnaces or 50-ton Bessemer converters coupled to a continuous casting machine provided an economic alternative. With this in mind, one authority suggested that it was 'at least possible that the trend towards larger units in the industry [might] be due for some change'.[11] At the time this statement was made there were no such systems in commercial use, but the view was expressed frequently and certainly as late as 1965.[12] The real question was how far this new process could be expected to replace the existing processes, or whether it was no more than a complementary supplement to a few large mills. The record of the industry was such that it is not possible to escape the suspicion that the process was first welcomed as a device to perpetuate the existing structure. If it was a complement, what was the new theoretically optimum structure for the industry? The general view within the industry was that greenfield developments were characteristic of underdeveloped economies, in which category the United Kingdom decidedly did not belong.[13]

F

Locational Effects of Technological Evolution

Throughout the 1950s as in the 1940s the first problem which faced the industry was that of satisfying demand. Improvements in efficiency were a secondary problem, and would remain so until such time as the balance of supply and demand should alter. This being so, it was expedient that the industry should continue to react by making piecemeal adjustments to its existing plant. Opportunities for repeated modifications abounded, and both the historical legacy of the industry and the intrinsic nature of its technology encouraged such policies and actions. Because all the British works had evolved rather than been planned, the position was that there was nowhere a perfect balance between all the departments in any one works. The nearest approach to such a balance was at Corby. Even when a balance was reached it was unlikely to endure for the reason that the experience of operating a plant uncovered areas for improvement. Once these improvements had been made the balance would be upset, and the stimulus to balance upwards again would be present. If that stimulus is reinforced by an unsatisfied level of demand it becomes transformed into an irresistible temptation. The very nature of iron and steel technology is therefore such as to create a state of continuous change, albeit at a slow rate.

In the previous chapter the experience of the ironmakers at Appleby-Frodingham and Clyde Iron was used to demonstrate the fact that although it is possible to make generalised predictions about the outcome of a technological innovation in this industry, the true merits of an innovation can be proved only in an operational context. This provides scope for online adjustments to disappointments and unexpected improvements. It was shown that the success of the sinter trials at Appleby-Frodingham caused the construction of the second pair of blast furnaces at South Works to be deferred. In 1952, however, the plan was revived and was modified to include a second and larger sinter plant and ore preparation on land recently released from ore mining operations. When the two new furnaces came into operation in 1954 the ironworks at Frodingham and at North works were closed with considerable gains in simplicity of works traffic. The hearth of the original No 9 furnace, renamed Queen Mary, had been increased from 22ft to 25ft diameter in 1951 and was to be increased to 27ft 6in in 1956. Queen Bess was rebuilt with a 25ft hearth, and the two new furnaces were built with hearths of 27ft and 28ft 6in respectively. Up to 9,000 tons of pig iron were obtained from one furnace in a week, and coke consumption fell from 23·3cwt to 17·3cwt per ton of pig iron produced as the percentage of sinter used rose to 95 per cent and above. The total results were that whereas in 1951 South Ironworks, with two blast furnaces, had produced 0·3 million tons, in 1960 production had been raised fivefold with the addition of two furnaces and a net reduction on the works as a whole of four furnaces. Furthermore, the limits of output from the new facilities had not yet been reached.

The locational implications of these developments were profound if they could be spread across the industry as a whole. In 1946, the common expectation had been that a large increase of output on the home ore fields must inevitably result in the creation of at least one new works. By 1960, however, it appeared that locational change upon this field was more likely to take the form of comparative change or negative absolute change. In practice, it became apparent that increases in pig iron output could best be obtained in home- *and* foreign-ore-using ironworks by the use of sintered ore, so that when Skinningrove opened its sinter plant in 1960 the only two integrated works in the country which lacked such facilities were Ebbw Vale and Park Gate. Part of the ore supplied to Ebbw Vale was sintered at Irthlingborough in Northamptonshire, but the only ore preparation at Park Gate was primary crushing. Across the industry at large as each furnace became due for relining the opportunity of enlarging the hearth, and thereby deferring the time when extra furnaces would be needed, was taken wherever it was possible.

There were, however, limitations to this process imposed by the size of the furnace foundation and the congestion created by the ancillary furnace plant. The clearest examples of this were at Dorman Long and Port Talbot. Dorman Long's first pair of modern blast furnaces at Clay Lane came into operation in 1956–7. With hearth diameters of 27ft 6in they dwarfed the 12–14ft hand-charged furnaces they replaced and the 18ft diameter furnaces rebuilt at Redcar in 1953. Their collective capacity was 0·7 million tons per annum and their efficiency was such that in the 1958 trade recession one of the Redcar furnaces was closed. This was but a foretaste of the permanent closure of that ironworks in 1961 as the total output of Dorman Long was centred on the three furnaces which were eventually built at Clay Lane.

At Port Talbot the three Margam furnaces were expanded to 23ft 9in and 27ft 3in (Nos 2 and 3) but in 1952 the second development plan included a fourth furnace with a hearth of 29ft 9in, the largest yet built in Europe. The congestion of the Margam ironworks required that this furnace should be built away from the original three and should be provided with its own stockyard. It came into operation in January 1956, and four months later the third development scheme which contained a fifth furnace (31ft 3in diameter) to be set alongside No 4 was announced. This final furnace came into operation in May 1959. With each furnace the capacity of the sinter plant was raised with the result that the total output of pig iron had been raised to 1·9 million tons in 1960—an increase of 450 per cent since 1952. The development emphasised the fact, however, that there was a conflict between short-term and long-term aims, a conflict of which the personnel at the works were well aware, witness the following statements by W. F. Cartwright and K. C. Sharpe:

> Port Talbot is not laid out as anybody would lay out a blast furnace plant today, starting with the knowledge of the desirability of crushing, screening and sintering ore, the use of self-fluxing sinter, and the high percentage of fines now present in most foreign ores. As a result an extremely complicated raw material layout has emerged . . .[14]

and

> The whole of this development was not foreseen when the first stage was contemplated, and consequently the layout is rather elaborate, being necessitated by the site.[15]

It was ironical that in the second largest continuous steelworks site in Britain the policies of progressive modernisation and expansion *in situ* should have led to congested operations. Nevertheless, a greater weakness was present in the form of an inadequate ore-dock.[16]

These important and locationally significant changes in blast furnace productivity had been achieved by a combination of modifications to the furnaces themselves (larger hearths and high top pressure) and by careful and extended burden preparation. There was no fundamental change in the process itself either at home or abroad, and the expectation was that the blast furnace would dominate the ore conversion process for the foreseeable future. Provided the correct location was chosen, there was little chance that capital investment in new blast furnaces would be regretted. In the melting shops, however, there were signs that the future course of technology was less certain: signs that technological as well as locational mistakes could be made. The revival of the basic Bessemer process at Corby and Ebbw Vale in the 1930s had demonstrated that there was an alternative to the open hearth for bulk steelmaking even under the total British trading conditions. However, the claims of the advocates of the process were largely discounted in the industry at large, and the output of the basic open-hearth furnaces was increased in absolute and relative terms.

Nevertheless, the converter process had been considered for the Port Talbot scheme in 1945, and in 1956 it was decided to replace the Margam I melting shop capacity and to expand total output with a new shop containing three 50-ton bottom-blown converters using a mixture of oxygen and steam. These came into operation in 1959 and in the following year a fourth vessel was added to produce a total capacity for the shop of 19,000 ingot tons per week. Significantly, two extra open-hearth furnaces were added to the Margam II shop in 1957. Also of interest is the realisation that the original plans for the Spencer Works at Llanwern were based upon one open-hearth and one basic Bessemer shop. The delay in developing this new works provided the opportunity to review these technical assumptions.

Elsewhere, the continued demand for extra steel and the need to balance the different parts of the works led to further innovations. At Consett, where the output of the melting shop had become a serious limitation for the works as a whole, the management resorted to the duplexing process. In this process the hot metal was first placed in an acid Bessemer converter before being brought to the final specification in the open-hearth furnaces. The aim, and the result, was to increase the output of the shop by 50 per cent, and it was pointed out that a new open-hearth plant of similar capacity would have involved three times the capital outlay. Furthermore, on that congested site there was no room to add such open-hearth furnaces as would have been required for the same net result. The general opinion within the industry, however, was that duplexing was an untidy process which sacrificed operational costs for capital savings. No other works used the process.

None of these developments, even if they had been on a larger scale, could have influenced the productivity and quality difficulties of the cold metal operations. American war-time and post-war experience, however, had demonstrated the effectiveness of the large arc furnace as a producer of alloy and carbon steels, but with only limited cost savings. The lower capital costs of the process were effectively nullified by higher operational costs, but the process held the promise of considerable flexibility.[17] The first British large arc furnace, of 60-tons tapping capacity, was installed at the Stocksbridge works of United Steel in 1954, and a second, larger furnace, 80 tons, was ordered the following year. Nevertheless, because of the limited cost savings, the full impact of this process would become apparent for the industry at large only when it should become necessary to replace the existing cold metal furnaces through their decay with age, or to build new cold metal works in order to expand output.

In 1956 Tube Investments decided to build two 50-ton arc furnaces in a new melting shop at Round Oak. Five reasons were given for the choice of this process, including its lower capital cost, its greater versatility, and the growing shortage of good producer-gas quality coals. The management also considered that fuel oil-firing of open-hearth furnaces could be no more than a temporary palliative, and that electric power was likely to become increasingly cheaper in comparative terms. The fifth reason was the increased bulk of scrap metal, which could be charged more quickly in the top-charging arc furnaces than in the side-charged open-hearth furnaces.[18] There was a further advantage in that the small building that was necessary to house the new furnaces could be more readily fitted within the site. It was the nature of the area as an old slag and refuse heap built over the preceding seventy years which created the difficulties rather than a shortage of space, but the smaller building rendered the task of reorganising the century-old railway system more straightforward and minimised the interference from the canal which bisected the works. The new shop came into operation in 1958 and raised the capacity of the works to above 0·5 million tons. In this way the twelve-year-old criticism of the works as being too small for efficiency was eventually laid to rest. There can be no doubt that in terms of availability of raw materials and of proximity to markets, the development took place on a site which had an admirable situation. In addition the development emphasised the space-saving facility of the electric arc process, which would enable it to be fitted into almost any steelworks site in Britain and still provide some margin of increased capacity. Large arc furnaces were, in time, installed in existing works, Parkhead and Cleveland, and in new works, Tinsley Park, and were used for hot metal refining at Brymbo; but the largest development was at Steel, Peech & Tozer. That development must, however, be seen in the wide context of United Steel and in the even wider context of the industry's attitude to new developments.

Resistance to Technological Change

Reviewing the period 1929–54, T. P. Colclough stated that it was significant that no vital new principle for the making of iron or steel had been discovered during that quarter-century.[19] The judgement was wrong even then, and 1954 was the last time that it could be made without immediate rebuttal, for the oxygen converter developments at

Linz–Donawitz in Austria had already been proved within certain limits and their greater potential was being realised elsewhere, if not in Britain. The use of oxygen in the converter was not a new idea—it had been suggested by Sir Henry Bessemer himself—but there were both economic and technical problems associated with its use. The economic problem of producing large quantities of the gas at low cost had been solved in Germany by 1930, and the technical problems had been solved in Germany, Belgium and Switzerland by 1949. Only the results of a large-scale commercial application were still awaited at the beginning of the fifties.

Neither the researchers nor the trade press in Britain were entirely unaware of these developments. As early as 1948 A. G. Robiette had stated that in his view the costs of oxygen were low enough for its use to be 'seriously considered both for combustion systems and for the refining of pig iron and the production of steel'.[20] In 1952, almost a complete number of *Stahl und Eisen* was given to reporting a conference devoted to the process.[21] In 1953, *Iron and Coal*, reporting on a conference at Liège, stressed that the type of pig iron being used in the LD was of open-hearth quality and concluded that although the process had not been perfected it clearly had considerable possibilities.[22] In 1955 *Iron and Steel Engineer* reported results on the process, and showed not only that the operating costs of the new process were lower but that on a 0·5 million ton installation the capital costs were $20·22 per ton compared with $39·61 for a new open-hearth shop. If the plant was larger—1·0 million tons—the capital costs were $12·67 and $33·71 respectively.[23] At home, an Institute abstract in 1956 stated:

> The manufacturing cost of LD steel is 55% of that of open-hearth steel. Over 1 million tons of rimming and fully killed steels, mostly for wire drawing, deep drawing sheets, and thin plates have been produced at Linz.[24]

It is difficult to be sure of the degree of attention that the British steelmakers were giving to these developments, but industry discussions over the years 1956–61 revealed marked scepticism and firm attachment to existing technologies. According to D. J. O. Brandt, in 1956, oxygen had been used in Britain in pilot-scale trials to dephosphorise molten pig iron prior to charging the open-hearth furnaces as long ago as 1945, but the advantages had been 'deliberately ignored by those responsible for directing research at BISRA because [they] did not accord with contemporary physio-chemical theory'.[25] In the discussion which followed the presentation of this paper the author was reproved for recriminating about the late start in using oxygen in Britain, and it was also stated that it was quite clear that Dr Brandt had for long been a 'strong protagonist of Bessemer's approach to steelmaking rather than Siemens-Martin's approach'. The implications of this view are not entirely clear, but the suggestion would appear to be that it was possible for a man's attitude to a technological innovation to be conditioned by his earlier attitudes. If this was so the steelmakers were not the first to discover this reality; presumably the criticism cut both ways.

In spite of these attitudes several British companies had already started along the path of experimenting with the use of oxygen, but the significant thing was that these experiments were adaptive rather than revolutionary. In that respect they showed a marked congruence with the prevailing ethos of the industry as a whole. The experiments were geographically widespread and were applied at different stages of the steel refining process. At Brymbo, Redbourn and Skinningrove experiments with the use of oxygen in the ladle as a desiliconising agent prior to the charge being placed in the furnace resulted in output gains of up to 30 per cent. At Dalzell, a 21 per cent increase in output was obtained, with a 14 per cent fuel saving, but at no cost saving on the 100-ton cold charged furnaces when using oxygen as an aid to combustion within the furnace. At Redcar, which operated the hot metal process, a 60 per cent increase in output was obtained and fuel requirements were reduced from forty to eleven therms per ton. Experiments with the fixed hot metal furnaces at Port Talbot resulted again in higher output, lower fuel consumption, but no cost reductions. The view which emerges is that oxygen in the 1950s took over from oil-firing in the 1940s as a means of providing immediately a higher level of output, and obviated the need either to build additions to the existing melting shops or to build new melting shops. The experiments were, therefore, locationally as well as technologically conservative. In view of this attitude and of the strong allegiance to the open-hearth process it is not surprising that the most interesting and satisfactory development in the use of oxygen, the Ajax furnace at Appleby-Frodingham, should be associated with the open-hearth. The development is interesting in terms of the display of technical virtuosity and ingenuity, as well as in terms of managerial conservatism and caution.

At this time there were two major problems confronting United Steel. Firstly, the cold metal furnaces at Steel, Peech & Tozer were old, and becoming competitively inadequate. Secondly, the extra output of only one new large tilting furnace (around 150,000 tons) was required from the Scunthorpe steelworks to absorb the increasingly higher outputs of the ironworks at one end and to supply the improved rolling mills, including the proposed continuous casting bloom plant for the new rod and bar mill, at the other end. Both projects would make financial demands upon the parent company, but the apparently smaller needs of Scunthorpe were overshadowed by the critical position which had been reached at Steel, Peech & Tozer. On the other hand, there was a greater potential at Scunthorpe which might have been realised by a Scunthorpe-oriented board. In due course the success of the Scunthorpe experiments rescued both works, but the effect of the rescue operation was the reduction of the growth rate of Appleby-Frodingham and the prolonging of its period of under-achievement by more than a decade. The company had considered the possibility of a wide strip mill at Scunthorpe, but this was rejected on the grounds of the size of the financial investment which would be required, and because it was 'felt that such a development would completely change the commercial and technical balance of the whole organisation'.[26] Clearly, such a radical change was thought to be undesirable.

In 1957 the Scunthorpe steelmakers wanted to build an oxygen furnace of either the Kaldo or Rotor variety, because it was already known that both processes could handle the high phosphorus pig iron of the district. It was thought that the maximum gains would be obtained from a 100-ton Kaldo vessel, but that such a vessel would produce more steel than was required. If such a vessel was built, other furnaces on the works, which were already producing more cheaply than most, would have to be scrapped, unless the total level of output was to be raised. This solution, along with that of building a new tilting furnace, was rejected. Developments outside the company were not, however, to be ignored, as it was decided 'to maintain a continuing interest in the new oxygen processes, against the time when a larger increase in production became necessary'.[27] Meanwhile, two technical steps would be taken. Firstly, an all-basic furnace would be built, and, secondly, further experiments with oxygen on the tilting furnace would be carried out. The results were immediate. The all-basic furnace produced an 11 per cent gain in output and the oxygen furnace added a further 38 per cent, or around 50 per cent in all. Furthermore, the new Ajax furnace returned lower costs when working with only 0·2 cwt of scrap per ingot ton produced compared with 3·5 cwt in the all-basic and conventional furnaces. If the Ajax furnace was to be used on a large scale the circulating scrap from the works would be rendered surplus. It was this new scrap surplus which would solve the problem at Steel, Peech & Tozer.

Many different proposals had been considered for Steel, Peech & Tozer including that of building blast furnaces at the works. Others had suggested the replacement of only the small Rotherham melting shop, with two 80-ton arc furnaces on the Brinsworth site; or the production of some of the works' ingots (the rimming steel qualities) at Appleby-Frodingham; or the transfer of hot metal or hot ingots from the same source. All these proposals were rejected and attention became focused on replacing both melting shops with one large shop containing seven 110-ton arc furnaces to be built precisely upon the existing and operating Templeborough melting shop. Such a shop would raise the output of the works from 1·1 million to a desired 1·35 million ingot tons. Technically, the plan was feasible but financially it could not be justified. However, the new scrap surplus at Appleby-Frodingham created by the use of the Ajax process, if transferred to Steel, Peech & Tozer, could replace the 33 per cent cold pig iron charge which had been used in the open-hearth furnaces and would provide a captive source of virgin scrap of known chemical constitution. In this way it would be possible to obtain the desired tonnage with six 110-ton arc furnaces instead of seven. On that basis, the new scheme, approved in 1959 at an estimated cost of £10 million, was economically justifiable and the Steel, Peech & Tozer dilemma was solved.

That did not mean that the men at Scunthorpe were happy with the situation, even though they remained justifiably proud of their accomplishment. Jackson himself admitted that in a greenfield situation with a demand for 0·5 million tons of one quality steel he would opt for a converter, but felt that the Ajax furnace was better suited to 0·1 to 0·15 million tons of varying qualities.[28] At an Institute discussion on steel processes a continued attachment to the open-hearth furnace within the industry as a whole was clearly revealed. T. P. Colclough felt that as long as only fifteen out of the eighty therms put into such furnaces for each ingot ton produced were actually used there was further room for considerable improvement in that technology.[29] R. Mayorcas felt that if the same amount of effort was directed at the open-hearth furnace as had been spent in developing the new converters, the results would be just as good, and he pointed out that there were 328 basic open-hearth furnaces already in the country to benefit from these improvements.[30] There was doubtless some merit in these statements, but it was not clear how many of those furnaces could be so adapted. At Shotton, for example, where Mayorcas directed steel production, the congestion within the melting shop prevented a full use of oxygen in subsequent years. On the other hand, an unlooked-for benefit of the Ajax process was that it deferred the time when a choice would have to be made between the new steelmaking technologies. Had the Kaldo been chosen in 1958 it would have been regretted by 1968. It was in 1958 that the important breakthrough in the use of the LD converter for high phosphorus pig iron was achieved at Dudelange in Luxembourg. This new process, designated LD-AC, sealed the fate of the Kaldo process, which had appeared to mark the way ahead for the high phosphorus pig iron users.

Even in retrospect it is impossible to say that the technological caution of the British industry was entirely misplaced, but by 1960 the original LD plants installed at Linz and Donawitz in 1952 and 1953 had been imitated at works in Canada, the United States, West Germany, India, Japan, Sweden, the Soviet Union and Luxembourg. In Britain, RTB had taken a licence to convert one of the converters at Ebbw Vale to the top blown process, and was installing the LD process at Llanwern, but the 'new' works at Ravenscraig and West Hartlepool were to use open-hearth furnaces. Elsewhere in Britain, Consett Iron had sent 500 tons of pig iron to Sweden and Austria to be processed in the Kaldo and LD furnaces and was deliberating on which to install. Stewarts & Lloyds were also considering the LD–AC for Corby. The comparative ease with which those companies that had had experience with the old pneumatic process took to the new is too obvious not to be noticed. They were not the only companies, but they led the way in Britain.

Even by 1960 the debate was not closed even if it was now clear that all cold metal operations would be based on the arc furnace. In 1961 A. J. Kesterton concluded that under British conditions the most economical proposition was a combined LD and open-hearth works.[31] A. Jackson, in 1962, correctly insisted that the LD should be compared not with the open-hearth as it used to be, but with that process in its most modern forms. The Ajax process had achieved increases in output of 70 per cent and was to achieve 100 per cent increases.[32] Capital costs had been reduced from £12 to £7 per ingot ton, and conversion costs were 68 per cent of previous *good* practice. These improvements were possible only because the 'own arisings' scrap from the Ajax-based works was consumed in the associated arc furnace works. Of considerable interest in this context, but of limited practical import in view of what had happened, was A. G. Robiette's view of the future technological pattern: electric arcs for cold metal, LD furnaces for hot metal. That view was expressed *in 1953.*[33]

Resistance to Locational Change

The prolonged discussions about the future course of technological development within the industry appear to have been characterised by the same set of influences which dominated forward thinking in all the industry's areas of decision. The great attachment to the open-hearth, for example, seems to have been matched by a similar attachment to established regional product specialisations and to individual locations. Neither set of attachments had given the industry bad service in the past, and the dominant conservatism had at least ensured a low rate of capital expenditure and good knowledge of the locations and technologies which were being used. But once again the question was one of willingness to give new ideas just consideration, and to make changes when there were reasonable expectations that they were required. In the nature of things it would be impossible to know beforehand that the correct decision had been taken.

As the demand for steel continued to grow beyond 1955 the industry began to find the operational constraints of its locational pattern irksome, and the question of locational changes began to appear. In its second Development Report the Iron & Steel Board distinguished between 'obsolescence of location' and 'obsolescence of plant', but concluded that location had to be, almost of necessity, a compromise solution.[34] It recognised that some 'sites' came closer to the ideal than others, but based its classification of productive efficiency upon the process used rather than the location. It was not until 1961 that the Board felt that location itself was of sufficient merit to warrant a separate chapter in its development report, by which time it had come to recognise the issue as being of 'fundamental importance to efficient and economic operation'.[35] In this respect the Board was in the vanguard of industry opinion, but in practice it lacked the means to implement its views.

With a liberal interpretation of the adjective it is possible to say that four 'new' steelmaking sites were selected for development during the prosperous years leading up to 1960. They ranged from the greenfield integrated works at Llanwern in Monmouthshire, through the cold metal works built on an old pithead site at Tinsley Park, Sheffield, to the major additions to existing works at West Hartlepool and Motherwell. Only the last can be considered a situational innovation in that it remade the raw material base and the product range of the Lanarkshire steel industry; the remaining three were locationally imitative rather than innovative acts. It seems to be a pertinent comment upon the British industry of the time that its sole situational innovation should be at variance with the trend for the world-wide industry where the established view was that imported-ore-based developments should be situated alongside tidal water.

To these four 'new' works should be added the decision by Tube Investments to redevelop the Park Gate works. The original announcement of this £55 million scheme in 1960 included a reference to a new ironworks to use home ore from the Midlands fields. It was described as a plan for the 'most advanced steelworks in Europe'.[36] Such a claim could not have taken account of the fragmented site upon which the works was to be built or the developing trends in raw material assembly costs, but must have been based upon the consideration of the choice of arc furnaces and Kaldo furnaces for the new melting shop, and upon the capacity of the new primary and bar and narrow strip mills. The ironworks was to have included one blast furnace and an ore preparation plant and the total capacity of the works would be raised to 0·875 million ingot tons. The whole scheme was in tune with the view that the level of output was more important than the cost of output, and presumably the new ironworks was a response to the unsatisfactory product of the existing blast furnaces supplemented with pig iron from Renishaw. The fact that it was 'also planned to accommodate future modernisation of the existing steelworks in perhaps ten or fifteen years' time' was sufficient evidence to indicate that no basic reassessment of location of even parts of the industry's processes was taking place.[37] Fortunately the Park Gate development was overtaken by events and the ironworks was deleted from the scheme in 1961 when the total cost was reduced to £33 million. The remainder of the scheme, along with the modernisation of the existing blast furnaces, was completed by 1965 (see page 150). It is difficult to see how Europe's 'most advanced steelworks' could have been built at a location whose site and whose situation for hot metal operations were already obsolete.

The same locational strictures do not apply to the English Steel Corporation's Tinsley Park development, because there was no reason to believe that the Don Valley was an obsolete location for a cold metal operation. The stimulus for this scheme lay in the congested site conditions of the River Don works. The Corporation had purchased the new site in 1954. In 1956 it obtained approval for a £15 million open-hearth-based heavy forge department, but made no progress other than clearing the site until in 1960 the scheme was reformulated to consist of three 100-ton arc furnaces and bloom, billet and bar mills to replace the forty-year-old plant at River Don and Stephenson Road. The period of delay had been long enough to show that the open-hearth was the wrong steelmaking process, and that the product growth areas were in billets and bars. The new £26 million scheme was the only greenfield cold metal plant to use conventional rolling technology built by the industry in the entire post-war period, but with an initial capacity of less than 0·3 million ingot tons it was below the desirable minimum set by the Productivity Team in 1952.

Yet another development to be initiated during this prolonged period of excess demand, but which also failed to come into operation until the 1960s when trading conditions had changed, was that of South Durham at West Hartlepool. By 1957 the capacity of that works had been increased by at least 100 per cent when compared with 1946, and the suggestion in the 1946 Report that the works should be phased out had been forgotten. The demand for wide plates was insatiable, and the company, under Mr Chetwynd Talbot, determined 'to get in as soon as, or sooner than anyone else' and to build at West Hartlepool the biggest works in the country.[38] Although the company already possessed an extensive tipping area at the south end of the West Hartlepool works, upon which it had long intended to build an ore preparation plant, a scheme which amounted to the construction of a new integrated works would require more land than was immediately available. After one false planning start, a 537–acre site on the disused Greatham airfield was obtained close to the south end of the North Works. On this site the company built an ore preparation plant and coke ovens to serve both the new South Works and the old North Works. It also added a melting shop with six 360-ton tilting open-hearth furnaces with a capacity of 1·0 million ingot tons and a slab mill. This was to serve the new 12ft 6in plate mill and the old 7ft mill, and was to take ingots from both works. Its capacity was 1·5 million tons.

The choice of the large tilting furnaces reflected the assumption that the new works would use ore from the company's 'Northants' field quarries and high phosphorus foreign ores. In view of the former assumption the apparently superior coastal situation of the works when compared with Consett and Dalzell, where plate mill developments were also under way, was largely discounted. In later years the time element in this 170-mile rail haul was cut by half, but even then it amounted to ten hours. One argument in favour of keeping this ore source was that the large slag volume was needed to offset the deleterious effects of the high sulphur coking coals, which the company was obliged to use. The main objection to the scheme, however, was that it must inevitably postpone for as long as a generation the time when the whole of the ingot capacity on Tees-side could be rationalised upon a single efficiently operated ore terminal. There is no evidence that Dorman Long was actively pursuing such a course of action, but the intense individuality of the separate North East Coast steelmakers would have been sufficient to prevent the completion of such a scheme even if it had been formulated. The result was that yet another major centre of steel production was constructed to the eventual disadvantage of all. Once the West Hartlepool scheme had been drawn up, the vigour of the Talbot family was sufficient to ensure its rapid completion. Had it been subjected to delay in the same way as Llanwern, it is possible that West Hartlepool might have been one of the first locations to use the LD–AC process rather than the last new works to be entirely dependent upon the open-hearth. Such a verdict could easily be made in 1971, but it was also being made in 1961 when the works came into operation. West Hartlepool's South Works is one of the clearest examples of the possibility of catching the very end of a technological train during a period of radical technological change. That it should be so at a works whose very existence was dependent upon a firm determination to remain independent seems to be only marginally relevant.

Ravenscraig and Llanwern

On 18 November 1958 Mr Harold Macmillan announced to the House of Commons that the extended national debate on the question of the location of the fourth strip mill had been resolved by the inspired decision to build two mills whose combined initial capacity would equal that of the one which had been sought. The source of the announcement was sufficient evidence to indicate the importance of the question, and the locations of the developments themselves bore witness to the continuing powers of the forces of equity, compromise and adaptation. Although the works at Llanwern was to occupy a greenfield site its selection was as much the result of these forces as was the Ravenscraig mill grafted on to the Lanarkshire industry.

The Ravenscraig sheet mill had its origins in 1953 when Colvilles obtained permission to build a new blast furnace ore preparation plant, coke ovens and melting shop on land adjacent to the Dalzell and Lanarkshire Steel works at Motherwell. The decision rescinded an earlier announcement to build a fourth blast furnace at Clyde Iron, which had been scarcely feasible in view of the existing congestion at the Clyde Iron–Clydebridge works. The new arrangement would permit

greater flexibility of operations at the two Motherwell works, and held out the distant promise of integrated operations at Dalzell where the replacement of the steelmaking facilities had become a matter of some urgency. The announcement was seen as the most recent and, it was hoped, the last instalment in the saga of the Clydeside works, for Sir Andrew McCance said that the decision 'presumably put paid once and for all to this old proposal'.[39] Such a hope seemed to rest on the assumption that the period of expansion and easy trading was to be a short one. If the location of an integrated works using foreign ore on an inland site made sufficient economic sense to enable the company to withstand the difficult conditions to come it did so only in the way in which it fitted into the existing framework of the company and into the social geography of Lanarkshire. In his study of the location of the Scottish industry, Warren came to the conclusion—seemingly with reluctance—that the company's claims that total marketing costs would be lower from Motherwell than from the Renfrew shore were valid.[40] In 1957 Colvilles announced their intention to build a second blast furnace and battery of coke ovens on the site, and to add a slab mill to replace the obsolete mill at Dalzell and a new four-high plate mill. The combined estimated cost of these schemes was £52 million.

The addition of these units was not physically difficult or complicating because the original plans had been designed so as to be capable of expansion to 'approximately three times their initial capacity'.[41] No one seemed to question whether a location which was suitable for the one size was suitable for the other. Perhaps no one ever seriously thought that the opportunity to expand would materialise. The development was, however, interesting in that full use was deliberately made of the slope of the site towards the north-west with the major movement of materials from stage to stage being down-slope. It was also the first large British works in which the new role of heavy road transport within a works, as a liberating factor from the strict control of a rail network, was realised. Road access to all the major items of plant was considered to be 'an essential requirement'. Both these features can be seen on page 150. The downslope is towards the camera. On the other hand, the choice of three 250-ton fixed open-hearth furnaces for the melting shop identified the works clearly with its heritage. The fixed furnaces, the largest in Europe, were chosen to complement the tilting furnaces at Clydebridge, for the Ravenscraig blast furnaces would use low phosphorus rather than high phosphorus iron ores and share with Clyde Iron the role of supplying the cold metal shops with pig iron. The 0·4 million ingot tons from Ravenscraig would lead to a net increase for the company of 0·2 million tons as obsolete plant in the Motherwell area was closed.

It was on this site, developed to offset the company's high dependence on scrap metal and to improve the efficiency of the Dalzell works, that Colvilles were persuaded, and agreed, to build a semi-continuous hot strip and light plate mill with a total capacity of 0·5 million tons per annum. The new cold reduction mill was to be located at the company's Gartcosh hand mills eight miles away. To support this new mill capacity, which was revised upwards to 0·675 million tons in 1959, it was necessary to add a third blast furnace, a fourth steel furnace in the open-hearth melting shop, and two 110-ton LD–AC converters in a second shop. It can be seen on page 150 that once again the additions presented no important engineering or works traffic problems, although the new works units were pressing against the limits imposed by the Dalzell mills and the deeply entrenched South Calder Water. By the time all these developments had been completed (1964) the company possessed a works the internal conditions of which were unequalled in Britain. The presence of the open-hearth shop, the only old-fashioned element in the picture, stood as a testimony to and a reminder of the date and original purpose of the works.

The speed with which these changes followed each other, each new stage being announced before the preceding one had been completed, was reminiscent of the succession of proposals and counter-proposals which had altered the end result at Port Talbot from that of its original concept. Once again the situational aspects of the location were ignored. At the beginning of this development Colvilles had reorganised their ore handling arrangements by transferring the point of entry from the Rothesay dock, with its limit of 10,000-ton carriers, to the General Terminus Quay, which could receive ships of up to 28,000 tons. The rail haul to Ravenscraig was fifteen miles and was scheduled to take 1 hour 20 minutes, but the congestion behind the quay created delays in assembling the trains, and the rail system required the use of small, two-axle wagons. Now the system would have to handle at least three times its original tonnage. These raw material assembly costs, coupled with the certain difficulty of obtaining coking coal from England if foreign coal could not be used, were, however, minimal compared with the additional marketing costs of a product 80 per cent of which would have to be sold outside Scotland.

The Ravenscraig works is the clearest example in this industry of a major development whose causative factors lay in the economic and social forces of the community as a whole rather than in the economic

G

forces of the industry itself. Of the parties directly concerned, Colvilles were the last to be persuaded of the desirability of the project, and much of the persuasion took the form of a £50 million government loan. As recently as July 1957 Sir Andrew McCance had given a negative response to an inquiry relating to even the possibility of Colvilles contemplating the financing of a Scottish strip mill, and he seemed to be looking as far forward as 1962.[42] The offer of the loan altered the financing aspect, and the pattern of trade during the recession had emphasised the weakness of the Scottish industry's product strategy. Presumably the company was not immune to the pressures of the Scottish MPs, the Scottish Council, and the trades unions, all of whom saw the creation of a Scottish mill as the essential first stage in the diversification of that country's industrial structure. The fact that the company chose a semi-continuous mill would suggest that it still held reservations about the likelihood of the diversification programme bearing much fruit. Nevertheless, the scheme was a locational innovation in that it established a major sheet steel centre outside Wales.

If the origins of the Ravenscraig mill can be traced back to 1953, the origins of the Llanwern mill must be found in the selection of Ebbw Vale in 1936. Unlike Colvilles, RTB had been active in seeking permission for a new mill since 1956, but they were careful not to specify a location. It appeared at the time that the operating limits of the ironworks at Ebbw Vale had been reached by the ability to operate all three furnaces together, but the hot strip mill which rolled 0·81 million tons in 1956 was still being supplied with slabs from Redbourn and West Wales, and the ironworks was still taking sintered ore from Irthlingborough. There can be no doubt that the company had already determined upon a development at Newport, but that it was willing to go through the motions of examining at least some of the fifteen alternative locations which were suggested.[43] Nevertheless, the first precise mention of Newport by the company made mention of no more than ore preparation, two blast furnaces, and two melting shops, one of which would use oxygen/steam bottom blown converters, while the other would use the open-hearth process. A hot strip mill, cold reduction mill and tinplate mill could be added later, but meanwhile the works would produce semi-finished steel. The blind, if that is what it was, could have convinced no one for the scheme was too large to operate for long in such a role. In reality, even though it was a forward bastion for Ebbw Vale, it was a part of the conditioning process whereby the company prepared the ground for the eventual acceptance of its views.

The debate was an empty one because the financial proportions of a new works, a minimum of £160 million, were sufficient to dissuade any other company from championing an alternative cause. As it was, the Federation was of the view that a fourth mill would not be needed before 1964 even though the Steel Board favoured 1962, and the other sheet steel companies were still formulating their own on-site development proposals. So it was that RTB had the field to themselves and were comparatively free to choose a location which best suited their own requirements, which were not necessarily those of the nation as a whole.

The layout of the Llanwern, or Spencer Works on its 1,700-acre rectangular site is to be seen on page 65. By the time the scheme had been formalised the LD process had been chosen as the sole steelmaking process, and the earlier idea of including a tinplate mill had been dropped. In these ways the works was to sever the major technological ties with the tradition from whence it came. It represented a technologically new phase, but in terms of its location it was doing no more than imitating the many moves which had taken the Welsh industry towards the coast and away from its inland locations. To be locationally innovative the company would have needed to go to eastern or southern England. The proposed capacity of the new works was increased by 40 per cent to 1·4 million ingot tons in 1959 and the proposals now included a continuous rather than a semi-continuous mill. But RTB had yet further ambitions which grew with the passage of time. In 1959 Mr Spencer suggested an ultimate capacity of 5·0 million tons, but by the end of 1960 this figure had grown to 10·0 million.[44] Although these suggestions were not taken literally it was true that the site conditions would allow for almost indefinite expansion, and the situation did not exclude the possibility either.[45]

A Fair-Weather Edifice

The 1950s ended on a note of previously unequalled optimism witnessed to by a resurgence in approved capital investment schemes, and supported by record levels of output and of profits. Between 1950 and 1960 the combined annual profits, prior to depreciation, of the twelve companies listed in Table 5 rose from £48 million to £167 million. All the companies shared in the growth, but there were some important changes in their relative performance. Most notably, the Steel Company of Wales by 1960 was returning the highest gross profits, but the high rate of depreciation on its mostly new plant pushed it into second place behind United Steel in terms of net profits. Similarly, it was

Table 5

COMPANY PROFITS: SELECTED FINANCIAL YEARS* £ MILLION

	1950	*1955*	*1960*
Colvilles	5·6	8·3	16·3
Consett	1·6†	3·7	4·1†
Dorman Long	6·3	11·7	14·0
Firth-Brown	1·4†	3·6	5·4‡
Hadfields	0·3	1·1	0·9
Lancashire	2·5	3·8	5·9
South Durham	1·5	2·8	7·9
SCOW	2·4	18·3	30·5
Stewarts & Lloyds	11·0	16·9	25·0
Summers	3·1	8·7	14·3
RTB	6·8†	11·3	14·8
United Steel	5·5	15·5	27·7

Sources: Various.
* Profits before depreciation for years ending September.
† Year ending March.
‡ Includes William Beardmore, purchased in 1957.

second to Stewarts & Lloyds in terms of profits per ingot ton produced, but in this respect was being pushed hard by both Summers and South Durham. The rapid growth of output and profits of the latter company, especially after 1955, was beginning to redress the balance of the two major producers on Tees-side, and by 1960 South Durham had fully consolidated its position as a permanent independent feature in the industry's structure.

The first effects of these raised profit levels were a reduction in the stridency of the comments of the habitual critics of the industry and an increase in each company's determination to pursue its own course. The general election of 1959 had removed the immediate threat of re-nationalisation, and resulted in a more favourable stock market attitude to the industry, thereby removing one possible inducement to contemplate new departures from the existing pattern.[46] Nationalisation would not, of course, have ensured such action, and it was possible that the removal of the threat would encourage foreign steelmakers or British steel-users to enter the British scene, but it is at least possible to believe, although not to prove, that the continuation of the threat would have maintained a heightened level of self-criticism among the existing steelmakers. It was true that the Iron & Steel Board had the formal right to initiate development, but in practice it possessed the powers of advice alone. Its consent was rarely withheld. As it was, only the most hyper-critical commentator would complain that when, for example, United Steel had raised its dividend from an equivalent of 11·5 per cent in 1957 to 18 per cent in 1960, management was failing to make the most of its opportunities.

At the same time, the leaders of the industry could point to the fact that they had made considerable progress in reducing the dependence on scrap metal, in building larger individual works, and in reducing the level of fuel consumption; three policies formulated in the 1946 Report.[47] Furthermore, British steel prices were still below those of the American and European countries, with the exception of France, and in sheet steel the British price was 9 per cent lower than the French. The Iron & Steel Board in one of its roles as protector of the consumer had enforced price reductions on British producers during 1959 as their profits began to rise, and although this action impinged most directly on the high-cost producers it affected the cash flow of all. The industry could argue that as long as it would never be free to make 'exceptional profits' it would never feel safe in taking 'exceptional action' and the fact that price reductions were possible suggested that traditional actions would suffice.

Nevertheless, and in spite of these gains, two important traditional weaknesses of the industry remained. First, and most important, little had been done to eliminate unnecessary duplication of finished steel capacity. In the heavy rail trade there were nine rail mills owned by nine companies to share a market which had shrunk to less than 0·5 million tons a year. There were four manufacturers of railway tyres, wheels, and axles, three of which were in the Sheffield district. Similarly, there were seven producers of colliery arches. Duplication of the more important products was to be expected, but it was doubtful whether the market existed to support the five wide-flange beam mills which existed or were being planned and developed, and it should have been possible to produce heavy plates in fewer than the ten works which shared this output, and medium plates in fewer than thirteen works.

The second traditional weakness was in the continued belief that certain products should be made only in certain areas. This was most apparent in the case of sheet steel, where, because of the growth rate in this sector, it was also the most important. The champions of a Scottish, North Eastern or Humberside strip mill had lacked practical support from within the industry, so that the debate had not been as real as it appeared to be. There was never much doubt that Wales would retain its dominant position in this sector of the industry, even if one of the plate makers should enter the steel trade. The effect of both these factors was to make the future as much like the past as possible.

Rationalisation of finished products would have resulted in absolute, comparative, and relative locational change of products as well as of ingot output, as would a breakdown of product affiliations with defined areas. Such changes could have been obtained without compulsion if the vision had existed, for the industry had been given a warning in the recession of 1958–9, but the warning was first ignored and then forgotten.

By 1960 it was possible that the industry would have to face up to the implications of the two additional developments: the new steelmaking technologies and the changing pattern of the international ore trade. The price of foreign ore had been declining since 1957 and the decline was accelerating with the increased size of the ore carriers which could be used. At the same time, the cost of home ore was rising. If these divergent trends were to persist, then the raw material base of the industry would be redrawn. Likewise, if the early promise of the new converters should be fulfilled it would be necessary to restructure the technology of the industry. At no previous time since 1932 had there been such a potentially powerful combination of changing factors, but in 1960 the power was no more than latent. During the 1950s the tactics employed by the industry had been frequently good, and occasionally excellent, but there had been an almost complete lack of strategy. It was a fair-weather edifice which had been built, and one which was not suited to endure, at any rate in all its parts, the onslaughts which the industry was about to encounter.

5

The Prelude to Nationalisation

THE FINAL SEVEN YEARS of the post-war period leading to the second nationalisation of the major part of the industry were unhappy ones. They did nothing to justify the optimism and promise which the steelmakers had experienced towards the end of the 1950s. The promise of 1961 was 34 million ingot tons installed capacity by 1965 to meet a total demand of 30 million tons. By 1962 it was believed that 30 million tons would be the average level of annual demand for the entire decade. Accordingly, the industry accepted the arguments in favour of providing a small margin of spare capacity to meet peak demands, and turned its attention towards striving after higher efficiency rather than output at any price. Such was the promise: the reality was an annual average level of deliveries at home and abroad of 26 million tons of ingot equivalent, for even the peak of 28·3 million tons in 1964 fell short of the looked-for average. The 1960 output level was surpassed in 1964 and 1965, and was matched in 1966. The financial performance was even worse as the combined trading profits, after depreciation, of the fourteen companies which were to be later nationalised declined from £104 million in 1960 to £23 million in 1967.[1] Their associated return on capital invested plummeted from 18·8 per cent to 1·9 per cent over the same period. Attention to cost cutting and improved efficiency, which had appeared to be merely desirable, had become essential.

The impact of the new trading conditions varied in its effects from district to district, from company to company, and from works to works. The diverse fortunes of the districts are portrayed in Fig 10, where the main contrast is seen to be between the North East Coast, which never again attained the 1960 level of output, and Lancashire and Deeside where a minor setback in 1961 was followed by successively higher levels of output until 1965. Of the remaining districts, Lincoln-

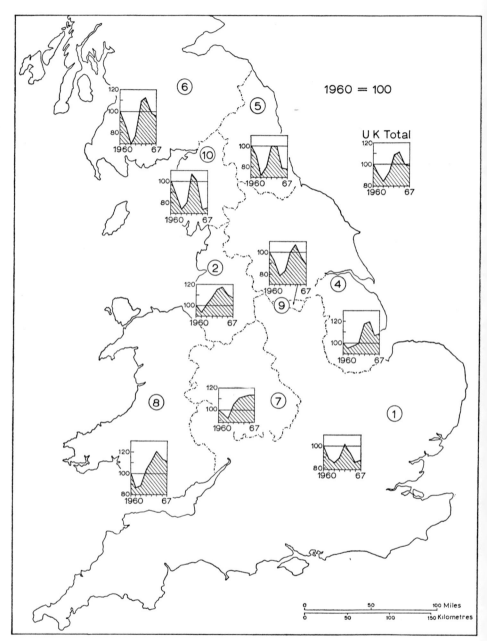

Fig 10. INGOT OUTPUT BY DISTRICT, 1960–7

shire, the West Midlands, and South Wales generally increased their output, while in Scotland, Sheffield and Northants output was generally lower. On a company basis 1965 or 1964 were record production years for all the major companies except SCOW and Dorman Long which never regained their 1960 levels of output. Only Consett Iron, South Durham and Stewarts & Lloyds ever surpassed their earlier record gross profit levels. At the individual works level, Llanwern passed the million-ton mark in 1964 as did Ebbw Vale and Consett in 1965. In South Wales the remaining cold metal open-hearth shops belonging to RTB and including Pontymister and Bynea were closed, as were the Port Talbot and Margam I shops in the Margam-Abbey works. Dorman Long closed the Acklam works in 1963.

The major cause of individual district and company deviations from the performance mean, represented by the total ingot level, was their adherence to one steel trade or another. The progress of four of the eight categories of finished steel for which the annual deliveries exceeded 1 million tons is plotted in Fig 11, from which comparisons with the trends in ingot steel production can be made. The main contrast was between the index for cold reduced sheets, which remained above the ingot index, and that for the light sections and associated trades which was consistently below. The strength of the sheet trades was such that its index followed a course independent of those of the remainder of the industry in the most difficult year, 1962. The regional specialisation in the production of this form of steel underpinned the total level of output in South Wales, helped to revive the fortunes of the Scottish industry after 1962, and, where it coincided with the production of rods as in North Wales and Lancashire, served to produce the most favourable production record among the major districts.

Within the wider control of product specialisation, variations in works efficiency or in raw material procurement and marketing costs were able to do no more than modify these trends. On the North East Coast, for example, South Durham based its production growth to 1·5 million ingot tons in 1965 on its participation in the pipe trade and attained export levels of 60 per cent in those products. On the other hand, the company found it necessary to pass its dividend payments in 1962, and, in spite of a change in accounting procedures, the high depreciation on the new plant kept the net profit level below that of 1960 when the 12 per cent dividend was restored in 1964. Within the company it was realised that the Cargo Fleet works, engaged in the production of sections and rails, would operate profitably only at the very best of times.[2] It now appeared that these would occur but rarely. In contrast,

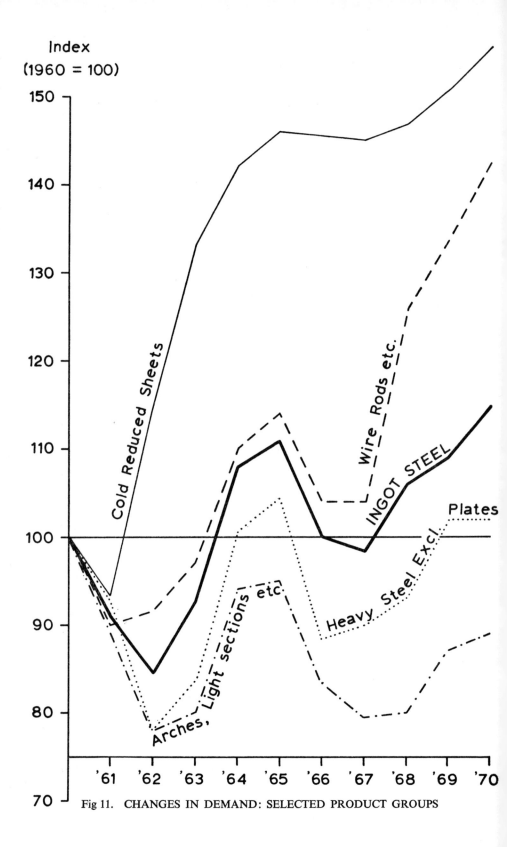

Fig 11. CHANGES IN DEMAND: SELECTED PRODUCT GROUPS

Dorman Long suffered reverses in output, return on capital invested, and profit levels, although the company always paid a dividend. In 1965, when 5 per cent of its output was sold in the ingot form, its output was 1·94 million tons compared with 2·27 million ingot tons in 1960. The return on invested capital fell from 17·4 per cent to 11·8 per cent and the net profits fell from £9·3 million to £5·9 million.

With the main exception of the Ravenscraig strip mill the investment decisions which had initiated the regional and company product specialisations pre-dated World War II, and subsequent developments had been elaborations upon that old-established pattern. To that extent the ability of the individual works to respond to the changing trade patterns of the 1960s was determined by decisions taken thirty years earlier. Market developments had, in the meantime, favoured some locations more than others. The clearest example of these changes followed upon the increased sheet steel prices announced by the Iron & Steel Board in April 1966. The expectation was that all sheet steel producers would raise their charges to all consumers by £2·62½ per ton, but against a background of declining home demand, increases in sheet steel imports, and rumours of hidden discounts, John Summers abandoned the system of uniform delivered prices and introduced new prices on a zonal system. The new maximum price was charged only in the South West of England. Prices in London and the South East were raised by £2·12½, in the Midlands by £1·62½, and in the North West and North Wales by only £1·12½. The other sheet steel producers responded with similar formalised zonal systems of their own, or by stating that they would match the quoted prices of their competitors at each location. Ultimately, it appears that a compromise solution was reached under which consumers near all the sheet mills were charged an extra £1·12½ and all other consumers were charged an extra £1·62½.

The ability of Summers to respond in this way was influenced by the growth of the motor industry at Halewood, Ellesmere Port, and Speke, and of other consumer industries in the North West. Similar developments in Scotland and South Wales had been on a smaller scale, and the large South Wales sheet steel producers were still heavily dependent upon distant markets in the Midlands and South East. The graphs in Fig 10 show that the most successful district in terms of crude steel output was the comparatively small West Midlands in which the continuous sheet steel industry was entirely absent. In that district the gross level of output for 1960 was passed in 1963 and continued to rise in each of the following four years. Moreover, the West Midlands was the only district in which the output of finished steel exceeded that of crude steel, with the re-rollers taking their raw material from South Wales and Sheffield and also from the North East Coast. All the sectors of the industry represented in the district shared in this growth, and three works, Bilston, Patent Shaft, and Round Oak, registered above-average rates of growth over the decade to 1967. Shelton had its own special difficulties. The district's share of national output rose from 5·2 per per cent in 1957 to 7·4 per cent in 1967, as total output was raised by some half-million ingot tons. Over the same period the output of the North East Coast district declined by a similar amount. The greater resilience of the West Midland producers seems to be associated with their central location within the most highly concentrated steel market in Britain, which also provided scrap supplies which were surplus to the local requirements. The siting of the works in the area had resulted, however, from nineteenth-century rather than twentieth-century decisions. Nevertheless, the proximity to major consumers seems to have benefited John Summers in the one case, and all the West Midlands producers in the other. Their success was a standing criticism of the location of the rest of the industry.

This introductory survey to the production record of the industry and of the financial record of the fourteen major private companies provides evidence enough of the increasing harshness of the trading environment in which the industry operated. In a period such as this, in which the actual trading experience of the industry fell so far short of the expected trading experience, it was inevitable that considerable tension should have been generated. The rapid technological changes which were taking place served only to augment the tension, and to remove from the range of theoretically possible lines of action the option of marking time and of waiting for the level of demand to rise again. As it was, the capital employed by the fourteen companies increased by £478 million from £750 million in 1960 to £1,228 million in 1967.[3] Even the comparatively small Lancashire Steel Corporation was spending over £2 million per annum throughout this period. Assuming, therefore, that it was essential to continue to invest over £50 million per annum, it was even more necessary that this money should be put into the right equipment at the right place, and that the pattern should not be distorted by company rivalry. It was argued in Chapter 4 that the apparent successes of the industry during the 1950s had blinded the companies to the need to reappraise their technology, their location and their structure, but it appears that as the financial difficulties intensified during the 1960s those blinding scales were gradually being removed. The future course of the industry without nationalisation can only be conjectured, but there is evidence to suggest that the organisational log-jam would have been broken, and that a more critical view of existing locations and technology was being taken.

The Coming of Oxygen Steel

The technological changes referred to above found their most evident expression in the hot metal melting shops where they took on revolutionary proportions. In contrast, the use of screened sinter, fuel oil, and oxygen-enriched blast in the ironworks was adaptive and evolutionary. Similarly, although more powerful motors installed in the new rolling mills served to emphasise the weaknesses of the older mills, they left the essential concept and plan of rolling mills unaltered. Even the potentially revolutionary principle of continuous casting was mostly adapted to present patterns of production. It was made the lynch-pin and saving mechanism of the obsolete works at Shelton, and a new scrap-using works based on arc furnaces and continuous casting was announced for Sheerness, in Kent, in 1964, but the project was repeatedly deferred. RTB installed a continuous casting plant at their stainless and alloy works at Panteg, and United Steel put their experimental plant at Barrow into commercial operation, but the two largest units at Port Talbot and Appleby-Frodingham were used as a means by which a small proportion of the total works output could by-pass the primary mill. The existing structures and locations of the industry were capable of absorbing the associated stresses without breaking.

In the cold metal melting shops large arc furnaces were installed at River Don, Parkhead and Park Gate, and at Stocksbridge an expanded electric arc shop replaced the open-hearth shop. Dorman Long placed two arc furnaces in the North melting shop at the Cleveland works, and United Steel and English Steel completed their schemes at Templeborough and Tinsley Park. These arc furnace developments, the operational advantages of which had been accepted in the 1950s, found a smaller counterpart in the completion of three developments using traditional open-hearth technology in the hot metal shops. At Bilston the reconstruction of the open-hearth furnaces was completed in 1961, and Dorman Long and Colvilles added the final furnaces to their Lackenby and Ravenscraig schemes. United Steel progressively converted five further furnaces to the Ajax process, and at Port Talbot some of the 230-ton furnaces in the Margam II shop were enlarged to 400 tons on the Maerz-Bolens principle. The significant point was that in practice the industry had already recognised that the open-hearth era for hot metal operations was drawing to a close, because those projects mentioned above were small when compared to the oxygen-using projects listed in Table 6.

Table 6

OXYGEN STEELMAKING PLANTS IN THE UNITED KINGDOM, 1965

Company	Location	Type of plant	No of furnaces and size (tons)	Start-up date	Annual capacity (million tons)
Colvilles	Ravenscraig Works	LD-AC	2 × 110	1964	0·84
Consett	Consett	LD	2 × 100	1964	0·84
		Kaldo	2 × 100		
Lysaght's	Scunthorpe	LD-AC	2 × 60	1964	0·50*
RTB	Ebbw Vale, Mon.	LD-AC	3 × 45	1960 1962 1963	0·67
	Spencer Works	LD	3 × 135	1962	1·57
	Redbourn	Rotor	1 × 100	1961	0·25
Stewarts & Lloyds	Corby	LD-AC	3 × 110	1965	1·68
Park Gate	Rotherham	Kaldo	2 × 75	1964	0·30
Shelton	Stoke-on-Trent	Kaldo	2 × 50†	1964	0·35
SCOW	Port Talbot	VLN	4 × 60	1959	0·95

Source: Steel Times Annual Review (1965), p. 73

  * Planned addition—vessels were interchangeable. The extra vessel brought capacity to 1·0 million tons.
  † Interchangeable vessels.

From that table it can be seen that the industry adopted both the LD process with its associated LD–AC derivative and the kaldo process, and that one works, Consett, chose both. The advantages of the kaldo were that it had already been proved capable of processing high phosphorus pig irons, and, with its slower operational speed, it could be relied upon to produce a greater variety of close-tolerance steels. The management at Consett had given close attention to both processes, and had adapted one of their acid Bessemer converters to the LD principle in 1958, but nevertheless opted for a fail-safe 'belt and braces' policy when they decided to install two 100-ton LD vessels and two 100-ton kaldos with a total capacity of 1·2 million ingot tons.[4] The new furnaces were built at the north end of the open-hearth shop and came into operation in February and May 1964, three years later than had been originally planned, as the open-hearth furnaces were progressively removed. The final melt was made on 1 January 1966. In May of that year one LD vessel alone produced more than 20,000 tons in one week, which was more than the ten open-hearth furnaces together had produced. By that time, greater experience with the LD, combined with the availability of lower phosphorus ores, had made the kaldo vessels almost redundant. One of those vessels was replaced with a third LD and the capacity of the works was raised, almost incidentally, to 1·4 million tons.

The result of these developments at Consett was twofold. Firstly, the operational bottleneck which had previously been at the melting shop was shifted backwards to the ironworks and forward to the rolling mills. A tentative scheme was therefore drawn up to expand the ore preparation plant, to rebuild and enlarge one blast furnace, and to add a rod and bar mill and a continuous casting plant for slabs. The depressed trading conditions of 1966 and the approach of nationalisation prevented the scheme from being implemented, but its existence acts as yet another reminder of the ways in which the momentum of an already existing operation can be harnessed to the pursuit of a balanced operation leading to higher and higher outputs without the locational merits of the works being reviewed or considered. In 1967 it was stated by a company director that it was 'entirely feasible' that Consett should expand to 3·5 million ingot tons at an additional cost of £40 million, and it was suggested that with the Tyne Dock being capable of expansion to receive carriers of up to 65,000 tons its location was not unsuitable for such a venture.[5] The second consequence of this development was that with the closure of the old plate mill and of the open-hearth melting shop an empty heart was being opened up in the centre of what had been, only twenty years previously, a highly congested works. The determination of the management had been such that the works had been provided, at a location whose transport deficiencies were locally approached only by those at the smaller Skinningrove works, with the most modern and efficient steelmaking plant of all. It was doubtful whether anyone outside Consett considered that expansion to 3·5 million tons was 'feasible', but the feasibility of Consett had long depended on the happenstance of its existence and the determination of its management. It was perhaps inevitable that when control of developments at this works passed outside to the British Steel Corporation this momentum should be lost, and these dreams should fade: no one had mentioned where the £40 million was to be found.

The kaldo process was also used as one of the supports of the Shelton redevelopment. By the end of the 1950s the mills and the open-hearth melting shop, with an output of 0·25 million tons, had reached a critical condition both technically and commercially, and it seemed as though closure was inevitable. The condition of the site, encroached upon on all sides by Stoke-on-Trent and bisected by the Trent and Mersey Canal, precluded the chance of a traditional reconstruction with a competitive volume of output, but it has been suggested that the decision to rebuild rather than close was partly activated by sentimental considerations as well as by objective measurements.[6] Be that as it may, the presence of a fully integrated ironworks and coke ovens, and a secure market in the Midlands for the surplus pig iron, appears to have persuaded the Summers management that if redevelopment was desirable at all it should incorporate a hot metal process.[7] The LD process was considered, but it was decided to install two 55-ton kaldos and to replace the primary mill with four continuous casting machines to supply blooms for the section mills and new universal beam mill. The cost was £20 million, and the capacity of the works was raised immediately to 0·35 million tons of finished steel. The production costs were reputedly among the lowest in Europe and the United States, and the operations were so flexible that most orders could be rolled in the week in which they were received.[8] Such flexibility, coupled with the works' central situation when related to the national markets, gave a greater competitiveness to the company in that it eliminated the customers' need to carry large stocks of steel. It was stated that the works was but a forerunner of many more 'pocket-sized' works which would be built to process locally arising scrap, and that such a profitable venture, built on a sixty-acre site, was conclusive proof that 'the minimum economic size for an integrated iron and steel works' was well under one million tons per annum.[9] If this were true there could be worthwhile savings from the national point of view in the elimination of hauls of steel from areas such as South Wales and the North East Coast to the Midlands and the South East. The scheme was the first practical application of the views of Sara and others in the mid-1950s, but it was nevertheless a hybrid in that it did not depend entirely upon locally arising scrap. Iron ore was still to be railed from Bidston on the Mersey. Like the Park Gate scheme the Shelton scheme was marred by a reluctance to abandon the blast furnaces already in existence, but here the mixture of the nineteenth century was even more apparent.[10]

The Normanby Park development demonstrates admirably the space-saving characteristics of the new processes, and the ease with which they could be fitted into existing works. In 1956 the works was producing 0·6 million ingot tons, but the demands on the mills resulted in a need for 0·75 million ingot tons. This need could have been approximately met by the construction of one extra open-hearth furnace, but there was no room for such a furnace in the existing shop, and it was not possible to enlarge the shop at either end. Furthermore, the congestion within the shop prevented a more intense use of oxygen on the existing furnaces. By 1958–9 the LD–AC process was becoming available, but it was not certain whether it alone could produce the complete range of steels which were required. It was clear, however, that if the process was to be installed, even with only two 50-ton vessels, the capacity would be expanded by at least 0·3 million ingot tons. The risk of having two melting shops operating below capacity levels was accepted, and it was decided to build a new shop alongside the open-hearth shop in a logical position between the blast furnaces and the ingot stripper shed. The maximum length of this new building was no more than 420 feet. When the process had proved itself it was found that if three 60/75-ton vessels were built, allowing any two to be used at one time, the capacity of the works *without* the open-hearth shop would be raised to 1·0 million tons. In Chapter 4 it was shown that in the 1950s such a level of output had been thought to be prohibitively expensive, and physically possible only by means of duplicating the open-hearth shop on the other side of Normanby Road. Only ten years later it was clearly shown both at Consett and at Normanby Park that almost any integrated works in the country was capable of being expanded to a minimum output of 1·0 million tons as long as the ironworks backing was present.

An obvious point from Table 6 is that all the developments were scheduled for existing works, or, in the case of Llanwern, for a works whose future existence had already been determined. In the case of Llanwern the new process was placed in a square melting shop measuring 1,000 feet by 1,000 feet which left ample space to the south to allow for a second such shop, should the long-term ambitions of the company be realised. This new shop, containing three 135-ton LD vessels, had a capacity of 1·6 million ingot tons, which should be compared with the six 360-ton open-hearths that South Durham had installed at West Hartlepool to produce no more than 1·0 million tons. It is doubtful whether any works in Britain, other than Llanwern, could be expanded to 3·0–4·0 million ingot tons and still retain a logical interior structure without a major reconstruction or reorganisation, and without using the new converters. Using the old technologies, and taking Appleby-Frodingham and Cleveland-Lackenby as representatives of those technologies, no fewer than eighteen open-hearth furnaces would be needed to produce 3·5 million ingot tons.

H

The last of the oxygen-based developments announced in the late 1950s to be completed prior to nationalisation was that at Corby, where it was decided to install one 90/100-ton LD–AC vessel in the open-hearth melting shop. This project was breaking new ground, not only locally but in the wider sense that vessels of this size had never been installed anywhere. The first vessel was built in 1960 and two more were added in the same shop in 1963–5 with an immediate target of 0·8 million tons. This was to replace a similar capacity from the Basic Bessemer shop in which the last blow was made on 22 January 1966. As the capacity of the vessels was raised, and as further operational experience was obtained, it became apparent that if the ironworks could provide sufficient backing there was a potential in the new process of around 1·6 million ingot tons, which was 40 per cent above the record output of 1960.

Although no more oxygen steel developments were completed under private ownership, two sets of proposals were approved by the Iron & Steel Board in 1965 and a third was deferred. The two approved schemes were for LD vessels at Lackenby and Port Talbot. The Lackenby shop was to be built alongside the new universal plate mill and was scheduled to replace the Redcar and Cleveland hot metal shops and a part of the Lackenby open-hearth shop. It was to have a capacity of 3·0 million ingot tons, and was to be fed with hot metal from Clay Lane. This fifth stage in the company's post-war development, which included extra stands in the plate mill and billet mill, was estimated to cost £23 millions. It cannot be pretended that the fifth stage had been contained as an embryo in the first stage, but the sequence of developments which had been announced in the twenty-year period all fitted roughly within the general strategy of the company as expressed in 1945. There had been local reverses as in the reconstruction and quick closure of the Redcar ironworks, and there were operational inefficiencies as in the comparative remoteness of Clay Lane from Lackenby, but the overall view is that the company was operating at a location which became increasingly favourable from the point of view of raw material assembly costs. In such a position, small inefficiencies could be easily absorbed. The weakness of the location was not in its site or in its technology, but in its range of finished products and its general remoteness from the Midland and metropolitan markets. Some progress towards diversification had been made to remedy the first weakness, but nothing could be done to eliminate the second entirely.

At Port Talbot the major item in the two-phase £42 million scheme submitted to the Iron & Steel Board in 1965 was the replacement of the four VLN furnaces with two 90-ton LD vessels and the addition of two 400-ton Maerz-Bolens furnaces in the Abbey melting shop. The second phase of the scheme consisted of an increase in capacity for the continuous casting machines, modifications to the hot strip mill, a new 56in hot strip mill, and a new LD melting shop with two 225-ton vessels. The result would be an increase in production of almost one-third to yield up to 4·0 million ingot tons. The first phase was approved by the Iron & Steel Board, but before any progress had been made on the project a revised scheme was proposed by the company. It was a clear indication of the speed at which the LD process was now being accepted and further developed, for the new proposal anticipated output of 3·75 million tons, all of which was to be obtained from two 270-ton converters. Both the VLN shop and the Abbey open-hearth shop would be closed. This willingness to abandon only partly depreciated plant revealed a more radical mode of thought in the Port Talbot management than was apparent elsewhere within the industry where the general tendency was to continue to use plant long after it had been fully depreciated. Both sets of attitudes have their appropriate times and places for application, but the Port Talbot attitude was the appropriate one for Britain in the mid-1960s.

The same attitude is detectable in the £80 million proposal put to the Iron & Steel Board by United Steel in 1966. The money was to be spent at Appleby-Frodingham on two LD vessels with a capacity of 2·0 million ingot tons, a new 2·0-million-ton slab mill, and an increase of light plate production to about 1·0 million tons. The South Melting shop would be retained, and the blast furnaces would be fed with a 50 : 50 Frodingham : foreign ore burden. The layout of the new works, which was to be built on the site of abandoned ore workings, would be designed to allow expansion to the level of 5·0 million ingot tons. Among the more interesting implications of this proposal was the revised place of Appleby-Frodingham in the total structure of the parent company. Investment of this proportion and production of this size must inevitably create a new balance within this Sheffield-based organisation. It represented not so much a break with the policy laid down by Gerald Steel as a realisation that efficiency in common steel production could be obtained only through growth. This had always been the case, but the scales had now been changed. It appeared that the Scunthorpe steelmen were to be forced to take the expansion which they had neither sought nor been allowed in 1958. At the same time, the decision to install LD vessels in Britain's only home-grown answer to the converters shows that, at long last, the argument within the British industry over the type of technology to be used had been resolved. Meanwhile, the Ajax process had won valuable breathing-space for the company. The third point was that the decision to use up to 50 per cent foreign ore in a works located on a cheap domestic orefield was an indication of the extent to which economic and technological considerations favoured the foreign material. With these enriched burdens the four blast furnaces would be able to support the expanded level of requirements of 2·5 million tons.

The proposals by Dorman Long and SCOW had been made at a time when the industry was not in the forefront of political attention, but this was not so when the Scunthorpe proposals were made. One section of the Labour party was using the argument that private ownership had produced too many small works as one justification for a policy which would nationalise in order to rationalise. Partly in its own defence against this argument the Federation had set up its rationalisation and co-ordinating committee under Sir Henry Benson; and A. J. Peech, chairman of United Steel, was a member of that committee. It was therefore probable that the timing of this announcement was dictated by the need to establish, firstly in the minds of the industry that Appleby-Frodingham was one of the locations upon which the industry would or should be rationalised, and secondly in the minds of the electorate that the private companies were aware of what was needed and also that they possessed the ability to satisfy that need—that nationalisation was unnecessary. The Iron & Steel Board deferred judgement on the scheme and asked that United Steel should not become fully committed to such a large scheme until the new Organising Committee had reported. This committee, under Lord Melchett, had been set up by the Labour government to facilitate the transition from public to private ownership. United Steel had no alternative but to agree to this suggestion, but it is doubtful whether it was in a hurry to implement and complete the scheme. It was the announcement of its intentions which was the important thing. Henceforward, all future plans for the industry, whether it was privately or publicly owned, would be compiled with the knowledge that a large development at Appleby-Frodingham was probable. Critics might suggest, as indeed they did, that the development should be located at Immingham, where the foreign ore was to be brought ashore, that it should mark the first step in a gradual transfer of the Scunthorpe steelmaking activities towards the sea, but the company recognised that Scunthorpe was already as close to the sea as were Consett, Ebbw Vale and Shotton, and furthermore it was not the intention to abandon the local ore field or the most efficient ironworks in the industry. In due course, the proposals were replaced by an even larger £130 million scheme which fully involved the Redbourn works, and to a lesser extent the Normanby Park works also. In 1966 the board of United Steel was unable to plan on such a broad canvas.

By 1966, therefore, it had been shown that the LD and LD–AC processes would provide the sole base for all foreseeable hot metal developments. At the same time there were reasons to believe that the 300-ton LD vessels to be built at Appleby-Frodingham marked the end of the period of rapid growth in these units. Table 6 shows that the vessels ordered for Llanwern in 1960 were each of 135 tons and that all the others were below 110 tons tapping capacity. In 1960 it had been thought that an ouput of 3·0 million tons would require two melting shops: in 1966 it was possible to obtain 5·0 million tons from one. In consequence the space requirements for steelmaking were being reduced, although the large vessels needed more ironworks support and larger rolling mills. The position had been reached in which it was theoretically possible to find either an LD or LD–AC vessel which would fit exactly into each works, and to produce steel at below open-hearth costs. If the 1960s had been a period of rapid growth in demand that policy could have been adopted. It would not have led to the lowest cost solution, because the larger works had cost advantages over the small even in the steelworks, but the policy could have been tolerated. A stagnant level of demand, however, required a different solution; one which certainly called into question the entire pyramidal structure of the industry, and possibly its absolute location. The optimum size for an individual works had become, once again, a crucial issue.

Optimum Works Size

Between 1955 and 1965 the proportion of British steel issuing from works whose individual output exceeded 1·0 million ingot tons had risen from 24 per cent to 62 per cent. By 1965, however, 1·0 million ingot tons was no longer a meaningful target. Nevertheless, apart from one reference to the desirable size of billet mills and hot strip mills in the 1961 Development Report of the Iron & Steel Board the question was not under active discussion in the industry.[11] Suddenly, in 1964–7, the issue became as important as the open-hearth versus converter arguments had been in the 1950s.[12] A common characteristic of all the contributions to this argument, with the exception of the *Benson Report*, was the reluctance to consider the question of location. This was logical only if the issue of works size could be detached from the locational problem, but implicit references to location were inevitable, as in W. F. Cartwright's paper, which compared the existing structure of the British sheet steel industry with a detailed ideal structure: two works instead of five.[13] The occasion of the paper's delivery was neither the time nor the place to say where those two ideal works should be located, but in practice Cartwright's company, SCOW, was already laying strong claims for further growth. Similarly, Dorman Long and United Steel were not prepared to observe the question of ideal works size in a locational vacuum.

By common agreement the industry was working towards a total capacity of 34 million ingot tons, but the Appleby-Frodingham development alone would equal 15 per cent of the total, or, if carried no further than the 3·0 million ingot tons level, approximately 10 per cent. The precise tonnages and percentages are not important, but, standing in the place of generalisations, they are indicative of the position to which the industry had come by 1965. There were twenty-two integrated works in operation in Britain in that year, counting Cleveland-Lackenby-Redcar as one, whose output ranged from about 0·25 million tons at Brymbo, Skinningrove and Workington to 2·7 million tons at Port Talbot. No fewer than ten works produced more than 1·0 million tons, and East Moors and Normanby Park were moving towards that figure. The arguments for expansion at Appleby-Frodingham, Lackenby and Port Talbot could be extended to Llanwern, Shotton and West Hartlepool, all of which had the necessary site space and all of which could obtain the necessary access to deep water as readily as Scunthorpe. If these six works were expanded to an average size of 4·0 million ingot tons they would be capable of producing 70 per cent of the *total* estimated requirements. (The argument leaves aside temporarily the associated question of product mix and the cold metal works.) Recent developments at Ravenscraig would require an output of about 2·0 million ingot tons, and there was a similar capacity at Corby. There, the difficulties of economically expanding the output of home ore were probably sufficient to place a limit at about that level. Congestion on the Cardiff site was likely to place an upper limit on pig iron and steel output at around 1·0 million tons. That level had already been reached at Ebbw Vale, and now that RTB had the much larger potential of Llanwern to uncover it was unlikely that there would be any pressure to expand production there. Assuming a limit of 1·5 million tons at Consett, and of 1·0 million tons at Normanby Park, these twelve works together could be made to produce 34·5 million tons, which was the target for the industry as a whole.

There remained, apparently surplus to requirements, ten integrated works with a collective minimum capacity of 5·0 million tons: Bilston, Brymbo, Cargo Fleet, Clyde Iron-Clydebridge, Irlam, Park Gate, Redbourn, Shelton, Skinningrove and Workington. In each case it could be argued, without recourse to community needs, that these works served a special industrial need either in the total steel industry picture, or in local terms, or in company terms, but these arguments applied most cogently to the mills rather than to their associated melting shops. If the argument was to be extended to embrace the local communities then it would be even more difficult to justify total closure, especially in the isolated communities such as Skinningrove and Workington. Moreover, even if large developments were to be carried out at only four of the six works which could be expanded to 4·0 million tons there would still be excess capacity in the industry at large.

Among the cold metal works the move towards giantism was less pronounced. Of the ten works mainly engaged in the common steel trade, Steel, Peech & Tozer produced 1·0 million tons and was expanding to 1·4 million tons. The other nine had a total capacity of 3·0 million ingot tons. The only likely candidate for closure without serious argument was Taylor Bros in Manchester, whose output was under 0·15 million tons. There remained the nine works engaged in the special steel trade, included within this study, with a combined capacity of 1·5 million tons. Development schemes to raise output to 0·5 million tons were being implemented at Tinsley Park, and this expansion would more than match the probable closure of the Northburn works at Coatbridge. All other companies could add a further 1·0 million tons, so that the industry was in the position in which large-scale development at six sites, marginal development at six others, and a maintained level of output at the remainder would provide no less than 47·0 million tons when no more than 35·0 million tons would be needed before 1975 at the earliest. No industry could view with equanimity a 35 per cent margin of excess capacity which was likely to endure for at least a decade unless some radical changes were made. Clearly the technological change in the steelmaking process had brought the industry to a crisis point even before the question of location was considered.

Situational Change

The question of location was with one exception ignored within the industry after the publication of the 1946 Report. That is to say, the locational framework in which investment decisions were made was assumed to be a given and fixed factor in the equation. The exception was to be found in the publications of the Iron & Steel Board, and most notably in its Development Reports. In the 1957 Report, as has already been seen, the Board observed that because 'there were few ideal sites for steelworks' their actual location was usually a compromise solution.[14] It did not specify whether the compromise was between conflicting cost factors and social factors in the present, or between the past and the future. Moreover, although it had the Orwellian insight to point out that some sites were more ideal than others, it did not specify whether the comparisons were to be restricted to sites which were already occupied, or between that set and the set of all sites, actual and potential. Even though the Board returned to this topic with an increased sense of urgency in 1961 it was virtually powerless to impose its views upon the industry, and it was obliged to permit major developments at both obsolete and obsolescent locations.[15] It approved and permitted the Llanwern development, and had no choice but to permit the Ravenscraig development, while doubtless disapproving of it on the grounds of industry cost effectiveness. The impotence of the Board was most clearly expressed in its inability to prevent the Millom Haematite Ore & Iron Company building a spray steelmaking plant to market up to 0·25 million tons per annum in 1966. It required other factors to stop that development and to bring about the liquidation of the company in 1969.

The issue of location was taken up in 1964 in an editorial in *Steel Times*, and by the Benson committee in its report in 1966. *Steel Times* attributed the 'geographical siting' of the British steelworks to an imaginary 'malevolent saboteur' who had successfully located them as far from the markets, the raw materials, and adequate land and sea transport facilities as possible.[16] It was an excusably pessimistic view of reality. The Benson committee was a little more sanguine in its assessment of the existing position and, in the so-called Benson Report, proposed a policy of comparative locational change coupled with the closure of certain works, while rejecting the option of a greenfield development for the hot metal industry.[17] The new concern with location was prompted by the realisation that there was a fundamental change taking place in the relative value of home ore and foreign ore, and in the different types of fuel which the industry was using and wished to use. The locational pattern of any industry which employs exhaustible sources of raw materials possesses an in-built element of insecurity, but the changes which affected the British industry in the 1960s were not only sudden but also the opposite of industry expectations. That the changes should occur at a time when demand was stagnant and when technology was being revolutionised was especially unsettling in that it removed yet another 'known' or 'given' factor in the decision environment.

Decline of the Home Ore Fields

The years 1960–7 saw the closure of two British ore fields, Cleveland and Oxfordshire. The former had been long in decline, and its closing was expected and of minimal importance in that the ores had been used exclusively at Tees-side works with ready access to ore wharves, and therefore to a foreign alternative. The Oxfordshire field, on the other hand, had been at the centre of a major planning inquiry in 1960 when RTB had sought an expansion in the level of output to meet the needs of the Spencer Works at Llanwern. Table 7 locates the areas of

Table 7

CONSUMPTION OF OXFORD AND SW NORTHANTS ORE
(000 tons)

Year	District 1 Derby Leics Notts Northants Essex	District 2 Lancs Denbigh Flint Cheshire	District 7 Staffs Salop Worcs Warks	District 8 S Wales	District 9 Sheffield
1960	211·4	94·1	389·0	594·6	21·0
1965	10·1	33·8	312·8	466·3	—
1967	—	38·1	118·6	150·2	—
1968	—	—	0·5	—	—

Source: Iron and Steel—Annual Statistics

consumption of the Oxfordshire ores. The principal trading weakness of this ore field lay in its lack of a captive local consumer, with the result that it was caught in the squeeze imposed by rising freight rates and costs of home ore and falling freight rates and costs of foreign ore. An additional factor was public resistance to an expansion of mining in this part of rural England, but the interest in this field manifested by the industry was not convincing. RTB closed its Irthlingborough mine, in the extension of this field into south-west Northamptonshire, in 1965. The closure of the field had a favourable rather than adverse effect upon the existing locational costs of the industry.

By 1967, therefore, the only large centres of home ore production were the North Lincolnshire field (4·7 million tons), whose output was used almost entirely in Scunthorpe, and the 'Northants' field (7·0 million tons). The figures in Table 8 show that the major consuming

Table 8

CONSUMPTION OF 'NORTHANTS' ORE

(000 tons)

	1960	1965	1969*
District 1	4,472	3,506	2,854
District 2	319	180	1
District 4	2,371	3,308	3,344
District 5	795	1,024	678
District 7	390	352	202
District 8	129	—	—
District 9	180	212	126
Total	8,656	8,582	7,205

Source: Iron and Steel—Annual Statistics

* The last year for which data was collected on this basis.

points for this ore were, firstly, upon the ore field itself, and, secondly, in Scunthorpe, but that 20 per cent of the ore had been used in other districts, including the North East Coast. The changes in the level of demand for these ores resulted from the closing of the small pig iron producers and the stagnation of Corby within the field itself; from the replacement of these ores by foreign ore on Deeside, and in Lancashire and South Wales; and from the growth of steel production at West Hartlepool and Scunthorpe. In consequence, Scunthorpe became the largest market for these ores, but it was also a market which was due to be lost to the foreign ore sources. At the same time, the market on the North East Coast could not be retained if the industry was radically restructured. It appeared, therefore, that the long-term future of the 'Northants' field was a level of production of about 3·5 million tons, with the precise level depending upon the size of the Corby works. It also seemed that production on the Lincolnshire field would stabilise at about 4·0 million tons.

This sudden decline of the domestic ore fields was anticipated neither by the Board nor by the Federation, so that when the company develop-ment proposals were being drawn up in 1959 it must have been assumed that this indigenous material would be used. Indeed, Stewarts & Lloyds planned a new quarry at Rothwell and larger operations at the Thistleton mine, and United Steel planned a new quarry at Stoke Rochford and a mine at Eston. The recognition of this assumption is further evidence for the belief that situational factors were never given great weight when arriving at development decisions. South Durham, for example, in 1961 was considering reopening its Twywell quarry in Northamptonshire to feed the expanded West Hartlepool works, and although one of the arguments used in favour of Llanwern as opposed to Kidwelly was its comparative proximity to the Oxfordshire field, the argument had the flavour of *post hoc* justification, for the company gave more than philosophical acceptance to the rejection of its plans for that field.[18] In 1958 the Iron & Steel Board had created a Special Committee on Home Ore, the main conclusion of which, appended to the 1961 Development Report, was that consumption would rise to 32 million tons of home ore in 1970 for an industry with an estimated ingot tonnage of 37 million tons.[19]

Increased Consumption of Foreign Ore

Such an expansion was forestalled by the combination of lower demand for steel and accelerated decline in the cost of foreign ore. The average c.i.f. value of all imported ores had already declined from its 1957 peak of 123 shillings per ton to 98 shillings in 1960, and was to decline to less than 84 shillings in 1965.[20] In contrast, the cost of home ore increased by 20 per cent between 1957 and 1962. In spite of the higher metal content of the foreign ores the immediate cost advantage nevertheless remained with the home ore user situated on an orefield.[21] Commenting on these costs, the Board estimated that in 1960 the average value per unit of iron in foreign ore delivered to the point of use was two shillings, and added that home ore was 'rarely' used where the delivered cost exceeded one shilling per unit of iron.[22] The price advantage of home ore was partly offset by the higher capital costs and fuel costs associated with its use, but the correct conclusion for the industry as a whole was a policy of specialisation with home ore users situated only upon the orefields and the other hot metal users located on or near the coast.

When the reversal in the trend of home ore production came, it came quickly. Instead of being one more step towards higher levels of output, the 1960 figure of 17·1 million tons proved to be a record. Nevertheless, in 1964, the year in which the gross tonnage of foreign ore used first exceeded that of home ore, the Board was still expecting that 19 million tons of home ore would be needed in 1970 for an industry whose estimated tonnage had been scaled down to no more than 30 million tons. The use of home ore declined as the industry firstly became aware of the cost advantages of using foreign ores and, secondly, began to implement various devices to improve its ability to obtain that material. Reference to Table 9, which shows the relative importance of the major foreign ore sources for selected years, shows that there were

Table 9

ORIGIN OF IRON ORE IMPORTED INTO UK
(% of total)

	1955	1960	1962	1965	1967
BY COUNTRY					
Sweden	32	27	32	32	22
Canada	11	19	13	16	19
Liberia	2	3	6	8	10
Mauritania	—	—	—	8	10
USSR	—	—	—	3	9
Venezuela	1	9	10	9	9
Brazil	1	3	4	3	5
Norway	—	2	3	4	4
Spain	6	4	5	3	4
Sierra Leone	5	4	4	3	1
Algeria	16	12	11	6	1
Morocco	*	5	2	1	1
France	5	3	3	*	*
Tunisia	7	4	3	2	*
BY REGION					
Scandinavia	32	29	35	36	26
W. Africa	7	7	10	19	21
Canada	11	19	13	16	19
Venezuela and Brazil	2	12	14	12	14
Spain and France	11	7	8	4	4
N. Africa	23	21	16	9	2
Total imported tonnage (million tons)	12·85	17·97	12·90	18·86	16·07

Sources: Iron and Steel—Annual Statistics, ISB and BISF.
* Less than 1%.

important changes in the tonnage involved and in the points of origin of that tonnage between 1955 and 1965, with most of the change taking place after 1960. The major threads in the pattern were the dominant position maintained by the Scandinavian sources, the increased importance of Western Hemisphere sources, and the decline of other European and North African sources offset by increased tonnages taken from West Africa. The grand result was an increase of 50 per cent in the total tonnage and a larger increase in the ton-mileage as the short-route sources became less important and the long-route sources became more important both relatively and absolutely. The data in Table 9 are, of course, only a summary of what the industry was able to do, and say little of what it wished to do, or should have done. To the extent that foreign ore is foreign ore wherever it may come from it would be possible to postulate a set of conditions under which these external changes need have no effect upon the internal operations of the industry, and upon its locational pattern in particular. Such a result would, however, be dependent upon a constant set of technical factors in ore transport, in the chemical constitution of the ores, and in the cost of the ores. In practice, constancy did not obtain in any of these sets.

The web of the British ore trade was woven from two strands: the historical and geographical happenstance that each ore-receiving port served one major works, and the overall control and co-ordination of the trade by BISC(Ore) exercised by the Federation. The first was the result of the scattered location of the British industry, and the second was a response to the trading conditions of the early post-war years. The role of BISC(Ore), which had been established during the war, was to obtain all imported ores for the British industry and to average the costs to all users, subject to minor price differences resulting from local operational efficiencies or inefficiencies. An almost inevitable consequence of this cost-levelling procedure was that it removed the impetus to perfect the local operations, because the financial gains would not be fully realised locally but would be spread throughout the industry. Capital investment in ore docks was, therefore, less attractive than investment within the works themselves, and would remain so until such time as the state of the ore supply system threatened to undermine the whole financial health of the industry. There was the added difficulty that improvements to the ore docks involved co-operation with outside bodies, negotiations with which were apt to be inconclusive, and certainly protracted.

Traditionally, the British, like all other ore trades, had been based upon tramp shipping, but in the 1950s BISC(Ore) had provided the industry with a fleet of purpose-built carriers, capable of carrying approximately half the industry's requirements. Against a background of escalating shipping costs these carriers were then chartered for periods of up to fifteen years. The philosophy underlying the design of this fleet was that the ships should be able to use the British ports as they existed. By 1955, nineteen such carriers were available or were on order, and of these twelve were of 8,500 tons capacity, and had been 'designed especially for the shallower ports, such as Port Talbot, Barrow and Workington'.[23] The three ports had much in common except for the tonnage which passed through them: a seemingly minor difference. By 1957 the total number of carriers available or on order had risen to seventy-two of which twenty-four were of the 8,500-ton size. The average size of ore carriers used in the British trade was 10,450 tons compared with 14,500 tons used by continental steelmakers and 21,500 tons used in the American industry. This resulted in higher c.i.f.

costs to the British industry compared with its continental competitors when using identical sources.[24] Wise though it seemed at the time, the system of long-term charters also reverberated to the disadvantage of the British industry. The system was therefore caught between the squeeze of above-average transport costs size for size, and an above-average dependence upon high-cost, low-capacity carriers dictated by the size of the British ports.

The advantages of the large carriers were that they made the use of distant ore sources economic, and gave to the industry which could use them greater bargaining powers with all ore suppliers. The British industry was partly aware of these advantages, and of the deficiencies of its existing arrangements, but does not seem to have been aware of the pace at which events were moving on the international scene; neither was it imbued with any sense of urgency. In 1959, for example, it seemed to accept the view that the optimum size for the British trade through to the middle or late 1960s was in the 20–25,000 dwt ton range because the 'slightly better' rates on larger carriers would be offset by the fact that there were 'very few ore exporting ports in the world' which could handle them.[25] That was true at the time, but it soon ceased to be so. The contribution of the industry to the *Rochdale Committee Report*, published in September 1962, showed that the tonnage figure had been uprated to 35,000 tons, while the view of the Committee was that 45,000-ton carriers should be used. In retrospect, the arguments at the time seem to have been circumlocutory: the ores imported into Britain came over short sea routes over which the largest carriers would yield no advantage, but the trade was confined to these routes because the British ports could not accept those largest carriers. The way out of this predicament was to put the question of the size of the port before the size of ore carrier.

Such a solution, however, posed further problems which stemmed from the prevailing one-to-one relationship between ore docks and iron-works. The established practice in the ironworks was to produce a furnace burden from a blend of ores: at Consett twelve different ores were in use, whereas the ironworks at Port Talbot used up to twenty-four.[26] This practice was partly a result of Britain's weak bargaining position in the ore trade, which was exaggerated in the Port Talbot case, but it also had a metallurgical foundation. The continuous arrival of small carriers from many sources helped to maintain a blend of ores, whereas the continuous arrival of large carriers to achieve the same result required the existence of large ironworks. The average consumption of ore at Port Talbot, the biggest ironworks, during the 1960s was approximately 3 million tons a year. If 60,000-ton carriers were to be used for that works no more than fifty arrivals would be required in any one year. Ten such shipments from a single source would be enough to raise that source to sixth place in the order of suppliers to the total British industry (using 1960 tonnages), which implied a change in ironworks practice and also a change in the whole of the ore shipping arrangements. Subsequent developments in Scotland showed that some changes were not impossible in that by 1967 76 per cent of the ores used in that district came from the Soviet Union, Venezuela and Liberia. Those ores were fed into two ironworks to produce 1·25 million tons of pig iron, which was more than was required from most individual British works. Assuming an average iron content of 59 per cent, an ironworks with an annual pig iron capacity of 1 million tons could be supplied with one 60,000-ton ship at approximately thirteen-day intervals. It was apparent that a good reason for not building larger ports in Britain was the small size of the individual ironworks which they supplied. This being so, it was not surprising that as late as 1965 the Federation should hold the view that 30,000-ton carriers would be adequate for the British trade with the exception of South Wales where provision for 65,000-ton carriers should be made.[27] Finally, in 1966, a more general acceptance of 60–65,000-ton carriers was given, by which time there were thirteen ore-exporting ports in the world which could handle ships of that size.[28]

In 1966 the largest ore dock in Britain, the Tyne Dock, could receive carriers of 33,000 tons, and there were three others, Glasgow, Middlesbrough, and Newport, which could accept ships of 21,000 tons. A firm commitment had also been made to build a 65,000-ton tidal basin at Port Talbot. The background to the Port Talbot decision had been long, complicated, and tortuous, and had involved almost every port authority in the Severn Estuary as well as the three major steel companies in the district. Doubts as to the ability of the original Port Talbot dock to supply the new works had been expressed in 1945, when there had been an attempt by the Iron & Steel Board to persuade the company to use the Kings Dock at Swansea. Barry dock had also been suggested. The first move to rectify the situation came in 1956 when SCOW entered into an association with the Cardiff works to acquire a site at Milford Haven suitable for the 'discharge and trans-shipment of ore from ships of the largest tonnage that can at present be envisaged'.[29] The necessary enabling parliamentary bill was pursued as far as the committee stage, but was then allowed to lapse. Whether Milford Haven was a suitable location for such a trans-shipment point or not, the existence of the scheme points to the fact that South Wales was the only district, with the exception of Tees-side, where it was reasonable to expect benefits from a common development to be shared between several works or companies. By 1961 the scheme had been abandoned, but the Iron & Steel Board in that year refused to permit an expansion of steel output at Port Talbot until provision had been made for carriers of over 25,000 tons: scarcely an ambitious figure.

By that time the Spencer Works was already under construction at Llanwern, and the ore supply mistakes which had been made at Port Talbot in 1947 were about to be repeated. The existence of the new works was also a complicating factor in planning the construction of a common ore dock if such a venture should be thought to be desirable. The principal point of entry for the new works was to be Newport Docks, situated on the west side of the river Usk. From there it was to be a two-hour round-trip journey to Llanwern. There was no provision for ore bunkers or stockyards at the docks so that the direct loading of the trains was slow, and the dispatch of the ships was delayed by the need to fit the ore trains into the local railway timetable and shift system. In later years RTB also made regular use of Barry Docks, twenty miles to the west of Newport. In 1962 RTB proposed to build a $3\frac{1}{2}$-mile jetty into the Newport Deeps from which to supply Llanwern directly by conveyor. The proposal encountered technical problems as well as objections from the Bristol Port Authority, and from the British Transport Docks Board which was anxious to keep the trade in Newport. A second, similar proposal received parliamentary approval in March 1965, but only after an active and bitter campaign by almost every voice of public opinion on the south side of the estuary. The jetty would receive 65,000-ton carriers, but all action was ostensibly forestalled by the decision of the government to ask the National Ports Council to report upon this scheme, on the parliamentary approved scheme for Port Talbot, and on renewed proposals for common ore docks at Milford Haven and also at Cardiff.

The Council reported favourably on individual developments at Port Talbot and at Newport in July 1965.[30] The reasons given included the closer overall control which could be exercised by the local works management, and the avoidance of potential difficulties and cost inflation associated with rail haulage from a common dock. The Minister of Transport gave approval for the Port Talbot tidal harbour in September 1965, and construction started in the summer of 1967. The original intention was to accommodate ships of 60,000 tons, and the estimated cost was £17 million, but by the time the work was complete in 1970 the project had been scaled up to 100,000 tons and the cost had risen to £20 million—there were advantages and disadvantages in delay.[31] Meanwhile, RTB, in conjunction with the British Transport Docks Board, had turned its attention towards considering an impounded basin at Uskmouth as an alternative to its already approved scheme. The receiving capacity for the new scheme was a minimum of 65,000 tons and eventually 100,000 tons. Once again, after opposition from Bristol, parliamentary approval was obtained but not until July 1967, the very month in which the industry was nationalised. This in itself was sufficient to ensure that no immediate action would be taken.

In 1967 the South Wales industry used 6·39 million tons of imported ore (as against 4·51 million tons in 1960), but because of its inadequate ore docks was taking this ore from no fewer than fourteen different countries. The inadequacy was highlighted, firstly, by its being almost the only district still using ore from France (average iron content 40 per cent) and, secondly, by the fact that Australian ore which was being used at Port Talbot had to be brought via Rotterdam. This trans-shipment had the effect of almost doubling the transport charges on the ore.[32] The North East Coast and Scotland, on the other hand, with their smaller tonnage requirements, but with their superior but by no means perfect dock systems, were taking ore from ten countries only.

Twenty years separated the decision to build the hot strip mill at Port Talbot and the beginning of the construction of an ore dock which could match it in terms of scale and efficiency. When seen from the outside, the delay may occasion dismay because the need for such a dock was so readily apparent, and its absence was an obvious cause of diminished levels of profitability. The need was also apparent to the men who operated the works, but it had to be placed within an order of priorities established by comparisons with other needs. This scale of priorities had existed in one form or another since the original choice of the Port Talbot site had been made. If the works had been placed in 1947 on a coastal greenfield site without access to a pre-existing dock, then a dock must inevitably have been included in the original scheme. Using the Middlesbrough wharf as a model, its capacity would have been 15,000 tons. But the priority of 1945 was the rehabilitation of the tin-plate trade within the confines of the industry's locational structure and financial borrowing powers. The prime need was for a mill, not for a dock. The subsequent and unforeseen history of the tin-plate and cold reduced steel sheet trades continued to place the level of output rather than the cost of output at the top of the list of priorities. Over the years

I

1953 to 1964 a minimum of £152 million was spent at Port Talbot and its associated works in order to meet that prior need.

When the new ore wharf was finally built the company's contribution to the cost was the comparatively small figure of £4 million. This sharing of the costs with outside interests contrasts with the total burden of cost carrying for investment within the works. The decision to build or not to build an ore wharf involved outside authorities as the allocation of costs indicates. It was therefore a more complex decision than that of building a new melting shop and was, in turn, the more likely to be deferred. Furthermore, as a minor partner in the scheme, in so far as the shouldering of the financial burden was concerned, the steel company could play no more than a subject role in the decision-making exercise. As a major customer, and thereby as a producer of revenue, its influence upon the decision was larger than its capital share, but as its own need for a harbour intensified it was joined in the queue of potential customers by the new Spencer Works. With the passage of time the problem became more complicated rather than simpler, and the final outcome had as much to do with the fact that Port Talbot's needs pre-dated those of Newport as it did with the inherent merits of the Port Talbot harbour itself. In this debate the Newport management, involved with the commissioning of a new works, was at a comparative disadvantage, even though its need for efficient ore-handling arrangements would in due course be as great. There was a scale of priorities at Newport as there was at Port Talbot, and in 1964 the ore arrangements were not at the top of that scale. Once the new Port Talbot harbour had been built it was certain that it would influence the precise location and sequence of new investment in the same way as the old dock had influenced the old. Such influences are an essential ingredient of investment in a mature industry and in a mature industrial economy.

Corporate Structure

The important issue of the industry's corporate structure began to receive attention at the same time as the problem of location, ie, 1964. In many instances the two questions were discussed together, suggesting that the answering of the second was dependent upon the reformation of the first. Thus the *Steel Times* editorial which had referred to the imaginary 'malevolent saboteur' of the industry's locational pattern blamed all the post-war governments for obstructing the formation of a rational corporate structure. Supposedly, under a regimen of relatively free capitalism 'the number of steel companies would have shrunk, by alliance and absorption, to the economically viable minimum'.[33] There was limited evidence to support such a view. It was true that it had been private initiatives which had created the Steel Company of Wales, and that it had been the Government which had insisted upon Trostre and Velindre when only the latter was sought by the company. It was also true that it was the Government which had insisted upon two strip mills rather than one in 1958. Likewise, the Government had denationalised the industry in the 1950s without giving serious thought to reforming its structure. On the other hand, the reforming moves initiated by the engineering companies in their policy of backwards integration, and by Firth Brown in its purchase of William Beardmore, did not lead to plant closures. The only examples of ownership changes resulting in rationalisation were the purchase of Bynea and Partridge Jones by RTB.

Indeed, the evidence points in the opposite direction. The workings of the Industry Fund, excused on the grounds of being in the national interest, had successfully prevented the free play of market forces, and the influence of powerful personalities had been ably demonstrated in the perpetuation of the separate identity of South Durham. There is also on record the insistence of Gerald Steel, the managing director of United Steel until his untimely death in 1957, that any expansion of that company should be vertical and not horizontal.[34] This policy was continued after his death, when the company took a 49 per cent shareholding in Ambrose Shardlow, a Sheffield drop stamper (GKN took 51 per cent), and, with Interlake Steel Corporation of America, acquired full control of Gerrard Industries, strapping makers, in which it already had a minority holding. In 1961, United Steel sold its holding in John Summers in order to help finance its Rotherham and Scunthorpe developments, and had thereby reduced its horizontal connections. Moving in the same direction, Stewarts & Lloyds acquired Wolverhampton and Birchley, and RTB acquired Whitehead Iron & Steel.

In 1965–6, however, Nial Macdiarmid, managing director of Stewarts & Lloyds, and also a director of United Steel, made an attempt to break the corporate log-jam. He suggested that the two companies should act together and take over South Durham.[35] The stimulus for this initiative was his desire to expand further the production of wide-diameter steel pipes, and his awareness that this could best be done at a coastal location. If United Steel joined the scheme they could take responsibility for the production of plates and sections, and could presumably partly rationalise the section and railway products trade by closing Cargo Fleet. The plan envisaged the expansion of iron and steelmaking at

West Hartlepool, and the construction of a continuous light plate mill for pipes. United Steel, however, saw the proposal as a threat to its own plans for Appleby-Frodingham, and therefore suggested that Scunthorpe should be the location of the joint venture. This counter-proposal was rejected by Macdiarmid, at first sight with good reason, because although United Steel might pretend that Scunthorpe was coastal this was evidently not a view shared by Stewarts & Lloyds. On the other hand, the West Hartlepool site was served by an ore dock which was already inadequate, and United Steel could rightly claim very low ironmaking costs at Scunthorpe. At this point the discussions were ended, but so far as is known there had never been mention of a complete union of the two companies.

The subsequent moves of the private companies did not involve United Steel except to link the company in rumour with the ailing Lancashire Steel Corporation. It is difficult to see how such a move would have benefited United Steel except for the fact that Scunthorpe was already becoming involved in the bar, rod and wire trades in which Lancashire Steel was almost entirely involved. There is very little evidence which would lend credence to the rumours, but they should not be entirely discounted. Meanwhile, Stewarts & Lloyds persisted in their endeavours to reach the coast. In June 1966 it was announced that with South Durham they were considering the construction of a new pipe mill at Greatham, adjacent to the smaller company's works. Chetwynd Talbot died in July 1966, and, whether by coincidence or not, the event was quickly followed by the announcement that the two companies were considering a full merger. In the autumn the range of talks was extended to include Dorman Long with the purpose of increasing the financial resources of the group, and of rationalising heavy steel production. The authorised capital of the three companies was £128 million, of which £60 million derived from Stewarts & Lloyds. In the previous financial year the trading profit of the three companies, after depreciation, had been South Durham £5·7 million, Dorman Long £5·9 million, and Stewarts & Lloyds £15·3 million. The merger was arranged to take place if the Government's nationalisation proposals were not implemented, and the new company with its head office in Middlesbrough was to be called British Steel & Tube. It meant, firstly, that Stewarts & Lloyds, which had made a major locational move in the 1930s, was now prepared to move the centre of gravity of its future operations yet again. Secondly, the merger would at last achieve the long-sought rationalisation of steel production on the Tees, but with the added merit of greater financial reserves and cash flow. It did not, however, mean that Corby, Clydesdale and Bilston would be closed.

Prior to this new arrangement, in 1964, Dorman Long had entered into an agreement with Consett Iron under which each company would provide for the other up to 2,000 tons per week of rolling capacity in their respective universal and sheared-edge plate mills. The Redcar plate mill would be closed. It was stressed at the time that no formal reorganisation of capital would ensue, but rumours to the contrary persisted.[36] The new arrangement with Stewarts & Lloyds now appeared to leave Consett Iron on its own, but it was possible that this company too would eventually be drawn into the net. A similar rolling agreement existed in South Wales between SCOW and RTB, under which slabs produced at Port Talbot would be rolled on the hot mill at Llanwern before being returned to the cold mills in West Wales. The trend in trading conditions prevented the agreement, which allowed for an interchange of up to 0·4 million tons a year, from being fully implemented. Other similar agreements, in lieu of company mergers, were perhaps possible elsewhere, but none was made.

By 1966 the weight of outside opinion was firmly committed to a policy of mergers, rationalisation and larger steelworks. *Steel Times*, becoming increasingly critical of the apparent inaction, referred deprecatingly to the policy of 'piecemeal revamping of works' by the companies, and suggested that if greenfield developments were financially beyond their individual means 'something really worthwhile' could be achieved if they 'merged their interests'.[37] It was against this background of thought, and against the background of a Labour government whose intention to nationalise the industry was thwarted only by the lack of an overall majority on this issue, that the industry set up the new Development Co-ordinating Committee. Its purpose was to examine the technical requirements for the period up to 1975, and to consider the organisational changes that would be required. In this latter important respect the 1966 Report would differ from that which had been published twenty years earlier. Once again, however, there would be no machinery to ensure the adoption of the proposals once they had been made. The Committee intended to publish the detailed results in a separate volume, but the general election of April 1966 ensured that the industry would be nationalised, with the result that only the technical survey emerged in the Benson Report. The committee consisted of three members from outside the industry, Sir Henry Benson, Sir Duncan Oppenheim, and Sir Peter Runge, and three industry leaders, E. T. Judge (president of BISF and chairman of Dorman Long), A. J.

Peech (chairman of United Steel) and Sir Julian Pode (chairman of SCOW).

There is no doubt that the publication of the Benson Report was an anti-climax, because it did no more than repeat what informed observers of the industry had already said was required. The area of real concern, difficulty, and controversy would have been covered in the Stage II Report. In most cases it is not possible to do more than guess what the agreements between the companies would have been, but the Stage I Report does give a fairly clear picture of the pattern which would have been required. In the first place, the Committee did not feel able to comment upon the activities of the engineering groups involved in steelmaking; thus it must be presumed that it envisaged the continued existence of Briton Ferry, Llanelly, Cardiff, Brymbo, Round Oak, Patent Shaft, and Park Gate (1967 output of around 2·7 million tons). Secondly, by direct implication of what was said, the Committee anticipated the cessation of iron and steelmaking, but not of rolling, at Ebbw Vale, Cargo Fleet, Skinningrove and Consett, and possibly even at West Hartlepool. Thirdly, it implied indirectly that Bilston and Irlam, and possibly Shelton, could be the location of cold metal workings only.

A policy such as the above, in which some works would continue to live as re-rollers of semi-finished steel, was suggested as an interim measure because it was believed that the savings on the higher capital costs of new mills were less attractive than those to be gained from the new steelmaking processes. However, the continued existence of these outlying mills would adversely affect the loading factor on the central mills during periods of recession. This policy also had the great social merit of phasing the closure of these outlying works over a period which would almost certainly extend to a generation. A policy of successive closures of departments at a works as opposed to a closure of the complete works at one time would reduce the impact upon the employment situation in the neighbourhood. Dorman Long had followed such a policy at Britannia, Acklam and Redcar. Inasmuch as most steelworks were located in development areas, this was a major consideration. However, such a policy would raise at frequent intervals the problem of how much capital should be invested in these re-rolling works in order to keep them in a satisfactory condition to meet the increasingly rigid specifications of the steel consumers. The development of shared facilities between neighbouring works where expansion was anticipated was recommended, and the policy of central ironworks and steelworks and outlying mills was but an extension of this policy.

The Committee did not decline to specify the amount of capacity which should be withdrawn (9·0 million ingot tons (paragraph 196)) nor those locations which should be chosen for further development. The Scottish industry was set aside as a separate unit to supply the requirements of Scotland and Northern Ireland, and the recommendation was that the industry should be concentrated upon *one* integrated plant with outlying mills. Again, Hallside, as an alloy steel producer, would presumably continue to make its own steel. By implication, the chosen location was Ravenscraig, because the Committee had rejected the possibility of greenfield developments (paragraphs 164–5). In England and Wales it was proposed (paragraph 176) that there should be one multi-product works at Scunthorpe (5·0 million ingot tons minimum), one *or* two on Tees-side (6·0 million ingot tons) and two in South Wales (8·0 million ingot tons). Deeside was considered to be suitable for development 'in the longer term' (paragraph 79) and should in the meantime operate at a level of 2·0 million ingot tons. Two or three cold metal works with a total capacity of 4·5 million tons would be required. 'A suitable nucleus for one' already existed in the Sheffield area, and the other(s) should be built in the London–Midlands–South Lancashire scrap-arising belt, possibly on the site(s) of existing integrated operations not scheduled for expansion. Finally, these proposals must be seen against the background of the Federation's reversion to its earlier policy that capacity should be commensurate with trend demand rather than peak demand, and that the extra peak demands should be met by imports (paragraph 64).

Nevertheless, the dominant impression which emerges from analysis of the Report was that caution was to be the touchstone of the future as it had been of the past. The Committee, in most cases with justification, had set itself against greenfield developments in favour of selective development on a large scale at no more than four or five (six, including Scotland) sites—Scunthorpe (Appleby-Frodingham), Port Talbot, Llanwern, and Lackenby, with the possible addition of West Hartlepool. This was not a bad decision because it recognised that even the 'malevolent saboteur' had not reduced the industry to the state in which all its locations were totally compromised.

In practice, the discussion and the action were curtailed by the act of nationalisation in 1967. Nationalisation was probably the quickest means by which the restructuring of the industry could be achieved, but although that argument was used at the time, the immediate stimulus for nationalisation was in the balance of power within the Labour party. The industry had, none the less, demonstrated that it was aware of its triad of problems, technology, location and structure, but it had not demonstrated that it had the financial resources or the will to solve all three. Whatever the reasoning which brought about the second nationalisation of the industry, the implications of the action were of such magnitude that 1967 must be considered the end of the era which had its beginning in 1932.

A New Industry in Old Locations

A valedictory survey of the locational pattern of the privately owned industry as it appeared in 1965, its year of record production, reveals that, subjective assessments notwithstanding, some notable changes had been produced since 1945. The most obvious of these was the reduction in the number of works operated by the twenty-three companies from fifty-two to forty-one, but of greater immediate and long-term significance were the changes in the size of individual works output. These changes have been summarised in Fig 12, which has been arranged to emphasise the diagonal movement of the industry across the years into what can be considered as the new territory of the multi-million-ton works, only the margins of which had as yet been colonised. This quasi-migration had been effected by the closure of eleven works in the first three classes in Fig 12, and of one, Acklam, in class 4; by the construction of two new works, Tinsley Park and Llanwern, in classes 5 and 11; and, most importantly, by the migration of works between classes.[38] The reduction of the population of class 2, for example, from thirteen to seven in the years 1955–65 was achieved by three closures and the migration of two members into class 3 and of one into class 4. The direction of migrations, which, with only three exceptions, was into the higher numbered classes, reflected the policy of almost universal growth. The longest migrations were achieved by the sheet steel works, but major moves were also undertaken by Consett Iron and West Hartlepool which migrated from classes 3 and 2 to 11 and 10 over the twenty-year period. It should not be forgotten that this latter pair had been designated as locations of limited growth or of imminent closure in the 1946 Report, and their final positions in Fig 12 are evidence of the dynamism which actually existed at those locations. Those were the notable migrations; elsewhere movement had been less perceptible.

The direction of these movements was an established fact, and its continuation into the future was mainly agreed, but the debate, as already seen in Chapter 4, concerned the speed and distance of future migrations. Using the proportion of each works in each of the thirteen

CLASS NUMBER	CLASS SIZE (000´tons)	1945	1955	1965
1	< 100	● ● ● ● ● ● ● ● ● ●	● ● ● ● ●	● ●
2	101– 200	● ● ● ● ● ● ● ● ● ● ● ● ● ● ● ●	● ● ● ● ● ● ● ● ● ● ● ● ●	● ● ● ● ● ● ●
3	201– 300	● ● ● ● ● ● ● ● ● ●	● ● ● ● ● ●	● ● ● ● ● ● ●
4	301– 400	● ● ● ● ● ● ● ●	● ● ● ● ● ● ● ●	● ● ● ● ●
5	401– 500	● ● ● ● ●	● ● ● ●	● ●
6	501– 600	●	● ●	
7	601– 700	● ●	● ●	● ● ● ●
8	701– 800			●
9	801– 900		●	
10	901– 1000		● ● ●	● ● ●
11	1000– 1500		● ●	● ● ● ● ● ● ●
12	1501– 2000		●	● ●
13	>2000			●
		n = 52	n = 47	n = 41

Fig 12. COMPARATIVE AND ABSOLUTE LOCATIONAL CHANGE, 1945–65

classes in Fig 12 as the measured characteristic, a significant difference between the form of the industry as it was in 1965 and as it had been in 1945 is indicated.[39] However, this does not mean that the changes had been large enough to satisfy the requirements of a minimum cost model for the industry. Indeed, the gulf which separated the industry from that ideal was as great as that which separated the actual forms of the industry in 1945 and 1965. The minimum cost model would suggest the complete evacuation of classes 1 to 10 by the integrated industry, and of classes 1 to 3 by the bulk cold metal producers. The recognition of the scale of the changes which had occurred is important in itself, but in the context of this study the full realisation that a 'new industry' now occupied the old locations is of even greater importance. It suggests that the relationship between location and technology may be so loose as to allow large-scale technological change within an existing locational pattern. Alternatively, it suggests that it is possible that movement at the technological and locational frontiers can be out of phase. However, it must follow that unless the location of industry is a random phenomenon the position must be reached, sooner or later, in which the existing locational pattern can no longer absorb the strains produced by new technologies and new patterns of demand.

The ability of an existing locational pattern to accommodate itself to the new demands which are being made upon it depends not only on the magnitude of those demands but also upon their velocity. If, for example, it had been the intention in 1945 to double the capacity of the industry over eight years rather than to raise it by no more than 37 per cent, greater attention must have been given to the issue of location: the Clydeside and the Midland ore-field works would have been built. As it was, the raising of output by 100 per cent was spread over sixteen years and was achieved by a series of incremental, cumulative decisions, no single one of which seemed to require a basic appraisal of the industry's location. Similarly, if in the years which followed 1962 the decision had been taken to close all home-ore workings rather than to adopt a policy of selective mining, the closure of the primary departments at Corby would have been certain, and of those at Scunthorpe would have been probable. In due course home-ore mining will cease, and such an action, *ceteris paribus*, will have sure consequences for Corby and will cast doubt upon the wisdom of the present Anchor scheme at Scunthorpe. A present awareness that these or similar doubts will arise is, however, no more than an argument for giving to present developments a maximum flexibility of response to future changes. It is not an argument for mortgaging the present to the distant future.

A major defect of traditional cartographic representations of industry, and of diagrams such as Fig 12, is that they give no indication of the capability of the existing pattern to absorb further change, and thereby fail to signal the proximity to, or distance from, the need to prepare for relocation. A system which is already fully stretched will succumb to the addition of even a small and gradual change, whereas one which is not so tense will be able to absorb even large and sudden changes. This applies to the industry as a whole, to its constituent sectors, to the individual works, and to the separate stages in iron and steel manufacture. However, it is improbable that a pressing need to relocate will simultaneously appear in each of these stages, sectors and works. The introduction of the continuous hot strip mill, for example, could have no effect upon the locational pattern of the steel sections producers, although within the relevant sector it caused the number of works engaged in sheet rolling to be reduced from at least fifty in 1937 to five in 1965. Apart from Blochairn, Britannia and Acklam, all the works which were closed during these twenty post-war years had been in the sheet steel sector: the remaining sectors had been able to adjust to the demands made upon them within their existing locations. Within the sheet steel sector, however, the ability to respond had varied from site to site. Thus the elasticity of the Shotton site had permitted a fourfold increase in output, whereas the constraints at Ebbw Vale had permitted a doubling of output but thereafter had made the search for a new location for expansion inevitable, as long as that expansion was to be under the aegis of RTB. In 1965 it was possible to believe that the period of absolute locational change for the sheet steel industry was over. Such a belief did not imply that the existing pattern was perfect, but it recognised that there was sufficient flexibility within the Ravenscraig, Shotton, Llanwern, and Port Talbot sites to allow for any future requirements. It seemed inevitable that the primary departments at Ebbw Vale would be closed, but this had been implicit in the selection of Llanwern.

The same continuity of the existing pattern of the other bulk steel manufacturing sectors into the future was not, however, assured. These sectors had escaped the technological revolution which had disturbed the old sheet mills, and had also experienced a slower rate of growth. The changes that had been required had, for the most part, been capable of absorption within the existing locational framework. Nevertheless, it seems that the traditional modes of iron and steel production had taken many of the existing members of these groups to the extreme limits of their capabilities. That is to say, that even without the new steelmaking technologies, and the new patterns of international trade in iron ore, further growth at many locations was unlikely because of the restrictions of their size of site. Bilston, Cargo Fleet, East Moors, Irlam, Lanarkshire Steel, and Redbourn had all absorbed the slack which had existed in their locations in 1945 and the list could certainly be extended. This did not mean that closure was inevitable but only that further growth would have to be located elsewhere. The severity of the locational crisis created by the LD process resulted from the fact that it demanded a reaction from a locational pattern in which many parts were already near to breaking-point. The freedom to adapt to these pressures within the existing structure was further reduced by the new patterns of ore trading and by the slower rate of growth that the industry now anticipated. It seemed that the blast furnace was almost the sole centre of stability, without which the industry would have been in a complete state of flux, but even there the small size of British furnaces was seen to be a handicap.

It has already been seen that the hot strip mill had resulted in a restructuring of the organisation of the previously fragmented sheet steel industry. Similarly, the tentative formation of British Steel & Tubes has been interpreted as the first response of the other steel companies to the need for change which had come to them almost thirty years later. The formation of the British Steel Corporation in July 1967 pre-empted that and all subsequent moves, and although it created difficulties of its own it made the overall planning and rationalisation of the British steel industry theoretically possible for the first time. It was, however, by coincidence that the ability to plan in such a way should have been granted at a time when it was most needed.

6

A Real Steel Industry?

THE BIRTH of the British Steel Corporation in July 1967 coincided with the lowest level of new orders for steel in any period since the last quarter of 1962. Since reaching a peak weekly average of 0·42 million tons of finished steel in the last quarter of 1964, demand had declined by an average of 0·29 million finished tons. Moreover, since early 1965 the level of deliveries had exceeded that of new orders, resulting in a shortening of the order book and increasingly difficult and expensive operations in the rolling mills. It was scarcely an auspicious time to embark upon a new venture, yet these very difficulties had been instrumental in persuading many who would otherwise have remained opposed to nationalisation that a new start was essential. Nevertheless, it was not an entirely bleak future which confronted the new organisation because the great imbalance between deliveries and orders which had characterised 1966, when the weekly disparity had averaged over 20,000 finished tons, had been reduced almost to vanishing point, and the hope was that the next demand cycle was about to begin. Subsequent developments proved that this was to be the case as the level of demand rose to new peaks in the first quarter of 1969 and again in 1970 (see Fig 13). The boom which was about to begin repeated the pattern of previous booms by carrying the industry to new production records, 27·8 million tons in 1970, but whereas the peak of 1965 had been 11·2 per cent above that of 1960, the 1970 peak was no more than 3·2 per cent above 1965. At the same time, the level of imports rose above 2 million tons in 1968 for the first time since World War II, and it stayed above that level so that by 1970 almost 12 per cent of steel consumed in Britain was contributed by foreign sources. This high level, which was partly offset by record export figures, was to be accounted for by interruptions to production at home, but also by the growth of excess

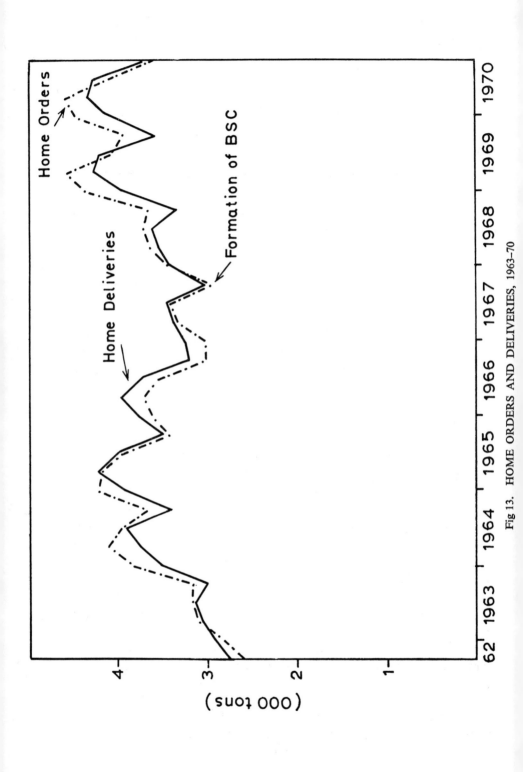

Fig 13. HOME ORDERS AND DELIVERIES, 1963–70

capacity world-wide and a subsequent softening of prices in export markets. The British share of world steel production declined to less than 5 per cent in 1970.

As the total demand for steel began to improve during 1967 it was apparent that the trends which had been developing since 1958 were to continue. Once again the upsurge was led by demand for cold reduced sheets, the output of which increased by 66 per cent over the decade, and continued to rise even through 1971 when the other sectors of the industry were yet again in recession (see Fig 11). Other growth sectors were found in wire rods and plates, whereas the other heavy trades and light sections enjoyed only marginally higher demand. The result was an increased polarisation of the industry between areas and works of prosperity on the one side and centres of depression on the other, with the possibility that a situation of overall excess capacity would coincide with local capacity shortages. Under such circumstances further comparative locational change was certain, and some absolute changes seemed probable with candidates for closure appearing among the heavy steel producers.

The British Steel Corporation

By vesting in the British Steel Corporation the securities of all British companies whose individual output had exceeded 0·475 million ingot tons in the year ended 30 June 1964 the British Parliament brought into being on 28 July 1967 an organisation which, in terms of output, was the second largest, and which in terms of sales or asset values was the third largest steel company in the non-communist world.[1] A movement among the steel companies of foreign countries to merge and to consolidate was already apparent, with notable examples being found in France, where the production of common steels was consolidated into two groups, in Germany, where August Thyssen Hutte acquired Huttenwerk Oberhausen, and in Japan where Yawata Iron & Steel and Fuji Iron & Steel were merging to form Nippon Steel. The negotiations in this last case were completed in March 1970 when there was brought into existence a company with a production capacity of 33 million tons, which represented one-third of the Japanese total. The creation of a large steel company in Britain reflected world-wide trends in steel technology and business organisation, but the consolidation of no less than 90 per cent of the nation's output in one concern was the direct result of political action. This political action at home provided the opportunity for the British industry to make the optimum adaptation to the commercial and technological forces that were affecting all industries. Ideology provided the opportunity, but it could not guarantee success: it had brought potential prizes, but it also brought its own problems. The prizes were to be won in the streamlining of commercial functions and in the rationalisation of production with consequential cost reductions in both cases. The problems were the creation of a financial structure suitable to a manufacturing industry, and the formation of an internal structure which would unarm the disrupting forces that inevitably existed within an organisation which had been formed through compulsion. The winning of the prize was the major task, but the priority task was the solution of these problems.

Capital Structure

The entire capital structure of the new Corporation took the form of fixed-interest-bearing debt, amounting to £834 million. This was the common pattern for the nationalised industries, but such a rigid financial structure was unsuitable for a manufacturing industry in which demand and the generation of profits were known to be cyclical. It was particularly inappropriate when it was also known that in its early years the Corporation would almost certainly produce a loss. The most that could be hoped for was a low level of profits which would leave a portion of the interest due unpaid and accumulating. This was quickly emphasised by the fact that in its first financial year the Corporation suffered a revenue deficit of £19 million (see Table 10).[2] Direct comparisons with the fortunes of the old private companies are not

Table 10

BSC KEY FINANCIAL AND OPERATING STATISTICS

	1968	1969	Financial years ending 1970*	1971	1972	1973
			(£ million)			
Turnover	1,071	1,196	682	1,457	1,292	1,478
Revenue surplus (deficit)	(19)	(23)	12	(10)	(68)	3
Capital expenditure	73	74	39	143	237	198
			(Million tons)			
Crude steel production	22·9	24·2	12·3	24·7	20·4	24·6
Steel deliveries	17·1	18·8	9·9	19·4	16·3	18·3

Source: BSC Annual Report and Accounts, 1971–2 and 1972–3.

* Six-month period October 1969–March 1970.

Page 149: *The Abbey site before and after development*

Page 150: *Park Gate* (above) *and Ravenscraig Works* (below)

practicable because, among other things, the Corporation adopted a fifteen-year depreciation period compared with the twenty or twenty-five years of the old companies and boasted of 'more stringent' accounting policies, but it was claimed that under the new procedures the aggregate loss of £3 million by those companies in 1967 would have amounted to £50 million.[3] Under these circumstances debt would have been piled inexorably upon debt, but in July 1969 it was determined that £700 million of this capital debt should take the form of Public Dividend Capital.[4] The new arrangement was intended to produce over the years the same level of interest, but gave the Corporation the discretion of fixing the dividend for each year. In this way it removed an inevitable source of frustration and argument, and solved the most tractable problem.

Internal Organisation

The second problem area requiring priority treatment, internal organisation, was left to the Corporation to solve. In this respect the operation was more akin to commercially motivated mergers rather than previous acts of nationalisation. The only statutory requirement was that the Corporation should publish a report describing its intended organisation within one year of Vesting Day. This report was issued on 1 August 1967, four days after Vesting Day, but, because this question had been one of the items considered by the Organising Committee, set up in 1966 and chaired by Lord Melchett, the speed was more apparent than real.[5] Three possible forms of organisation were considered. A single pyramidal structure with all authority centred in a single head office was rejected as being too cumbersome, and this left a final choice between divisions defined on a product basis similar to the ICI model, or a number of groupings organised on a regional basis. Each system had its advantages and disadvantages, but the wide geographical spread of almost all sectors of the British industry made it impossible to consolidate the advantages of both in one working model. The choice of product divisions would facilitate the rationalisation of production, as the order book for each sector could be allocated to the most efficient mill. But each management group would be concerned with mills which were, in some cases, as far apart as Llanelly and Gartcosh, or Glengarnock and Cardiff, with obvious difficulties of communication. The regional groupings, in contrast, would simplify inter-works communications, and would allow a sensible pattern of raw materials and products handling to develop. The disadvantages

K

were that each group would make many products and that there would
be extensive areas of overlap between groups, despite the fact that there
already existed some regional specialisation. The final decision was to
adopt the regional grouping system shown in Fig 14.

There can be no doubt that this choice reflected the historical orientation of the British industry towards production, and that in this respect
it was at variance with the stated intent of the Corporation to be
'market oriented'.[6] Furthermore, in a situation of world surplus
production capacity, to the extent that the two sides can be separated
the major problem was that of selling rather than of producing steel.
Although this was recognised at the time, explicit mention was made of
the desirability of maintaining 'strong technical rivalry between the
individual managements in order to secure the cheapest production by
the best practices'.[7] Competition could not, of course, extend to price,
and it seldom had in the previous decades, but the statement also
suggests that the lowest production costs could be obtained regardless
of location. The choice of a regional model may have reflected a
reluctance by the organising committee to make full use of the powers
which nationalisation had provided, for the hope existed in some
quarters, even within that committee, that in due course the industry
would be returned once again to private ownership. It would be a
comparatively simple matter to restore complete autonomy to the
regional groups. Similarly, references to competition between the
groups could be interpreted as attempts to allay the fears of consumers
faced with an apparently monolithic supplier. Whatever the truth of the
matter, the creation of geographical groups was certainly the quickest
way to initiate the process of control, and was probably seen from the
very beginning as no more than an interim arrangement. The task of
welding fourteen manufacturing companies, plus Skinningrove in which
the Corporation had a 90 per cent share, and thirty-one important
works producing forty major types of steel into one organisation, was
immense.[8]

Subsequent events, however, were to show that this first model
failed to reduce the intense regional rivalries which had bedevilled all
previous attempts to rationalise the industry. It was but a minor
satisfaction to realise that long-term planning was to be conducted by a
committee chaired by the chairman of the Corporation.

The change from private ownership to state ownership was not, of
course, accompanied by a comparable change in management personnel, and the need to reconcile management to its new environment
made the adoption of the conservative regional organisational model

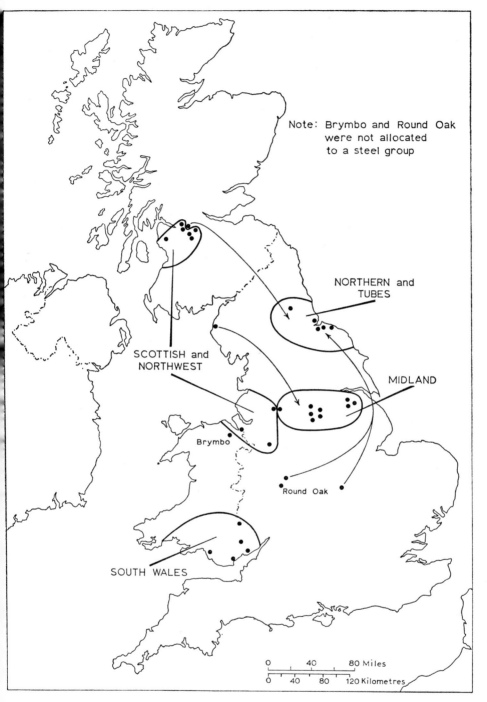

Note: Brymbo and Round Oak
were not allocated
to a steel group

NORTHERN and
TUBES

SCOTTISH and
NORTHWEST

MIDLAND

Brymbo

Round Oak

SOUTH WALES

0		40		80 Miles
0	40	80	120 Kilometres

Fig 14. BSC REGIONAL DIVISIONS, 1967–70

almost inevitable. A complete reconciliation, assuming that such was possible, would take time, but events were soon to show that the old jealousies were persisting. This first became apparent in the relatively minor problem of choosing the location of the regional headquarters offices. But the complete failure of the regional organisational model to dissolve the old parochialism, and to resolve the problem of finding an overall development programme, became publicly apparent in the summer of 1968 at a press conference called by the Colvilles division. It was assumed that the purpose of the meeting was to reveal the Corporation's intention to apply for permission to build an ore terminal at Hunterston, on the Clyde, capable of receiving carriers of up to 150,000 tons capacity. Instead, the meeting became the platform from which the division announced its desire to build in three stages at Hunterston a fully integrated iron and steelworks at an estimated cost of £300 million. The capacity was to be 5·0 million ingot tons, with a completion date set at about 1983. Meanwhile, the ore dock was to be built by 1973 and an interim level of capacity at 2·5 million ingot tons would be reached by 1978. The proposals were built on the assumption that the Corporation's total capacity in 1983 would be a minimum of 35 million ingot tons, and that Scotland would share in this expansion. The scheme, if completed, would reverse the conclusions of the Benson Committee on the feasibility of greenfield sites in general, and on the size of the Scottish industry in particular. Such a reversal was not necessarily wrong, but the details of the scheme implied a willingness to follow the Llanwern practice of imposing heavy initial capital costs upon a new works over a prolonged period of incremental expansion. Of even more import for the financial health of the Corporation was the fact that the announcement contained all the elements of a pre-emptive bid and was one which was certain to collect the backing of all sides of Scottish industry.

In the light of this precedent it was scarcely surprising that within six months the Midland Group should unveil its own capital programme of £312 million to be spent at Scunthorpe and Sheffield, and also at Workington where increased blast furnace capacity was to be complemented with LD converters. This programme was basically an expanded version of the old United Steel 'Anchor' Scheme, but it is hard to imagine that the Workington proposal was intended to be taken seriously. Neither the Scottish nor the Midland proposals should be dismissed out of hand as intrinsically counter to the well-being of the industry, but a situation in which local groups could make public statements seemingly designed to embarrass the London headquarters

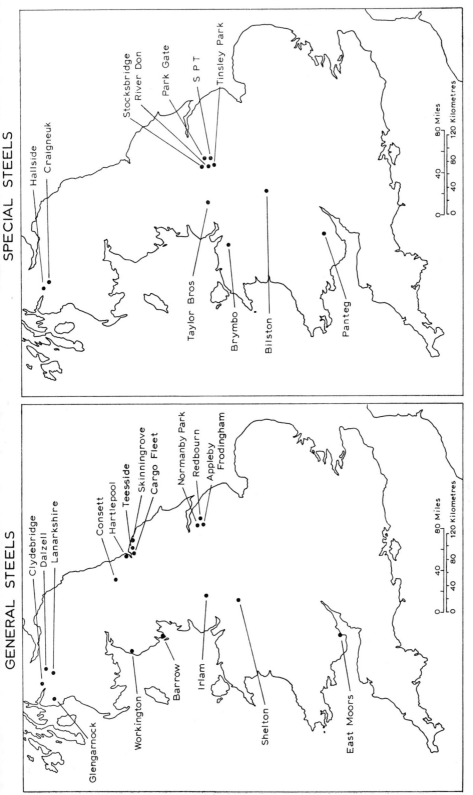

GENERAL STEELS

Clydebridge
Dalzell
Lanarkshire
Consett
Hartlepool
Teesside
Skinningrove
Cargo Fleet
Normanby Park
Redbourn
Appleby
Frodingham
Glengarnock
Workington
Barrow
Irlam
Shelton
East Moors

80 Miles
120 Kilometres
0   40   80
0   40   80

SPECIAL STEELS

Hallside
Craigneuk
Stocksbridge
River Don
Park Gate
S P T
Tinsley Park
Taylor Bros
Brymbo
Bilston
Panteg

80 Miles
120 Kilometres
0   40   80
0   40   80

Fig 15. BSC PRODUCT DIVISIONS, 1970 *(continued overleaf)*

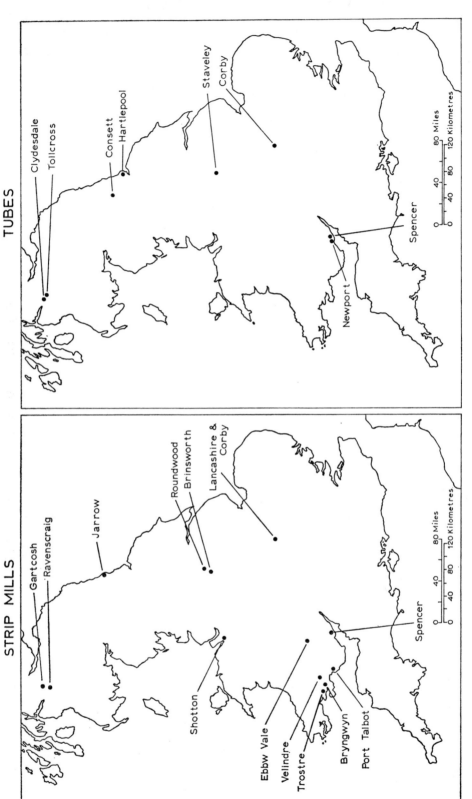

Fig. 15—*continued*

could not be allowed to continue. A solution would be to increase the power at the centre by the scattering of the foci of interest in the out-lying groups.

By the time the Midland Group had made its plans public the issue of organisation was already being formally reconsidered by a Corporation committee. The deliberations of this body, which was set up in January 1969, were revealed in two reports published in March and December.[9] The first revealed the view that regional groupings impeded rationalisation and thereby the best utilisation of assets, and indicated that despite some disadvantages the balance of merits and demerits lay with a system of product groupings. The contents of the final report could therefore be anticipated, but it was hoped that local anxieties about the loss of control would be soothed by the promise that special attention would be given not only to Scottish and Welsh interests but to regional interests also.[10] In due course four new steel divisions plus Constructional Engineering and Chemicals divisions were brought into operation on 29 March 1970 with each one operating as an individual profit centre. These divisions were sub-divided into groups assembled on the basis of both product specialisation and geographical proximity to each other. The comparative size of each division can be seen from the operational and financial statistics in Table 11, and the major works

Table 11

BSC PRINCIPAL OPERATING STATISTICS

Product division	Deliveries (million tons) (%)		Financial year 1970–1				Employees (000)
			Trading surplus* (£ million) (%)		Capital expenditure (£ million) (%)		
General Steels	8·5	44	41·0	34	75	53	89
Special Steels	2·6	13	31·2	25	14	10	42
Strip Mills	6·9	36	36·0	30	39	28	67
Tubes	1·4	7	10·3	9	9	6	41
Constructional	—	—	0·4	} 2	2	} 3	10
Chemicals	—	—	2·0		2		2
Total	19·4	100	120·9	100	141	100	251

Source: BSC Annual Report and Accounts, 1970–1.

* Before depreciation.

in each division are shown in Fig 15. These figures give a clear indication of the size of the problem of organising the industry according to product divisions, but such an organisation was essential if a rational structure and a reorientation towards the market were to be achieved. In general terms, each works was allocated *en bloc* to one division or another, although some rolling mills had to be detached from their quondam melting shops. So, for example, the Brinsworth, Roundwood and Jarrow mills were allocated to the Strip Mills division, whereas the works of which they had been a part became members of the Special Steels and General Steels divisions. It was impossible to exclude all overlaps, but the only confused margin was between the Special and General Steels divisions. In turn, the overlap between the public and private sectors was greatest in the case of the Special Steels division. This overlap was epitomised by the ownership of Round Oak, which was owned jointly by the Corporation and by Tube Investments. From Fig 15 it can be seen that the new organisation destroyed the vestigial traces of the old companies. The new system came into being on the same day as the old company names were formally abolished, and the Corporation ceased to present separate financial accounts for those companies.

Almost three years had passed since Vesting Day, but it now seemed that the final working framework had been reached, and the new masters of the industry could begin to reap the potential fruits of nationalisation. All that was needed was a period free from outside interruptions in order to consolidate the ground. A plea for such a period provided the final paragraph of the December 1969 report.[11]

The Struggle for Autonomy

These early experiences of the Corporation, following the history of the private industry since 1945, proved that the provision of a suitable organisation of the industry was an essential prerequisite of reconstruction. But a new form of organisation was not, in itself, a guarantee that a rational reconstruction would be possible. Accordingly, the plea for freedom from outside interference extended within the Corporation to other and larger regions to include the vital issues of steel prices and the future size and locations of its activities. Autonomy in these matters had been foregone by the industry since the 1930s in exchange for tariff protection, so the new plea was for no more than a greater degree of freedom. But after the change of government in June 1970 even the structure of the Corporation was placed in doubt once again. Mention was made of 'hiving-off' the ancillary activities such as chemicals and structural engineering; of denationalising the Corporation's interests in special steels; of reintroducing private capital according to the so-called 'BP Model'; or even of dividing the Corporation into two or more separate and competing multi-product groups. These suggestions, which were not confined to political circles, persisted into 1972 but declined markedly in 1971 with the drop in demand for steel and the consequent increase in the size of the Corporation's operational deficits, and the organisational pattern now appears to be resolved.[12] On the other hand, the issues of steel prices and investment have retained their central position in public debate, where they are likely to remain.

With the benefit of hindsight it is possible to see that the course of the Corporation's development policy turned upon the events of the early months of 1971. These uncovered in a dramatic manner the fundamental weaknesses of the Corporation, and also forced the Government to agree to restore to its only nationalised manufacturing industry some of the freedoms which such an industry required. The public enactment of the drama which was to change the operational circumstances of the Corporation began in February 1971 when it became known that an increase in steel prices averaging 14 per cent was being sought. If granted, these would be the fifth round of increases since June 1969, the most recent of which had been introduced in October 1970. Steel prices had remained constant between April 1966 and June 1969, however, and the rapid succession of increases had been partly in response to that long period of declining profitability. Moreover, each of the four increases had been delayed by prolonged negotiations with the Iron & Steel Consumers Council, or with the Prices and Incomes Board, or by deliberately dilatory ministerial action. The Steel Consumers Council had a statutory right to advise the minister on steel prices, and he in turn was required to explain his reasons to Parliament if he decided to act against that advice. It was, however, no more than customary rather than obligatory for the Corporation to obtain ministerial approval for price increases. In this ill-defined situation, confusion was probable and delay in implementing the latest round of price increases inevitable. In contrast, although European and American producers were subject to government pressures over prices, the Common Market producers were under a statutory obligation to give no more than forty-eight hours' advance notice of their intention to raise prices.

By mid-March, when Parliament came to debate the industry, no decision had been taken, but it was clear that the sickness of the Corporation had become acute, and that an appropriate remedy was required. In 1969 the Corporation had predicted a profit of £200 million, before charges, for the financial year 1970–1, which was about to end. By March 1970 the predicted figure had been reduced by 50 per cent, and was thereafter reduced to £37 million in July, to £15 million in August, and to a loss of £7 million in October. The 5 per cent price increase granted in that month was estimated to increase revenue by £27 million, but by January 1971 the estimated loss for the financial year had risen yet again to £20 million.[13] The proffered explanation for this loss, which eventually proved to be £10 million, included continuous increases in raw material costs, industrial unrest inside the industry and among suppliers and customers, delays in commissioning new plant, and the breakdown of old plant which had been starved of investment in the early 1960s.[14] Of even greater importance, however, were two sets of continuing factors which stemmed from the constitution of the Corporation and the system of price controls. Firstly, in the absence of capital reserves any costs which were incurred from accelerated depreciation of plant or from plant closures had to be included within the Profit and Loss Account. In 1970–1 these amounted to £18 million. Secondly, the situation in which British prices were fixed below foreign prices had placed the Corporation at a serious disadvantage in a year in which the balance of supply and demand had swung quickly from one extreme to another. At the beginning of the financial year, in an attempt to satisfy a high level of demand at home, the Corporation had diverted steel from the temporarily more lucrative foreign markets and had purchased foreign steel to supply its home customers at an additional cost of £10 million. At the end of the year, when demand at home and abroad had declined, and when international steel prices had weakened, it was faced with competition from foreign steel at home. These switches were inevitable after two decades during which capacity had been installed to meet no more than trend demand, but they were aggravated when, firstly, the installed capacity could not all be used, and, secondly, when there was little freedom to adapt prices to market conditions.

Somewhat surprisingly, the parliamentary debate failed to produce a government decision on steel prices, but was spiced by the statement that the remedy for the sickness would have to await the result of a 'deep-seated review' of both the financial position of the Corporation and its future capital investment policy. The first part of the review, dealing with the financial position, was promised quickly, and emerged in two parts in June and December 1971. Meanwhile, on 1 April, the Corporation announced that it intended to implement a 14 per cent price increase immediately in order to raise revenue by £165 million in a full year and to produce a profit of £30–£40 million in the financial year 1971–2. The Government's reaction was prompt, and took the form of directing the Corporation to limit its price increases to an average of 7 per cent. In so doing, it acknowledged that a further loss of possibly £70 million would be inevitable, and implicitly sanctioned a continuation of the policy of deficit financing of a state-owned industry in order to subsidise the export of manufactured goods.

The principal elements in the first part of the Government review resulted in a reduction of the public dividend capital to £500 million, and the write-off of £150 million of long-term indebtedness to the Exchequer with the intention of providing up to £110 million for the general reserve. The Corporation was given greater freedom over individual prices, but was still restricted to a 5 per cent average increase from April 1972, and was left comparatively free to negotiate with private industry on the disposal of some minor activities, tool steel production for example, and on the re-drawing of the boundary between the public and private sector in the stainless steel trades.[15] Furthermore, it was anticipated that the Corporation would return losses of up to £100 million in each of the financial years 1971–2 and 1972–3. As it transpired, the loss in 1971–2 was £68 million, but this was followed in 1972–3 by a profit of £2·8 million. In August 1972 the outstanding debt to the National Loans Fund was reduced by £150 million, which amount was credited to the general reserve for the financing of future losses. At the same time, the Corporation was given a target of achieving an average 8 per cent return on net assets during the years 1973–4 to 1976–7. This would mean annual average profits of about £96 million in those years.

The fixing of this target brought to an end the financial aspect of the review which had been in progress for eighteen months, but it is worth considering whether the difficult trading conditions of 1971–2 had not marked a turn-around in the fortunes of the industry. It should not escape notice that the budgeted loss of £100 million for 1971–2 had been based on an assumed level of sales of 15 million tons, whereas the realised loss of £68 million was achieved on sales of as little as 12·6 million tons. This would suggest that the rationalisation measures were beginning to take effect; but, these hopeful signs notwithstanding, it is difficult to see how a level of future profitability of £100 million could be fixed when it had not yet been decided whether future capacity should be 36 million ingot tons or 28 million ingot tons, or somewhere in between. Nevertheless, a restoration of profitability was essential, and the level of that profitability would have as much influence on future location decisions as the choice of wise locations would have on profits. It is impossible to pretend that the Corporation has won complete autonomy as long as its development programme is subject to governmental review and approval, but the degree of autonomy will be increased as the British industry becomes subject to the Treaty of Paris. The Steel Commission has powers to investigate the monetary arrangements by which development is financed and to veto them if necessary, but it has no power to prohibit development as such in either gross or fine detail. Although the Corporation will remain state-owned, the direct control exercisable by the Government will be no larger than that exercised by the shareholders of any large corporation. That is to say, it will be minimal, but the indirect control which is exercised by all western governments will remain. That is considerable. One estimate of the cost to the Corporation of this outside control was £150–£200 million over the period July 1967 to March 1973.[16]

The Heritage Programme

The questions of an acceptable financial structure and an operational internal organisation for the Corporation were settled by the end of 1971. By contrast, it was not until the end of the following year, five years after the fourteen companies had been first brought together, that the outline development strategy for the 1970s was finally agreed with the Treasury. Meanwhile the Corporation planners were forced to make a series of interim decisions which, it was hoped, would not vitiate that strategy. The corpus of those decisions came to be known as the 'heritage programme'. When assessing the merits of those decisions it is, therefore, essential to recognise the large element of uncertainty that surrounded the entire undertaking.

The twin objectives of the heritage programme were the identification and removal of the weaknesses in the inherited businesses, and the identification and fortification of the strengths. This second objective was as important as the first, for although the Corporation had inherited a multitude of problems it had also received some valuable and developable assets. It was as important to find what was right with the existing plant as it was to find what was wrong. At the same time it was essential that the interim policy should not prejudice the long-term programme. On the question of works size, for example, it was known that British works were too small, even though the 'best' size for Britain had not yet been determined. But it was equally well-known that the new capacity already installed had never operated at maximum efficiency. This was particularly true of British blast furnace practice. This low productivity stemmed from the combined effects of the low driving rates of British furnaces imposed by inadequate cooling facilities, and from the use of inferior burden material, especially of high sulphur coking coals.[17] If these problems could be solved, productivity could be increased by 50 per cent or more, and the size of the largest works would be increased. Such exercises in 'fine tuning' could not eliminate the costs of working at high-cost locations, but by substituting partly depreciated plant for new investment they could buy a period of respite for the better existing works. The danger was that new equipment would be installed at obsolete locations.

The consolidation of the base under the heritage programme involved the use of three sets of processes: integrating adjacent works, consolidating the output of certain products on selected works, and one single case of a major expansion. Even though the three sets are interacting, an attempt has been made in this analysis to define the principal characteristics of each scheme, and to allocate them accordingly. In Chapter 5 it was argued that twenty years' devotion to similar policies had brought the industry to a position where the slack in the locational pattern had been largely absorbed, and subsequent events were to show that this was indeed so. Nevertheless, even before the regional groups were disbanded there was room for some adjustments, and more was found when the formation of the production divisions had been completed. Furthermore, the experience of finding that it was possible to squeeze marginally higher output from old equipment over short periods of time was repeated, and this experience provided potential ammunition for the defence by local groups of this equipment when threatened with possible closure, but in every case the record outputs depended upon temporarily favourable factors which could not be maintained over long periods. For example, in the early months of 1970 the open-hearth melting shops at Irlam and Bilston established record levels of output, but these could not be equated with contemporary records at Stocksbridge and Tinsley Park, where new arc furnaces were in use. Similarly, successful experiments with natural gas in the open-hearth shop at Round Oak, and progressively higher outputs from the Ajax furnaces at Appleby-Frodingham, could not prevent the eventual replacement of these furnaces with arc furnaces and LD furnaces respectively. Space does not allow a fuller cover of these and many similar 'dying-gasp' achievements.

Integrating Adjacent Works

The new pattern of ownership presented unmistakable opportunities for integrating neighbouring works in Scunthorpe and Rotherham, but also provided less obvious possibilities on the North East Coast and in

South Wales. Progress in this direction was made in all these areas as early as 1968 and has continued with gathering momentum. At Scunthorpe a system was developed whereby surplus hot metal at any works could be transferred over British Rail lines to deficit works in the town. Although the use of the traditional 'out-of-gauge' jumbos called for strict controls of this traffic, the first exchanges were made in July 1968 between Appleby-Frodingham and Normanby Park. In subsequent months hot metal and sinter were exchanged freely between Appleby-Frodingham and Redbourn. This new-found flexibility made it possible to carefully formulate a collective policy of blast furnace development to meet the forthcoming Anchor project steel requirements at a time when the demand from the mills could otherwise be met only by buying ingots from other British and continental sources. In 1969 three blast furnaces at Appleby-Frodingham were exceeding the previous levels achieved by four furnaces, and the fourth furnace was not used until the Redbourn No 3 furnace was blown out in 1970. By the end of that year South Ironworks was producing at an annual rate of 2·2 million tons. Thereafter, developments in the three ironworks were to be explained by reference to the Anchor scheme rather than to the exigencies of current requirements.

A similar exchange of hot metal was introduced on the North East Coast in 1969. In 1968 the kaldo vessel at Consett had been replaced by a 150-ton LD converter, thereby raising the steelmaking capacity beyond the capabilities of the works' blast furnaces. The deficit was made good by transporting hot metal in purpose-built torpedo vessels over 63 miles from Cargo Fleet via Stockton, Ferryhill, Leamside, Pelaw and Gateshead, provision being made for transporting 600 tons of metal seven days a week. The irony of the arrangement was intensified as plans were announced for the closure of the riverside Cargo Fleet works (iron and steelmaking ended in 1971-2) while blast furnaces and coke ovens were rebuilt at Consett. In 1971 the first two LD vessels at Consett were replaced with a single 150-ton converter, and iron and steelmaking were brought back into balance. This decision assured the mid-term life of the works and was tacit recognition of the fact that when comparisons are made between existing works, technical inefficiencies at one plant can more than offset the locational inadequacies of another.

The integration of Park Gate and Steel, Peech & Tozer in Rotherham was a more protracted process. The separate identities of the two works were formally merged in April 1970, but before that date the movement of ingots to the Aldwarke primary mill from Templeborough, and of cold pig iron to the Templeborough melting shop from Park Gate, had become well established. The problem was that both works were unbalanced. At Park Gate, for example, the kaldo and electric arc melting shops produced a record 0·56 million tons in 1969, but the primary mill rolled 0·81 million tons. In contrast, the Templeborough melting shop was producing at annual rates of 1·5 million tons, whereas the associated mill, under the most favourable conditions, could reach no more than 1·3 million tons. Moreover, the kaldo vessel at Aldwarke, even at its highest level of output, remained a high-cost producer. The capacity of one arc furnace at Templeborough was raised to 180 tons in 1968, and in 1969 it was decided to raise four of the remaining five to the same level to procure a minimum annual output of 1·8 million tons. This work was originally scheduled for completion by August 1972, but in March of that year it was decided that one of these arc furnaces would be conveyed to the kaldo shop at Aldwarke, already scheduled for closure in 1972–3, and that a second would be transferred to the electric arc melting shop also at Aldwarke. Meanwhile the major items of expenditure on the rolling mills were £0·7 million on the Templeborough billet mill, £5·5 million on the Roundwood 11in mill, and £1·4 million on billet inspection at Aldwarke. It is therefore clear that as the original Park Gate site is abandoned through the closure of the open-hearth melting shop (1968) and the blast furnaces (1971–3) an equal balance between the two centres of this 2·0-million-ton complex is being established. Elsewhere in the works, Park Gate lost its three hand-operated bar mills and its colliery arch plant, and Templeborough lost its Morgan strip mill. In the Ickles works the press shop was closed and the work transferred to the River Don works, the railway wheel orders being placed on the Trafford Park mill in Manchester. In exchange, Ickles became the sole producer of tyres and rings. This was the type of rationalisation that nationalisation was supposed to achieve, but in 1971 the Corporation was still protesting that Aldwarke was one of the four loss-making centres that had been acquired at unrealistically high prices.[18] The closure of the ironworks and hot metal steel processes, together with increased production of special steels, would eventually reverse that position.

Consolidating Production

The policy of integration is geared to producing greater flexibility in the system. Consolidation is designed to remove redundant duplicate facilities. For example, the emerging pattern at Rotherham will allow the interchange of ingots from one part of the complex to another if or when this is necessary, whereas the decision to close the coke ovens at Shelton (1968) and to supply that works with coke from East Moors, Cardiff, removes the chance of a reverse flow and represents an act of consolidation even though it integrates the works more closely than had previously been the case. The difficulty lies in achieving a balance between flexibility of response and efficiency of output. The initial regional organisation adopted by the Corporation allowed integration of works, but in practice appeared to obstruct a thorough policy of consolidation. Nevertheless, it was under that regime, in its first year of operation, that the Corporation, endorsing the conclusion of the Benson Committee, announced that even an annual output of 34 million ingot tons would not require the construction of any greenfield works before 1975, but that that level could be achieved by judicious expansion of existing works. Consolidation was to be the keynote of development policy. At the same time, the degree of consolidation was put in doubt by the contemporary announcement that 'major closures of complete works' were not envisaged before that date either.[19] At first sight it therefore appeared that the industry would remain virtually unchanged, but in reality this depended upon the interpretation of the words 'major' and 'complete'. Some confusion was inevitable at that date, but as the policy of consolidation was implemented announcements of intention to close some sections of works employing over 4,300 men were made, with Irlam and Cargo Fleet for example stripped of all functions other than their finishing mills.[20]

Outside the special steels sector the only obvious location for a major consolidation of production and of growth was at Lackenby and its neighbouring works. The LD melting shop planned by Dorman Long was scheduled to come into production before the end of 1970, but in October 1969 a £17 million scheme which included the addition of a third converter, a two-strand continuous casting machine to produce 0·9 million tons of slabs a year, and extra facilities for the coiled plate mill, was announced. The immediate aim was to double the output from the Lackenby shop to 4·0 million ingot tons, to close the Redcar, Cargo Fleet and Skinningrove open-hearth shops, and to supply those outlying works with semi-finished steel. At the same time, £1·7 million was to be spent on the Skinningrove mills to capitalise on their growing reputation as producers of special sections and bulb flats. After April 1970 and the formation of the Product Divisions an extra £11 million was allocated for an eight-strand continuous casting machine for blooms and associated equipment to supply blooms to these plants.

Page 167: *Visual contrast: Consett Works* (above) *and Sheephouse Wood Mill, Stocksbridge* (below)

Page 168: *Irlam* (above) *and West Hartlepool, South Works* (below)

Workington was brought into the same scheme when it was decided to close the melting shop and to supply the rail mills with Tees-side blooms. The Workington blast furnaces are to serve the market for merchant pig iron, and the production of ferro-manganese is to be transferred and consolidated on the Bessemer blast furnaces in the Cleveland works. At the same time, it was decided to close the seven-foot plate mills at West Hartlepool and Appleby-Frodingham and to consolidate the output, which amounted to over 0·3 million tons, at Lackenby.

These decisions were in the tradition of Dorman Long, but were now being made on a larger scale. In July 1969 final approval was given to construct at a cost of £16 million an ore terminal capable of receiving carriers of 150,000 tons at Redcar, where the initial capacity can be expanded from 7 million to 10 million tons of ore a year. The purpose is to serve Tees-side and Consett, but it was also suggested that it could supply Ravenscraig and Scunthorpe.[21] With such distances in mind the extra cost of the four miles to the Clay Lane blast furnaces could apparently be accepted with equanimity. The savings on the use of large carriers would more than offset this new local haul.[22] Nevertheless, with this arrangement the South Tees-side works, as the total complex was now called, was retreating from its tide-water position. Between May 1969 and August 1972 No 3 and No 1 blast furnaces at Clay Lane were rebuilt with enlarged hearths of 29 feet diameter and were provided with improved furnace screening facilities, to raise the annual output from the ironworks by 0·6 million tons to 2·4 million. At a total cost of £3·6 million, this extra tonnage was obtained for as little as £6 per annual ton. A new rail track system was installed between Clay Lane and Lackenby to allow the use of torpedo hot metal ladles. All these developments were in operation by the end of 1972. The low capital cost of £55 million spent on all the stages from the ore terminal to the continuous casting machines was one example of the logic which lay behind the policy of growth through consolidation.

In 1964 W. F. Cartwright presented a paper which set out the cost benefits of operating two sheet steel works in Britain in place of the five works which the industry suffered.[23] This, as the author recognised, was a counsel of perfection which for financial and political reasons could never be adopted in its entirety. The major problem in 1967 was to bring the Llanwern and Ravenscraig works to a profitable position, but this was compounded by the need to decide the course of future developments at each of the remaining three works. The immediate future of the Port Talbot works had already been determined, and the programme was interrupted in detail only by labour and technical

L

difficulties. The VLN melting shop was closed after only ten years of operation in July 1969, three months before the LD converters began their difficult run-in, and the open-hearth melting shop was finally closed in November 1970. The ore terminal, with a capacity of 4·0 million tons a year, was opened in 1970, and opened the door to suggestions for future growth. The ingot-making capacity of the works was now 3·25 million tons, but preparations had been made in the new melting shop to install a third converter which would raise the capacity to 6·0 million tons. The presence of the ore terminal would suggest that this was advisable, but the works was already out of balance inasmuch as the mills could not roll all the steel produced in the melting shop, and growth to 6·0 million tons would require a new blast furnace, which implied a minimum annual production of 1·8 million tons. Continued technical progress in the ironworks had made the smallest furnace at Margam surplus to existing requirements, but had not progressed to the point where, even regardless of cost, the 5·0 million tons of hot metal needed to support the larger melting shop could be obtained from installed ironworks equipment. This type of problem had never been so acute in the open-hearth era when the addition of one extra furnace added no more than 0·25 million tons to the pig iron requirements. Expansion by sall inmcremental steps was no longer a practicable option.

At Llanwern the annual level of working had been raised to 2·0 million ingot tons by early 1968, and was consolidated at that level in the subsequent year without making full use of either the melting shop or the hot strip mill. In March 1969 a £7·5 million scheme to raise output to 2·2 million ingot tons was authorised. The significance of this scheme was that the money was spent entirely on ancillary equipment. Provision was made for oil injection in the blast furnaces. Improved cranes and larger ladles were installed in the LD shop to enable a full weight of 155 tons, as opposed to the current 135 tons, to be charged in each vessel, and extra annealing and pickling capacity was built at the finishing end of the mill. This so-called 'B' scheme was a stop-gap measure which typified the investment practice of the Corporation at that time, but within nine months, in January 1970, a £42 million development programme was authorised to raise the ingot capacity to 3·5 million tons and the throughput of the mill from 1·9 million to 3 million tons. Included in this scheme is a new 5,000 tons per day blast furnace, costing about £9 million, which is as yet the only new blast furnace to be finally authorised by the Corporation. This extra ironworks capacity will be needed to supply the replacement LD vessels of 165 tons. Assuming that the first two blast furnaces were to be retained, there threatened to emerge a surplus of ironworks capacity, and this was especially so in view of the statement that the hot mill would roll 3,500 tons per week of coil from outside slabs and 1,000 tons per week of coil from stainless steel ingots. The future of the scheme was put in doubt by the financial crisis of March 1971, but the Corporation was given government authorisation to proceed on 29 April 1971.

The new blast furnace brought to the fore again the issue of ore supply and the question of the Uskmouth scheme. Ever since the Redcar ore terminal decision had been taken the idea of supplying Llanwern from Port Talbot had been allowed to develop in the collective consciousness, until in May 1972 a scheme to install a third unloader at Port Talbot was quietly unveiled.[24] This will raise the annual capacity to 7 million tons, and the fifty-mile rail haul to Llanwern is to be completed using purpose-built 100-ton wagons. When the arrangement is in full operation five trains, each carrying 2,500 tons, will be needed each day. No running cost figures have been given, but they must amount to a minimum of £0·88 per ton of ore, which in turn would approximate to £1·50 per ton of finished steel.[25] The total costs will be lower than those of the previous arrangement in that the savings obtainable from the use of 100,000-ton carriers at Port Talbot, rather than 30,000-ton carriers at Newport, will more than offset the cost of the new rail haul. It is idle to wish that the common ore terminal had been built at Newport rather than at Port Talbot, but the timing of the event had been fine, and it is a wish that will inevitably occur to most informed, well-wishing observers of the British industry over the coming decade. It is a wish which will also be shared by some practitioners within the industry, because the result has been the same as locating the works fifty miles inland, without the possible counter-attraction of a neighbouring market.

Within three months of the authorisation of the Llanwern 'C' scheme the closer integration of Llanwern and Port Talbot was extended to include Ebbw Vale. In 1969 a third electrolytic tinplate line with an annual capacity of 0·25 million tons had been opened, and the future role of the works was now seen to be that of a specialised sheet steel producer. In March 1970 a £45 million mill development programme was announced including a new cold reduction mill and a fourth electrolytic line to roll strip up to forty inches wide, producing differential coatings as required. Extra provision is to be made for rolling silicon steels, to be produced at Port Talbot, and for galvanised steel. The galvanised line at Bryngwyn in West Wales had already been

closed to make room for a second 'color-coat' line at that works, and
Ebbw Vale is destined to take up this galvanised sheet market and to
share the tinplate market with Trostre and Velindre. As these developments are phased in, the primary iron and steel departments are to be
phased out, with the loss of 1·1 million tons of steelmaking capacity.
This loss will be made good from production at Port Talbot and
Llanwern, with the more distant of those works being the major
supplier. This is a logical result of a policy of consolidation.

Table 12

MAJOR CLOSURES ANNOUNCED UNDER THE HERITAGE PROGRAMME

Works	Estimated recent annual output (million tons)		Year of final closure
	Pig iron	*Ingot steel*	
Appleby-Frodingham	—	1·59	1973–4
Ebbw Vale	0·70	1.10	1974–6
Redbourn	—	0·81	1972–3
Irlam	0·45	0·70	1971–3
Redcar	—	0·40	1971–2
Cargo Fleet	0·32	0·38	1971–2
Skinningrove	0·17	0·24	1971–2
Workington	—	0·23	1972–3
Taylor Bros	—	0·01	1971–2

A similar, but less radical policy of specialisation has been adopted
at the Shotton works where approximately £32 million has been invested
between 1968 and 1973. The major component in this expenditure is
designed to raise the output of cold reduced sheet from 1·1 to 1·6 million
tons. It is intended that the present practice of rolling bought-in hot
rolled coils will be expanded until 0·35 million tons of other works' hot
rolled coils will be processed at Shotton each year. Almost £5 million
has been spent on raising the annual output of aluminium-coated
sheets, zintec, and stelvetite to a combined annual level of 0·5 million
tons. Each of these schemes recognises the favourable market situation
of the works. Expenditure of £7 million was made on a new battery of
coke ovens completed in 1971, but the new policy of fifteen-year
depreciation rates can presumably be modified so that this department
is amortised within five or six years, and does not imply that the works
will retain its primary departments. Under the Heritage Programme the
policy for Shotton has been that of building upon the works' obvious
strengths, while leaving the issues of raw material supply largely in
abeyance.

At Ravenscraig £60 million of expenditure was authorised in a series of plans announced over the long period from January 1970 to June 1972. Taken together they allot to Ravenscraig the twin roles of a major producer of hot rolled coil (2 million tons) and of a supplier of ingots and slabs to the Scottish works in the General Steels Division. The annual output of the works will be raised from 1·5 million to 3·1 million tons. This will be achieved by operating all three blast furnaces and batteries of coke-ovens, by the addition of a third LD converter and the construction of two continuous casting machines for slabs. The largest converter will have a capacity of 200 tons, which is below even the new English and Port Talbot vessels, and the modified blast furnaces will produce no more than 2,100 tons per day, which is again below par by international standards, only two-thirds of the output being achieved at the modified Margam works No 5 furnace. In February 1972 the Corporation finally announced its intention to build an ore terminal at Hunterston capable of receiving carriers of 250,000 tons, and of being expanded to 350,000 tons if required. The adjoining stockyard will hold 1·0 million tons of ore, and the annual throughput of the terminal could amount to 10·0 million tons. As Scottish annual ore requirements cannot exceed 5·0 million tons before 1975 a policy of trans-shipment from Hunterston, or of only part-unloading prior to the carrier moving on to other European terminals, is implied. The cost will be £26 million, which is double the suggested cost of the schemes that were being mooted in 1969. Ore will be railed to Ravenscraig under similar conditions and over similar distances to those which prevail between Port Talbot and Llanwern. A new stockyard and ore preparation plant will be built at Ravenscraig, and the open-hearth furnaces at Clydebridge, Glengarnock, Lanarkshire Steel and Dalzell will be closed by 1977. The furnaces at Clydesdale, in the Tubes Division, are to be replaced with electric arc furnaces, and the capacity is to be raised to 0·35 million tons. No statement has been made, but it is implied that the blast furnaces at Clyde Iron, which produced a record 0·72 million tons in 1970, will also be closed. In this manner the policy of integrating works and consolidating activities begun by Colvilles in the 1930s will be complete. Unless further additions are made there will be one land-locked primary works and a series of out-set finishing mills. The result will be an improvement over that which has gone before, but in terms of technology employed and of location the Scottish industry will be below the standard of international competitiveness, with the only cost compensation being derived from the continued use of depreciated sites. Hunterston has been described as a 'symbol of the future', but Ravenscraig is a symbol of equal significance which shows that that future will

be as much the child of the Scottish black band ores as it will be the child
of the super ore carrier.[26]

Major Schemes: the Anchor Project

The policy of consolidation involved expenditure of up to £80 million
in individual locations and resulted in 'balancing up' costs at Llanwern
and Ravenscraig of approximately £40 per annual ingot ton. In contrast,
a greenfield project on traditional lines would cost £100 per annual ingot
ton. Between these two schemes is the Anchor project, the tentative
beginnings of which were described in Chapter 5, which will cost
£230 million.[27] In 1970 the combined output of the three Scunthorpe
works was 3·3 million ingot tons. The initial target for the three 300-ton
LD converters is 4·4 million tons, to which should be added 1·1 million
from Normanby Park. With modifications, but at an unspecified cost,
the Anchor project can be expanded to 5·25 million ingot tons producing
a grand total of 6·35 million tons, or a net gain of 3 million tons. On
this reckoning the costs per ton will exceed £52. When United Steel
first proposed the scheme it was at an estimated cost of £80 million.
The larger, modified scheme approved by the Corporation in 1969 had
an estimated cost of £130 million. Since then the cost has risen by 77
per cent, through inflation, modification and additions to the project.
The important point is that although the investment decision was taken
at £130 million and costs have since risen to £230 million, the first steps
towards this decision were taken at an even earlier stage.

In an address to the Lincolnshire Iron & Steel Institute in 1967 Mr
J. D. Joy, general manager of Appleby-Frodingham, made the point
that capital development is a continuous process with no beginning
and no end. He argued that the three elements in the Anchor scheme,
an ore terminal at Immingham, oxygen steelmaking, and a continuous
plate mill, had all been present in company thinking when the Temper
project had been authorised in the late 1950s, but although they had
been rejected as inappropriate for the time they had remained 'firmly
planted in their minds'.[28] The formulation of Anchor I between March
1966 and February 1967 emerged from this background. He also argued
that there existed 'both a moral and an economic obligation' to pursue
the course set by the founders of the industry and that the choice lay
between developing 'our own plant' or of being overtaken by people
elsewhere. The difficulty, however, lies in defining the future direction
of that course, or in determining whether the best course for Scunthorpe
lay in development at home or by moving to Immingham. This very

question had been considered by the BISF Development Committee, the Iron & Steel Board, the Benson Committee, and the Ministry of Power, and they were unanimous in their decision in favour of Scunthorpe.[29] There were four reasons for this unanimity. Firstly, there was the presence of the Appleby-Frodingham ironworks whose replacement value equalled £70 million, approximately the same amount as the first estimate for the Anchor project. Secondly, the use of 3·5 million tons of Frodingham ore instead of a 100 per cent foreign-ore burden would save £5·25 million in foreign exchange each year. Thirdly, a move to Immingham would involve extra haulage costs on coke and other materials from the west, and, fourthly, a coastal location would create additional marketing costs. Taking these four sets of factors together it was 'easy to prove' that development at Immingham 'would not be of financial benefit to the *country*' (my italics).[30] By this time, April 1968, a third converter had been added to the two in the original plan, and additional capacity for medium sections, billets, bars and rods was envisaged. A continuous plate mill was still included in the scheme, but the works was now expected also to roll stainless steel in thick strip coils for Shepcote Lane in Sheffield.

Anchor III, announced in July 1969, contained major internal changes, while leaving the external issue of the Immingham ore terminal unresolved. The continuous plate mill was dropped and was replaced with a bloom and billet mill with an annual capacity of 2·5 million tons to feed a new medium section mill, the Appleby-Frodingham rod and bar mill, and external customers. A four-strand continuous slab casting machine would be the sole source of supply for the Appleby-Frodingham 12-foot plate mill which would be modified at a cost of £25 million. The scheme was scheduled for completion by the end of 1972, and the three Appleby-Frodingham and Redbourn melting shops are being phased-out during 1973–4 together with the slab mill, light plate mill, and light section mill at Appleby-Frodingham and the bloom, billet and bar mills at Redbourn.

Preparation of the 1,000-acre site, on abandoned ironstone workings to the east and south of the old works, commenced in February 1970. A decision on the Immingham ore terminal was still awaited, and meanwhile it was suggested that a lower-cost alternative might be found in hauling the imported ore 107 miles from Redcar. If this really was possible then the anticipated operational costs at Scunthorpe must have been low indeed. The final outcome of the investigation was approval for the Immingham terminal, with an ability to receive 100,000-ton carriers, linked to Scunthorpe by a 'merry-go-round' system employing 100-ton gross hopper wagons. Ore stockyards of 0·6 million tons capacity have been built at Immingham and at Scunthorpe where the first stages in ore blending will be implemented. The annual throughput of foreign ore will be six million tons, involving thirteen train-loads each day.

The change in emphasis from plates to billets has improved the competitive position of the Scunthorpe works by effectively moving it closer to its markets, but at the same time the freedom to import coking coal, and the increasing use of oil injection, have moved the cost structure in the direction of Immingham. The continuity between past and future is maintained by the use of local ores and the ten blast furnaces already in the three works. The use of so many furnaces, and separate batteries of coke ovens and sinter plants, will inevitably lead to complications in daily operations and make the attaining of the desired aim of standardised blast furnace practice difficult in the extreme. A mixed burden of imported and Frodingham ore has been used at Normanby Park since the end of 1968, but the output of the LD converters at that works is more specialised than that which is anticipated from the Anchor works, whereas both are to be supplied from the same stockyard. A four-mile conveyor system has been built to link the Anchor ore preparation plant with Normanby Park. There can be no doubt that in view of the extensive modifications that have been completed in the three ironworks, total capacity will be more than adequate, but there must be doubt whether the hot metal will be so consistent as to produce the best internal operating costs. In the absence of precise cost data the outsider is left with his own thoughts as to whether the economic argument was won so easily by Scunthorpe, but the fifteen-year depreciation policy implies that even major developments can now be viewed as being no more than a part of a temporary solution. The economic scale is not the sole scale for measuring relevance, but the Anchor scheme has been sold on economic terms, and the preservation of the 'garden city' of Scunthorpe has been presented as a happy corollary of the argument.[31] It is possible that the Corporation has taken the view that the rate of technological change is now so great that by 1988, when the new plant is fully depreciated, all blast furnaces will be obsolete, or that the pattern of world trade will have changed to the extent that bulk steelmaking in Britain will be no longer economically or socially worthwhile. Meanwhile, the Scunthorpe ore field and blast furnaces will suffice. Any announcement of major new expenditure at Scunthorpe during this period will inevitably lead to the suggestion that in 1969 the best long-term policy was sacrificed to a satisfactory medium-term policy.

A Strategy for the 1980s

Between Vesting Day and March 1973 the capital expenditure of the Corporation totalled £764 million. This investment was necessary to maintain the overall level of output already achieved by the former companies and to improve efficiency. The first signs of success for this programme were the lower-than-expected deficit (£68 million) for 1971–2, and the small surplus (£3 million) for 1972–3. The 'heritage programme' provided the Corporation with between 26 and 27 million tons of modern capacity. By careful planning this could be stretched to 29–30 million tons. But, unless further investment was permitted, future increases in demand for steel in Britain would have to be met either from existing high-cost equipment or by growth in the private sector. A more radical long-term policy would be to leave the export trade *and* allow future increases in home demand to be met from imported steels. These issues were the component parts of the 'deep-seated review' which was carried out during 1971–2.

An outline of the results of this review was given to the House of Commons in December 1972 and published in a white paper the following February.[32] The major points were that agreement had been reached to spend up to £3,000 million during the following ten years, and to thereby give the Corporation the freedom to install capacity of 36–38 million tons by the middle 1980s. At first sight this appeared to be a victory for the Corporation, but in reality it was a triumph for compromise and caution, albeit judicious compromise. For, whereas the Corporation had been freed from the limit of 28 million tons which had been one government view in 1971, it had also been compelled to retreat from its own earlier targets of 40 million tons by 1980. Furthermore, only one-third of the £3,000 million was scheduled for expansion because the maintenance of 'the existing asset structure', it was admitted, 'would cost up to £200 million a year'.[33] Under the new regime of continuous planning this expansion can be forestalled if the supposed larger market for the Corporation's products is seen to be not forthcoming. The new procedure is that the Corporation annually prepares a five-year investment programme in which the expenditure for the second and subsequent years is no more than provisional.[34] In this way it should be possible to avoid a second planning hiatus similar to that which had occurred in 1971–2, and at the same time give maximum flexibility of response to changing conditions. Indeed, flexibility was now the hallmark of right thinking, but flexibility was not to be identified with indecision. The object was to avoid the Charybdis of high unit costs which would result from no expansion and the Scylla of 'foolhardy' over-expansion and to steer the middle course of 33–35 million tons by 1980.

Although the choice of this course had been based upon a supposedly more careful estimate of future demand than any that had gone before, no more than a superficial view of this critical part of the argument was revealed in the white paper. But the brief glimpse that was given contained two basic ideas. First, it was estimated that demand in Britain would grow by 2·6 per cent annually. Second, world demand would grow even faster. The hidden reasoning behind 33–35 million tons must have been that the share of the British market (estimated to be 30 million tons by 1980) taken by foreign suppliers would remain constant, and that the British producers would also retain their share of international trade. On that basis imports would be approximately 4 million tons and exports 9 million tons. Assuming a 3-million-ton total capacity for the private sector, and an average plant utilisation of 90 per cent, the Corporation would need a capacity of approximately 34 million tons. These figures are conjectural, but the Corporation has expressed its own view that although membership of the Common Market will increase the volume of trade in steel the net effect on crude steel production will be minimal. The greatest effect of membership will be increased specialisation, and changes in gross imports and exports will balance out.[35]

In contrast a very clear view was given of the likely effects of the agreed development strategy on 'plant configuration'. The production aspect of this view, summarised in Table 13, is composed of four general categories of works. The hot metal base load will be supplied by the five major works already developed under the 'heritage programme' with capacity at Port Talbot being approximately doubled. Present levels of production at Corby have been assured 'at least for the rest of the present decade' and a new works is to be built at Redcar, adjacent to the Lackenby works.[36] Redcar will be developed in two stages, each of about 3·5 million tons capacity, and at a total cost of over £900 million. This is the nearest that the Corporation will come to building a greenfield works, but the ability to dovetail this development with Lackenby and the already completed Redcar ore terminal is estimated to produce an *annual* saving of £20 million.[37] Furthermore, by developing the site in two stages the Corporation is retaining considerable flexibility. A greenfield works at Maplin or on Southampton Water, standing on its own, must have been rapidly developed to at least 5 million tons.

Table 13

BSC PLANT CONFIGURATION 1980

Ingot Steel—million tons*

1	*Base-load works (expected capacity)*				
	A	*Basic oxygen steel plants*			
		Heritage Works			
		Ravenscraig	3·55	Anchor	5·00
		Port Talbot	5·75	Lackenby	5·00
		Llanwern	3·65		
		Others			
		Corby	1·20	Redcar	7·00
	B	*Electric Arc*			
		Hallside	1·00	Clydesdale	0·35
		Sheffield area	2·80	Panteg	0·12
2	*Marginal works (present capacity)*				
		Normanby Park	1·10	Irlam†	0·50
		Consett	1·10	Bilston†	0·70
		Cleveland arc	0·75	Shelton†	0·40
3	*Disposal to private sector (present capacity)*				
		Brymbo	0·35		
4	*Works to be closed (present capacity)‡*				
		Clydebridge	0·55	Shotton	1·60
		Dalzell	0·40	Hartlepool	1·00
		Glengarnock	0·30	East Moors	0·80

Source: British Steel Corporation: Ten Year Development Strategy (Cmnd 5226).

* Long tons. Figures obtained from various sources.

† Existing process to be closed. One works a possible mini-mill site.

‡ For earlier announced closures see Table 12.

The cold metal base load will be carried by the Rotherham, Tinsley Park and Stocksbridge works in the Sheffield area, together with a new electric arc plant of up to 1 million tons capacity 'which is likely to be put at Hallside' in Lanarkshire.[38] In due course this will probably be supported by a direct-reduced pellet plant at Hunterston. The cost of these two Scottish developments will exceed £70 million.

In the second general category are seven works whose future is uncertain. On technical grounds alone they fall into two groups. The BOS plant at Consett and Normanby Park and the electric arc plant at Cleveland do not require new capital investment, but the steelmaking processes at Irlam, Bilston and Shelton are high-cost and obsolete and must be closed. The future of the one group hinges on the pattern of trade and that of the second upon a decision to provide a new steelmaking process. Irlam, Bilston and Shelton are still seen as 'possible sites for any further electric arc steelmaking plant that might be needed' but it is unlikely that more than one of these, if any, will be rescued in this way.[39]

The third general category contains one works only, Brymbo. The delay in returning this works to GKN was occasioned by a disagreement on price, but agreement on a figure of £20 million was reached in August 1973.

The fourth category contains those works where steelmaking is scheduled to end before 1980 and where redevelopment is not anticipated. The white paper confirmed the earlier proposals to end steelmaking at the Scottish open-hearth plants and at Ebbw Vale, but added two major closures, West Hartlepool and Shotton. The timing of these closures is, in part, subject to local negotiations and the provision of alternative forms of employment. At Ebbw Vale, for example, the open-hearth shop and the hot slab mill were scheduled to begin to close in March 1976, but it is now proposed by the Corporation that this beginning should be deferred for between twelve and eighteen months. In all these instances the timing is flexible, but the basic intention remains firm.

By 1980, therefore, the Corporation intends to reduce the number of ingot-making works to a nucleus of thirteen or fourteen, the exact number depending upon whether Consett is still in production. The primary mills at these locations will be complemented by finishing mills at most of the works where ingot-making will cease. Specific assurances for continued operation of the mills at Glengarnock, Dalzell, and Shotton were given in the white paper but it was suggested that the plate mill at West Hartlepool might be closed.[40] The integration of the complete system can be illustrated by the expected pattern of disposals from the Anchor works. Of the 3·25 million tons produced from the bloom and billet line 30 per cent will be sold to outside customers, 45 per cent will be processed further at Scunthorpe, and the remaining 25 per cent will be used elsewhere within the Corporation, mainly at Irlam.

Before the final strategy was chosen, twelve major strategies were simulated in the Corporation's computerised economic planning model. This was designed to consider overall profitability based on estimated values of sales, and production costs, social and regional effects, and consequences for the national balance of payments.[41] Nevertheless, profitability was the paramount consideration for the Corporation took the view that it 'was meeting the public interest' by running efficiently, and declined 'to do something purely for social and regional reasons which [it] would not have done for purely business and economic reasons'.[42] In aggregate terms the argument was that the workforce must be reduced to 180,000 in order to guarantee the continued employment of those 180,000. The regional effects of plant closures were not, however, totally discounted and one justification for the choice of building the Redcar works was that the Northern Region was carrying the brunt of redundancies produced by rationalisation.[43] The final choice, however, was not one of the original twelve, but a compromise solution between the most profitable and the most 'robust', that is, one which did not depend upon everything going according to plan.[44]

Despite the intricacy and sophistication of this planning process the chosen strategy bears a remarkable resemblance to the broad-brush plan suggested by the Benson Committee in 1966. There is the same configuration of basic oxygen and electric arc plants based on existing locations, and the same rejection of a greenfield development. There are, however, two important differences. Firstly, the unity of the British Steel Corporation has provided the freedom to implement this plan, and to remove the areas of uncertainty. For example, the one or two plants suggested by the Benson Report for the North East Coast have become the single Lackenby-Redcar complex. Similarly, the possible hope for development at Shotton has been denied. The second difference is that the rigour of the planning process has enhanced the feeling of confidence in the rightness of the chosen solution. It can be claimed that everything but the unforeseeable has been considered.

The 'Ragged Frontier' and the Private Sector

Further important consequences of nationalisation were the dissolution of the BISF and the Iron & Steel Board, and the formation of a new organisation called the British Independent Steel Producers Association (BISPA). This organisation had a membership of about 110 companies, employing 95,000 people, and producing over 2 million ingot tons from about 160 works. Producing mainly special steels, these companies accounted for approximately one-third of the annual financial turnover of the British industry. By definition they were each producers of less than half a million tons annually, and the primary interest of most was in engineering, but there was no statutory obligation placed upon these companies to remain small or specialised, although major expansion plans had to be approved by the Minister and could be investigated by the Corporation itself. The dissolution of the Federation removed from the industrial scene the only central clearing house of ideas and development plans. Nationalisation had the effect of driving a wedge between the two parts of the industry, leaving the private companies to pursue their own developments subject to national and local planning dictates, and to accept as price leader a Corporation over which they lacked any direct influence.

The wedge is neither clean-cut nor straight, and is more aptly referred to as the 'ragged frontier'. Frontiers are inherently unstable and historically their realignment has been a major cause of dissent. This one has partaken of that inheritance. Actual or anticipated movements in the position of this ragged frontier have been variously described as nationalisation via the back door or pragmatic adjustments to economic and operational requirements, according to the political standpoint of the commentator, but movements have taken place in both directions. A limited extension of the Corporation's territory was seen, for example, in the purchase of Wellington Tube Works at Tipton in 1970 for £3 million. The closure of this works, which took its raw materials from Corby, was announced in April 1971 as part of the rationalisation programme. As part of the same programme the Corporation has chosen to close the Birchley re-rolling mill at Warley during 1973–4 rather than sell the mill to the private companies which were reputedly interested.[45] These actions inevitably lead to accusations of the use of *force majeure*. Conversely, the Corporation has sold the Openshaw tool steel business, to Edgar Allen & Company.

The most tortuous part of the frontier passed through the stainless sheet mill at Shepcote Lane. Two-thirds of this works had been owned by Firth-Vickers, and one-third by United Steel, with control of the works allocated on that basis. But Firth-Vickers had been owned on a 50:50 basis by Firth Brown, which remained independent, and by English Steel which became a part of the Corporation. As a result the Corporation, through United Steel and English Steel, had a majority interest in Shepcote Lane but minority control. In all the other instances of joint ownership, Templeborough Rolling Mills, Sheffield Rolling Mills, Alloy Steel Rods, etc, the Corporation's control was equal to its holding, but the potential for conflict between the owners had been increased by the new disparity in power.

The protracted discussions with Firth Brown over Shepcote Lane involved the future of the Corporation's River Don and Grimesthorpe works, and continued over a period of three years, reaching their most critical stage in 1971 when it seemed that the closure of the loss-making River Don works was inevitable. Although the Ickles heavy forge had been closed, the low level of orders from the heavy electrical plant manufacturers was still insufficient to give profitable support to River Don. An appeal by the Corporation to the major customers to provide

£10 million for developing the works was quickly rejected, but the need to retain one producer of 200-ton forgings in Britain has resulted in what appears to be a compromise solution. In May 1972 Firth Brown agreed to acquire the entire assets of Firth-Vickers, plus the River Don interests in closed die and medium-size alloy die forgings, but to sell back the Shepcote Lane mill to the Corporation for £2·5 million. The company is now free to develop its interests in stainless steel billets, bars and castings, and the Corporation possesses a near-monopoly in the production of stainless steel flat products. This monopoly does not, however, extend from production to supply and herein lay the final inducement to the two sides to reach an agreement in realigning this sector of the frontier. In 1971, 50 per cent of the stainless steel sheet used in Britain was imported, and the task of the Corporation is to reduce that figure to the level at which it can begin to approach full utilisation of its already installed capacity. This it has sought to do by entering 'loyalty' agreements with the leading stockholders, and the release from the statutory requirements to adhere to its printed price lists will give additional strength, but the surplus of capacity is world-wide and stainless steel is readily transported over long distances.[46] The Corporation's production capacity in Sheffield, Stocksbridge and Panteg exceeds the current UK demand for flat stainless products of 80,000 to 90,000 tons each year, so the restoration of capacity working will not be readily achieved. This complex decision with Firth Brown, from which it is hoped that both sides will benefit, did not necessarily safeguard the future of the River Don melting shop, but in July 1972 a £1·12 million capital programme was announced which will result in only partial closure. The alternative solution of bringing steel from elsewhere has been rejected, and the number of potential redundancies has been reduced from 4,500 to about 500. One more British steelworks has been saved.

The Private Sector

At the time of nationalisation it was hoped that further consolidation and rationalisation of production would also be achieved within the private sector, but most moves in this direction have taken place within rather than across company boundaries. Duport, for example, has closed the Briton Ferry mill and nine hand mills in the Midlands, building up the annual capacity of its London Works at Warley to a level of 85,000 tons of bars and sections and of the Llanelly mill to 60,000 tons. The Llanelly and Briton Ferry cold metal melting shops still operate the open-hearth process. In January 1973 Duport, in a move towards greater vertical integration, took over Flather-Halesowen, a Sheffield-based bar and wire maker, and a major customer of the London works. At Patent Shaft modifications to the open-hearth furnaces and the mills have raised annual plate capacity to 240,000 tons and bar capacity to 35,000 tons. The market-oriented location of the works has ensured that an above-average level of utilisation has been achieved during the last two recessions, but a decision by the Corporation to close the Shelton blast furnaces, which supply Patent Shaft with cold pig iron, could lead to the need to reassess the steel-making technology and thereby the existence of the works. At Round Oak, which is jointly owned by the Corporation and Tube Investments, £9 million is to be spent to replace the five open-hearth furnaces with two 110-ton arc furnaces and to replace the heavy finishing mills. The new plant will be installed in the existing buildings, and the intention is to raise the quality rather than the quantity of steel produced.[47] On a smaller scale, Samuel Osborn, using £1·75 million loaned by the IRC, have reduced the number of operated sites from thirteen to three and have concentrated their activities mainly on a 33-acre site at Ecclesfield, outside Sheffield.

The few attempts to rationalise production across company boundaries have usually met with failure. Most of them have, in one way or another, involved Dunford & Elliott. In 1968 this company, owned by bankers William Brandt, paid £4·7 million for the larger but ailing Hadfields since which time £2 million has been spent on modernising the Heccla works with electric arc furnaces and a new bar mill. Meanwhile the company's annual pre-tax profits have increased from £0·26 million to £1·53 million.[48] Armed with this above-average record of achievement the management has attempted to extend its range of operations. In December 1972, after an unsuccessful attempt to reach a private agreement, a market bid of £24·6 million was made for Firth Brown whose profits had fallen from £4·3 million in 1970 to £2·2 million in 1972.[49] The rationale for this bid towards horizontal integration was that the two companies complemented each other and that together they would make a company big enough to operate successfully in the European market. This argument was coupled with adverse comments on the managerial efficiency of Firth Brown as indicated by the declining profit record. Firth Brown's defence was that whereas the bidding company had already reaped the benefits of its own modernisation programme, the fruits of its own £6 million programme were only beginning to appear and that annual profits exceeding £5 million were forthcoming in the medium future. Moreover, by concentrating on high-value steel production and processing, and on high-technology products, Firth Brown had moved into a more profitable and less cyclical business, and was no longer competing with the Special Steels Division of the BSC which was the major competitor of Dunford & Elliott. Both companies' arguments were valid—the area of overlap was confined to alloy forgings, forged steel rolls, and some qualities of billets and bars—but the real issue was that of independence. If the Dunford & Elliott bid, which was eventually raised to £35 million, had been successful, there seems little doubt that the separate identity of Firth Brown would have perished with the Firth Brown board. In the event, Firth Brown accepted a counter-bid from Richard Johnson & Nephew, controlled by Jessel Securities, which guaranteed a continued independent existence. This agreement was also supported by the Firth Brown workforce in Sheffield and Glasgow which had opposed the Dunford & Elliott bid through fears of redundancies resulting from a more streamlined operation. Firth Brown therefore remains as an independent steel producer even though financial control has passed into the hands of City interests. Rationalisation of Sheffield steel production now appears to be even more unlikely than it did before.

Financial interests originating outside the steel industry have revitalised Dunford & Elliott and, through the imposition of stricter financial controls, are likely to revitalise Johnson Firth Brown, as the company is now called. It is probable that either or both companies will attempt to acquire some smaller special steel producers in the future. The obstacles which they must overcome are the intense feelings of company identity which are now shared by management and workforce, and the realisation by these companies that an alternative to merging is to move into engineering and stockholding. Thus the chairman of Arthur Lee, in his 1970 statement to shareholders, explicitly stated that the company intended to remain independent and to expand its interests in stockholding rather than lose its identity through inter-company rationalisation at the ingot and semi-finished steel stages of production. The same philosophy has been demonstrated on a larger scale by the hitherto thwarted attempt by GKN to acquire Miles Druce, the largest independent stockholder. This move, which would consolidate in one organisation almost 25 per cent of the British stockholding market, has been presented for approval to the Commission of the ECSC.

The largest Sheffield producer left outside these moves towards consolidation is Brown Bayley Steels Ltd. In 1969 the IRC acquired a 51

M

per cent holding in this company, which was already completing the first stage in its own reconstruction and expansion scheme. The IRC was seen by many as a catalyst in the reorganisation process, and there were talks between Brown Bayley and Dunford & Elliott to that end. These appear to have foundered in 1970, and the only subsequent move by Brown Bayley was the purchase from Leeds Assets, another Jessel Securities satellite, of the Rotherham-Tinsley rolling mill in December 1971. Although the annual capacity of Brown Bayley has been raised to beyond 0·15 million tons, the financial performance of the company has suffered more than most of the independent producers through the pricing policy adopted by the BSC. Brown Bayley now appears as a likely battle-ground for the private parties seeking to restore the prosperity of the industry, with the Department of Trade and Industry, the inheritor of the IRC interests, being cast in the role of referee.

Given the longevity of the steel companies and their reluctance to combine, the only additional agent for change is the formation of new companies, but births of this kind have been notably absent from the British steel scene in the post-war years. The principal obstacles to entry have been low profitability and the required scale of operations. Nevertheless, the advent of the combination of arc furnace and continuous casting machines in the 'mini-mill' concept has made such entries both possible and practicable. The plans of Raine & Company of Newcastle-upon-Tyne to build such a works at Sheerness, in Kent, approved by the ISB as long ago as 1962, finally bore fruit in 1972 with the opening of a works to produce 0·18 million tons of reinforcing bars. The financing and the construction were supplied by North American interests directly involved in the construction and operation of similar plants in Canada and the United States, where more than thirty 'mini-works' are now in operation. At a cost of £9 million the capital cost per annual ton at Sheerness is as low as £50, but this could be reduced to £30 if the installed equipment was duplicated at a cost of £3 million. The present mill will consume 0·21 million tons of scrap, which represents about 15 per cent of the scrap arising in the London area.[50] In 1971 the Norwegian company Christiania Spigerverk was encouraged by the Department of Trade and Industry in its search for a site to build a similar works in Britain, but its application to locate the mill at Chesterfield was rejected. The initial response of the company was that location in a development area would be uneconomic, but interest was revived after the changes in investment grants and treatment of depreciation contained in the 1972 budget proposals. The company obtained planning permission for land in South Wales, but has abandoned that location in favour of a site in Manchester.[51] In June 1972 F. H. Lloyd Holdings Ltd and Cooper Industries Ltd formed a joint company to build a 'mini-works' on Lloyd's Grazebrook Foundry site at Netherton, Dudley, in Worcestershire. Estimated to cost £2·5 million, the plant will consist of a 30-ton electric arc furnace and a four-strand continuous casting machine to produce 70,000 tons of billets for use in the parent companies' mills. The aim was to make the companies 'less dependent' upon existing suppliers, defined as 'outside sources' by Cooper Industries and 'the British Steel Corporation' by Lloyds. The complaint was that the Corporation's price structure on materials and products was having a serious effect on the profit margins of these independent producers.[52] Elsewhere, the Glacier Metal Company is to build a 75,000-ton mini-mill at Hartlepool, and Richard Johnson & Nephew and Hall Engineering are to build a 150,000-ton mini-mill at Birkenhead. The output of both mills is destined for the building and civil engineering industries. Finally, in 1973, GKN decided to build a 400,000-ton mini-mill at Cardiff to support its 600,000-ton rod mill. The total cost of these projects is estimated at £30 million. This is the largest of these projects scheduled for Britain and will provide the company with a captive market for the scrap from its engineering works.

7

Geographical Perspectives

SPATIAL PATTERNS of human activities are the expression of human choice and decisions. It therefore seems probable that the key to the understanding of the pattern of industrial activity is most likely to be found, as Stafford has suggested, in the study of the producers, not the product.[1] Over the last decade there has appeared, as a complement to the locational literature based on the normative concept of Economic Man, a growing number of empirical studies describing the spatial behaviour of firms and individuals, as they are rather than as they might be supposed to be.[2] As complementary ventures, the two approaches share the common goals of valid generalised explanations of the pattern of industrial activity. The strength of the new approach is that it treats people as though they were human beings. This, as Harre and Secord have argued, is the only *scientific* way of treating them.[3] The weakness of the new approach is the lack of precision, hitherto, in its findings. Nevertheless, this weakness may yet prove to be its enduring strength, for human decisions are not based on precise calculations and exact knowledge. The decision-maker cannot confine his attention to those problems which are already well-defined, and which can be solved in their entirety. He must take his problems as they appear, and accept that his proposed solutions are tentative, piecemeal and possibly altogether inappropriate. He will still, in most cases, act rationally even though he knows that he is acting in a world permeated with uncertainty. This uncertainty is born of his inability to predict external changes precisely, and its effects are compounded by his own changing aspiration levels over time, coupled with his own inherent imperfections. The general problem for the decision-maker is to match a subjective view of reality—where do we wish to go from here—with objective reality—where is it possible to go from here. The specific problem for the British steel producers throughout this post-war period has been that of taking the inherited structure, reshaping it to meet the needs of the time, while satisfying their own aspirations.

With the benefit of hindsight it is possible to define three major groups of problem with which they were confronted. The first was the need to adjust to the long-term trend of increasing demand. This was complicated by the cyclical nature of that demand, so the search for long-term solutions was often confused by the need to accommodate to short-term declines. The second was a rate of technological change unparalleled in this century. The third stemmed from the need to substitute imported ore for domestic ore. Each problem impinged with varying degrees of intensity, and at different times, upon the separate steel-producing sectors. Thus almost unremitting demand was felt most acutely by the sheet steel producers, whereas the makers of railway products faced a decline in demand for their products. Again, the sheet steel producers were already grappling with a technological revolution, the continuous hot strip mill, when the period opened, whereas the other hot metal users escaped problems of similar magnitude until the entire industry had to face the consequences of the basic oxygen steel-making revolution from the late 1950s onwards. The scrap-metal users were not directly affected by that change, or by the changes in the ore trade, but they had to adjust to the large arc furnace. But these producers, more than any others, now face the problem of anticipating the likely effects of the increased demand for scrap metal generated by the so-called 'mini-mill', and the changes in the organisation of the scrap trade following submission to the Treaty of Paris in 1973. The first steps in finding solutions to all these problems had to be taken while the problems were still emerging. They were taken tentatively, often with reluctance, and with knowledge shaped by the historical and geographical perspectives of the time and place.

These perspectives or points of view were, and remain, of central importance to an understanding of what was done, and of what is likely to be done in the future. It is certain that perspective shaped the answers that were given but it would also appear that perspective defined the questions. For example, the industry was British-owned and was manufacturing almost exclusively in Britain. The world scene was viewed from Britain—that was the distinctive perspective. The questions asked were defined in British terms. Even if the industry thought in terms of least-cost solutions, which is doubtful, the quest was that solution not for the world steel industry but for the British steel industry. Perspective defined the problem and also imposed severe constraints upon the range of possible answers. Similarly, each company had its own view of the British scene. Although there was a large area of common ground shared by all the companies there was, in practice, no single question confronting them all, and therefore they were not united in seeking a single common answer. In contrast, the critics of the industry's performance had the great advantage of being able to take a single view of the whole scene, and of supplying a single and total answer to their single, and total, question. A recognition of the existence and persistence of a number of question posers and solvers is essential to the explanation of the variety of response.

Industry Perspectives

Before this internal variety is examined the major features of the common ground should be summarised. In the forefront was the common assumption, which was also shared by the critics of the industry, that the manufacture of steel should be continued in Britain. The acceptance of this view implied that the world-wide spatial margins of profitability had not yet shifted so dramatically as to exclude the British Isles. In subsequent years there was no critical reappraisal of this assumption which thereafter underlay all investment decisions. A variation on this assumption, but one which was not accepted by all outside opinion, was that certain steels should be made in certain districts within Britain. The outstanding example of this attitude related to the location of sheet steel production in general and tinplate in particular. The proper place for these products was deemed to be Wales. As sheet steel was the strongest growth sector of the industry this attitude had a profound influence on the pattern of locational change at the regional level. It influenced the choice of Port Talbot in the 1940s and of Llanwern in the 1950s, and enabled the Welsh producers to discount the occasional hints from the steel plate producers that they were considering entering this trade. It was an outside decision-maker of greater power who broke this pattern and created the means and the initial drive for a Scottish sheet steel industry.

The second shared belief was that overall development should be cautious, and that peak demand should be allowed to exceed supply marginally. This attitude, as seen in Chapters 3 and 4, dominated thinking for the first post-war decade and was relaxed by all producers together in the late 1950s. But caution also extended to the view of the methods of steel production. The accepted view was that the open-hearth process was the 'correct' method of producing steel in Britain, and the merits of the basic Bessemer process, which was used at Corby and Ebbw Vale, were ignored in the industry at large. This cautious approach to markets and technology which had its roots in the history of the industry made the attainment of an escape from that history difficult in the extreme, even if such an escape was desired.

A cautious approach to the present and future was also reflected in the adoption of a basic policy of minimum competition which was extended to a policy of mutual co-operation and support. The practice of minimum competition was revealed at the general level in the habit of accepting the maximum prices, imposed by the Iron & Steel Board and others, as the only prices. This practice broke down in the early 1960s in the sheet sector (see Chapter 5) but after a brief period of disorder the sheet suppliers all levelled their prices downwards to the same extent and the usual pattern of behaviour was resumed. On a more specialised basis, each company allowed its own development policies to be modified by the knowledge of the other companies' policies. For example, in 1945, the effects on the other structural steel producers of the universal beam mill to be built at Lackenby were not ignored, for it was said that Dorman Long had 'a *rational* outlook on the matter' and were prepared 'to consider schemes whereby other beam producers may enter into certain arrangements' (my italics).[4] In practice South Durham, a major producer of beams, thought that a competitive product could be fabricated by welding, and the twelve-year delay in bringing the new mill into operation made such arrangements unnecessary, but the important thing was that the industry accepted such a willingness as an expression of a 'rational' pattern of behaviour. The extension of this policy of minimum competition into the realm of co-operation and mutual assistance was made explicit in the operations of BISC (ore) and the Industry Fund (Chapter 3). In the light of these facts it is proper to consider the companies in many important respects as colleagues rather than as competitors. Location theory built on the assumption of competition is unlikely to yield an accurate explanation of their activities. The industry had its own pattern of rational behaviour which may or may not have been better suited to local and national requirements.

This cautious approach to the future and co-operation between colleagues gave rise to a pattern of behaviour which was given direction by what might be termed the principle of minimum disturbance. In its extreme form this reads: the future must be satisfied by the present. This is the principle adhered to by all conservatives of all political colouring at all times. In behaving in this way the steelmakers were not at odds with the expectations of British society. In a modified form the principle was seen at work in the 1940s in government insistence that the first tinplate mill should be built at Trostre to absorb the labour released from the hand pack mills, and again in the late 1950s in United Steel's decision not to disturb the balance of the company by building a strip mill at Scunthorpe.

The same principle of minimum disturbance appears to be operating in the selection by the British Steel Corporation of the basing points for the new pricing system which came into operation on 1 May 1973. Under the terms of the Treaty of Paris the previous system of uniform delivered prices had to be replaced by a system whereby a base price is quoted at a chosen location and transport costs to the consumer are added according to distance. The base point can be the works where the product is rolled, or, subject to certain provisos, any other point. Some change in the existing system was therefore necessary, but the Corporation has chosen 'basing points which are likely to cause the least possible disturbance to its customers and at the same time likely to be acceptable to the European Commission' (see Fig 16).[5] With its wide variety of products and the widespread distribution of its works the Corporation was able to use discretion in selecting these points, but with the exception of tinplate and railway materials it opted for points away from the works. The marketing of any particular product is, however, also affected by the decision to opt for either a single basing point or several. All carbon steel billets, for example, are sold from the single base point, ex-Sheffield Midland Railway Station (see Fig 17a). The general effects of this arrangement can be ameliorated by the Corporation's new-found freedom to offer discounts to large customers. For customers ordering over 0·4 million tonnes of billets annually and accepting them in minimum loads of 75 tonnes the discount is 3·7 per cent—marginally exceeding the transport cost of 130–40 miles. (There are smaller rebates for smaller annual tonnages.) The rebate scheme does not negate the intention of the basing point system, but it means that major consumers as far away from Sheffield as Cardiff, ie GKN, are minimally disturbed. An example of a multi-basing-point product, universal beams, is shown in Fig 17b. Here there is no quantity rebate scheme, and the transport cost gradient is steeper than for billets, but the selection of three basing points helps mitigate the distance factor.

The statutory obligations of the Treaty of Paris were sufficient to prevent the Corporation locating some base points in South East England, but trends in the organisation of steel marketing on a world scale make such points less necessary. In the case of cold reduced sheets

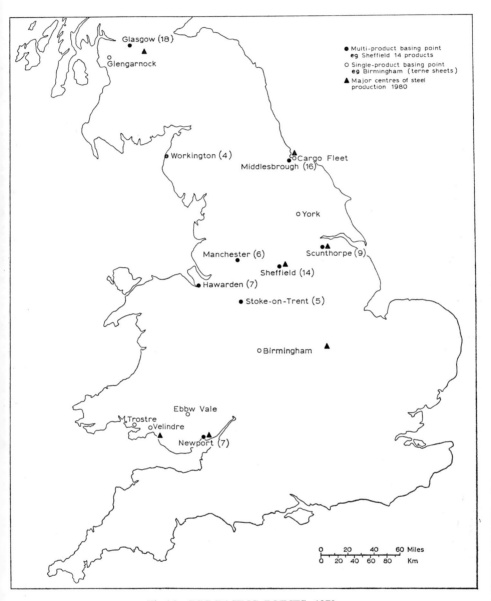

Glasgow (18)

Glengarnock

● Multi-product basing point
  eg Sheffield 14 products
O Single-product basing point
  eg Birmingham (terne sheets)
▲ Major centres of steel
  production 1980

Workington (4)

Cargo Fleet
Middlesbrough (16)

York

Manchester (6)

Scunthorpe (9)

Sheffield (14)

Hawarden (7)

Stoke-on-Trent (5)

Birmingham

Ebbw Vale

Trostre
Velindre
Newport (7)

0   20   40   60 Miles
0 20 40 60 80   Km

Fig 16. BSC BASING POINTS, 1973

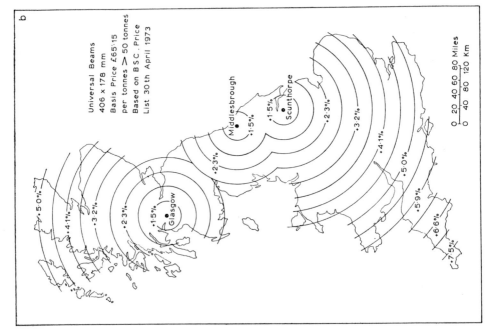

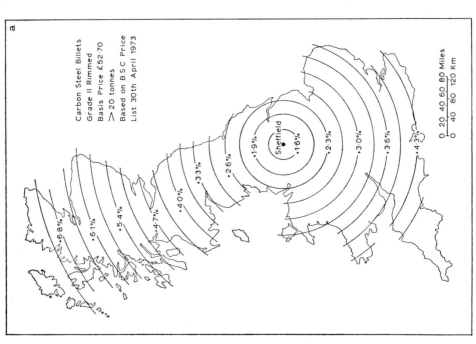

Fig 17. EFFECT OF BASING POINT PRICE SYSTEM ON SPATIAL COSTS OF
(a) CARBON BILLETS AND (b) UNIVERSAL BEAMS

the base points are Glasgow, Hawarden Bridge, and Newport, Mon. These safeguard the Port Talbot mill from the full effect of its isolation, but the entire Corporation is itself safeguarded by the reluctance of continental steel producers to engage in price-cutting in the English market.[6] In recent years European, American and Japanese steel producers have been prepared to modify their individual actions in order to preserve the existing principal features of the world steel industry.[7] Besides the overt political influences to which they are subject, the world industries share a common anxiety over their individual and collective ability to finance future steel developments.[8] Direct co-operation in cost-sharing across international boundaries is illustrated in the involvement of August Thyssen-Hutte, of West Germany, and Usinor and Wendel-Sidelor of France in the new works being built at Fos, near Marseilles. Closer co-ordination of investment policies on a world scale seems inevitable, and as it develops it will be matched by direct co-operation between individual companies or between national industries through the International Iron and Steel Institute or through trading agreements.[9] By degrees the world steel industry, which has hitherto been compartmentalised along political lines, is taking on the characteristics of controlled competition common to the already established international industries. The decisions now being taken by the British Steel Corporation must be seen in the light of this newly emerging world-industry perspective. The progress of steel development around the world is now controlled by the problem of capital availability rather than by direct market forces.

Company Perspectives

The views and attitudes that constituted the British industry's perspective—caution, mutual co-operation and support, and minimum change—defined the broad outline of the course for the post-war era. But, in the absence of any over-riding centralised control over investment, the responsibility for progress along that course rested with the companies. In this way their separate perspectives came into play in the posing of questions and the formulating of answers. The immediate question for each company was not where do we, the industry, wish to go from here, but where do I, the company, wish to go. If they thought in terms of least-cost solutions, which again is doubtful, their quest was for that solution for the company first, and, perhaps, for the industry second. The relevant unit when decisions were being taken was the company. It was not the industry and neither was it the works. For that reason the companies were classified in Table 1, at the beginning of this book, according to whether they owned one, or two or more works, rather than by the size of output or the type of steel they produced. For the single-works company the identity of works and company was synonymous, but for the multi-works company the identity of each works was submerged, to a greater or lesser extent, within the identity of the company. The industry perspectives shape the perimeter of the companies, but within these perimeters the companies operate their own individually planned economies. It is at this internal scale that spatial costs are seen to influence decisions directly. Nationalisation has not changed this salient point.

It is, therefore, possible to observe a consistency in the pattern of behaviour of the British Steel Corporation, its antecedents, and its privately owned contemporaries. Under private ownership the identity of each company was preserved, and works closures took place *within* company boundaries. For example, Richard Thomas & Baldwins preserved its identity while closing ten works acquired at various stages in its history. In contrast the resilience of the Skinningrove and Consett works, admittedly in different circumstances, can be largely explained by the fact that they composed the entire decision field of the companies to which they belonged. At Consett the offices in which the decisions were taken were located between the ironworks and the steelworks, and the identity of works, company and town coincided perfectly. Since 1967, nationalisation has had the effect of merging the previously separate identities of the fourteen companies into one. The relevant unit for decision-making is now the Corporation, but this was initially obscured by the regional-based organisational structure which the Corporation first used and which tended to obscure the identity and create separate confusing identities. Under the development programmes already announced the steelmaking activities of no less than four of the original companies will end before 1979—Skinningrove, Lancashire Steel, South Durham and John Summers. Such a radical change would have been difficult to effect under the old regime, but it has been achieved by exactly the same process of rationalisation *within* company boundaries as was practised before.

Much of the conflict that surrounds the Corporation's rationalisation programme stems from the inevitable difficulty of creating a new corporate identity throughout its wide-flung interests. This new identity can be gained only by the sacrifice of the old identities. Such a process would be difficult even if the short-term interests of the Corporation and of each of its works were identical. That they are not identical can be illustrated by reference to the plans for the ex-Summers works at Shelton and Shotton, where the primary departments are scheduled for closure. In each case local action committees have drawn up alternative schemes designed to reduce, although not to eliminate, redundancies. At Shelton, however, the local anxieties were fed by the conviction that the local voice was not being heard along the labyrinthine channels of communication which connected Stoke with London via Glasgow. At Shotton it was felt that the Corporation was deliberately dilatory in answering the voice which no one doubted could be heard. In both cases the Corporation's case was eventually put at specially convened meetings. In both cases the Corporation has argued not that production cannot be profitable at these locations, but that their continued existence would lead to lower levels of profitability and undermine the long-term aim of achieving sufficient profits to finance the continuing development programme for the Corporation at large.[10] Clearly the two sides are not asking the same question, and it should therefore occasion no surprise that the answers are different. Nevertheless, now that steel production is planned on a national scale the same solution for Shotton has been adopted as was advocated by the critics of the Federation's report in 1946: finishing departments supplied with semi-finished material from works located at points with low raw material assembly costs.

In all these respects the forces currently altering the appearance and substance of the steel industry are the same as those at work in all industries organised by multi-plant corporations. The quarrels which arise between the central authority and the outlying branches are based on genuine conflicts of interest originating in the desire of each group to act according to its distinctive view of the situation. The level of conflict may be raised through the feelings of alienation and neglect which arise in the branches, but attention to improved communications can remove only those parts created by ambiguity and misunderstanding. It cannot dissolve a quarrel whose source is a genuine difference of objectives. It is significant that feelings of alienation are not confined to those plants in the British Steel Corporation that are scheduled for closure, but are noticeable at some of the growth points where the question of massive redundancies does not exist. In former days the board of the United Steel Companies showed a sensitive awareness of this problem in holding periodic board meetings at the works which it controlled. But similar behaviour by the British Steel Corporation can be expected to have only a marginal anodyne effect in view of the radical changes which are now in progress.

The large corporation is a solution to the problem of industrial organisation based upon the logistics of individual industries. An alternative solution might be found in the co-ordination of many industries through a single organisation which had an identifiable regional allegiance.[11] Such a solution would coincide with the individual's perspective and with those of local society. These are rarely national. With the existing forms of organisation a distinct 'branch plant economy' has emerged in areas such as South Wales. There it is especially ironical in that a social philosophy used the political process to nationalise the local traditional industries, but thereafter these were rationalised on a nation-wide basis along the lines of industrial logic. The industries have benefited, as has the national economy, but the local communities have carried the burden. When the controllers of many of the new industries which colonise these areas are resident in Europe or North America, as is now the case, London might seem comparatively accessible and sensitive to local issues. The resolution of these matters requires a new social initiative before areas such as these are infected by a 'branch-plant mentality', and the conflict between industrial and social logic becomes acute.

Continuity of Spatial Patterns

The apparently flexible locational requirements of industry encourage the belief that a fresh initiative to join together these diverging aims of industry and society could succeed. In the short history of steelmaking there have been notable changes in the balance of forces which define the most profitable location. The first steelworks were established in situations already selected by the coke-using iron industry on the iron-bearing coalfields. The range was subsequently extended through the use of scrap metal which transformed some of these into market-oriented locations, and through improved fuel economy to ore-field locations and coastal locations near the coalfields. Each locational innovation was a comment upon the old, but seldom resulted in complete evacuation. Locational change therefore took a crab-like course as new sites were pioneered in new situations and some older sites were later abandoned. Each new wave added to the variety of locations in use. Vestigial elements of the earliest stages can be seen in the present spatial pattern of the industry, and the later stages are influencing the decisions which are now being made for the future. In this succession of changes new processes have been habitually set down in old locations.

The inherited, and often unquestioned, geographical perspective of the industrial decision-maker is one important factor in the explanation of the slow pace of locational change. Thus, the production of tinplate passed from the use of iron to steel sheets in the hand-pack mills, and then to the continuous mill, without the situation of the industry being critically examined. Similarly, the industry which was originally attracted to Tees-side by the availability of Cleveland ores and Durham coking coals has been replaced *in situ* by an industry using imported ore and increasing proportions of imported coal. All the growth points in the British Steel Corporation's development strategy have their origins in the late nineteenth century, for even Llanwern owed its selection in the 1950s to the existence of Ebbw Vale. But it is doubtful whether the Corporation was free to consider new locations for its major developments, even if these might prove to be profitable.[12] Thus a mature society, with its even more restricted geographical perspective, encourages the industrialist when he preserves the existing pattern, and defines for him a very narrow field of choice. An example of this encouragement was the rejection by all sectors of Lanarkshire society of the Clydeside project in the 1940s. This antipathy to relocation still appears in Scottish tacit acceptance of the decision not to build a multi-million-ton works at Hunterston. An unconvincing case for this works was made in the *Oceanspan* report, but unless Scotland was to see a massive expansion the 10,000 jobs which Hunterston would have provided would have been won at the cost of at least an equivalent number in Lanarkshire.[13] Retrenchment, in employment terms, at Ravenscraig, Clydesdale and Hallside, with its degree of limited disturbance, appears to meet with greater approval.

These desires for limited change can be gratified for an expanding industry only if the relationship between industry and site is flexible. That this is often so can be seen in the sequence of events at Port Talbot and Redcar. The first was chosen for a *modern* industry when the anticipated level of output was 1·25 million tons or less. By the 1980s the same site will produce 6·0 million tons. When the Redcar site was abandoned in the 1960s it had a capacity of less than half a million tons. By the mid-1980s it will produce 7·0 million tons. Not all sites have this flexibility, but the process of locational change broadly controlled by situational factors and patterns of ownership is directed precisely by the geography of site. In all these cases there is a compromise between the ideal and the available, for if the ideal location had to be found before any action were taken action would give way to inaction. Conversely, if all other locations were abandoned whenever a better location were found, human existence would be constant turmoil. Although there are many favourable situations even for heavy industry, favourable sites are rare, and once chosen tend to endure. The ultimate purpose of industrial enterprise is the preservation and preferment of the society which it serves. It is, therefore, a happy verdict that the spatial pattern of industry has a greater continuity through time than the manufacturing processes which operate within.

Acknowledgements

THIS BOOK has grown out of an interest in the industry developed through a three-year period in which I worked for the United Steel Companies and by subsequent years of reading and teaching within the field of industrial location. My indebtedness to colleagues and acquaintances past and present is inestimable, and at the risk of excluding some who should be mentioned I would like to express my especial gratitude to Mr Ronald Peddie and Mr Donald Calder, who introduced me to the industry, to Mr John Spooner, Mr Henry Waters, Mr Jack Dunsmore and Mr Alastair Moncur, who provided a stimulating working environment within the industry, and to Dr Kenneth Warren and Mr Tony Moyes among my academic colleagues for their participation in discussions on this industry and on industrial development. My thanks are also due to Messrs D. A. Allen, C. R. Blick, I. R. Chamberlain, B. Goodyear, T. Griffiths, J. H. Groocock, F. Jones, D. H. Nixon, R. D. Robson, E. T. Sara, K. D. Thompson, G. Westland, G. Wilson and P. Wright and to Miss J. Francis for giving generously of their time in answering my general and specific questions, or for indicating where a solution to a problem might be found. I am also indebted to the many writers on technical and financial developments within the industry without whose contributions my task would have been impossible. For technical help in preparing the manuscript I must thank Mr D. Griffiths, Mr M. Hughes and Mr E. James of the Geography Department at Aberystwyth. My wife has been a constant source of encouragement and her efficiency has been largely instrumental in bringing this enterprise to its conclusion. Finally, I must thank the makers of my 1962 Austin Cambridge, tempered with British steel, which has selflessly taken me to and from the farthest corners of the scattered domain of the British Steel industry, parts of which seem inaccessible by public transport.

References

CHAPTER 2

A Varied Inheritance pages 21–42

1 It is not suggested that there might be frequent need to travel from Workington to Consett although in the late nineteenth century Consett Iron had been using Cumberland hematite ore. Workington was a supplier of hematite pig iron to the Sheffield area works of United Steel

2 Roepke, H. G. *Movements of the British Iron and Steel Industry 1720–1951*, Illinois Studies in the Social Sciences, Vol 36 (1956)

3 See Andrews, P. W. S., and Brunner, E. *Capital Development in Steel* (1951)

4 BISF 1945. *Statistics of the Iron and Steel Industry of the United Kingdom for the Year 1945*, Tables 3 and 14

5 See Smith, W. *The Economic Geography of Great Britain* (1949). Warren, K. 'The Steel Industry', in *South Wales in the Sixties*, ed G. Manners (1964). Warren, K. 'Locational Problems of the Scottish Iron and Steel Industry Since 1760', *Scottish Geographical Magazine* (1965), pp 20–37 and 87–103

6 For details of this and other cost equalising schemes see Burn, D. L. *The Steel Industry 1939–1959* (1961), pp 345–58. This is an invaluable source of information and opinion for students of the industry. Not all the opinions expressed therein were happily received by the steelmakers

7 BISF 1945. *Op cit*, Tables 32 and 49

8
$$P_i = \sum_{j=1}^{n} \frac{Mj}{dij}$$
where P_i = the index of potential at place i
Mj = the aggregate income at place j within the field
dij = the 'cost' separating i and j

9 Clark, C. 'Industrial Location and Economic Potential', *Lloyds Bank Review*, October 1966.

10 These are arbitrary units

11 Company information. Identity withheld by request

12 *Times Review of Industry*, August 1948, p 30

203

13   At Shotton (Hawarden Bridge) John Summers owned 10,000 acres of
     mostly developable land. The area being used had already expanded
     from 60 acres in 1910 to about 600 acres

14   Mardon, H. H. and Terrington, J. S. 'The Layout of Integrated Iron
     and Steelworks', *Journal of the Iron and Steel Institute*, Vol 156 (1949),
     pp 327–59

15   Ibid, Table X

16   The East Moors works also took semi-finished steel from Scunthorpe
     (Lysaghts) and could operate only three of its four blast furnaces
     together

17   Scopes, Sir Frederick. *The Development of Corby Works* (1968), p 33

18   Elliot, G. *Ironmaking at the Appleby-Frodingham Works of The United
     Steel Companies Ltd*, ISI Special Report No 30 (1944), Tables III,
     IV, VI, VII

19   Brisby, M. D. J. 'Traffic in Iron & Steelworks', *Iron and Coal Trades
     Review* 165 (1953), pp 629–35

20   Watkin, E. R. S. 'Railway Traffic. An Analysis at Appleby-Frodingham',
     Iron and Steel (1953).

21   *The Times*. Leading article, 8 May 1946. See also Burn, D. L. *op cit*,
     p 184 footnote 3

22   The process was well suited to the production of rails from hematite
     iron, but had been abandoned elsewhere in Britain

CHAPTER 3

Sufficient unto the Day pages 43–75

1   *Reports by the British Iron and Steel Federation and the Joint Iron Council
     to the Ministry of Supply*, Cmnd 6811 (May 1946), henceforth cited as
     the 1946 Report

2   Burn, D. L. *The Steel Industry 1939–1959* (1961), p 173

3   Ibid, pp 73–112 and 172–90. A contemporary view of the Report can
     be found in the *Economic Journal* (1946), pp 487–99, by B. Tew, a shorter
     summary in *The Economist*, 11 May 1946

4   See page 136

5   1946 Report, pp 27–8

6   *The Times*, 8 May 1946

7   *The Economist*, 11 May 1946, said one: *The Times*, 8 May 1946, said two

8   *The Economist*, 11 May 1946

9   Cole, G. D. H. *Why Nationalise Steel?* (1948)

10   See, for example, Shone, R. 'The Iron and Steel Industry Development
     Plan: Some Statistical Considerations', *Journal of the Royal Statistical
     Society* 110, Part IV (1947), pp 283–309

11   Summers, Sir Richard. John Summers & Sons Ltd, *Annual Report 1946*

12   Summers, Sir Richard. John Summers & Sons Ltd, *Annual Report 1947*. Stewart, A. G. Stewarts & Lloyds Ltd, *Annual Report 1947*

13   *Economic Survey for 1947* (Cmnd 7046)

14   *Times Review of Industry* September 1947, p 13

15   Dorman Long, for example, lost 79,611 tons of production in the year ending September 1947, 54,743 being attributed to wagon shortages and rail-traffic embargoes. These seem very precise figures, but the company was prone to precise statements

16   Herbert Morrison, by no means a proponent of nationalisation, blaming the industry in a speech at Smethwick on 17 October 1947

17   *BISF Statistical Bulletin*, October 1948

18   *Iron and Coal Trades Review*, 160 (1950), p 41

19   James, Sir John, *Iron and Coal Trades Review*, 160 (1950), p 1264; Chetwynd Talbot Annual Report, *South Durham Steel & Iron Co* (1949)

20   *Iron and Coal Trades Review*, 161 (1950), p 781

21   In 1946 the scrap users subsidised the pig iron users to the extent of 35s per ingot ton (*The Economist*, 26 January 1946, p 143). In 1951 imported scrap at £20 per ton was being sold to the industry at £6 per ton (*The Economist*, 23 August 1952, p 464), the difference being made up from the Industry Fund. In 1949 the ingot levy was increased from 25s to 51s per ton. D. L. Burn, op cit, p 209

22   Warren, K. *The British Iron and Steel Sheet Industry Since 1840* (1970), pp 188–243. Disagreement with some of his conclusions has been expressed by industry sources, but until these are substantiated his account must stand as the definitive statement of what happened

23   Cartwright, W. F. 'Production Control in an Integrated Iron and Steelworks', *Journal of the Iron and Steel Industry*, 195 (1960), pp 137–44

24   The cold reduction mill at Margam was not approved until December 1947

25   A recurring theme in D. L. Burn's criticism of the industry as a whole at this stage was that it failed to face up to the likelihood that imported ore would be expensive regardless of these additional factors. D. L. Burn, op cit, pp 103–4 and 203–6

26   For a thorough examination of the pervasiveness of compromise in land-use decisions see Firey, W. *Man, Mind and Land*, Free Press of Glencoe (1960)

27   *Times Review of Industry*, December 1947, p 29

28   Stewart, W. *Iron and Coal Trades Review*, 155 (1947), p 927

29   Strauss, G. *Iron and Coal Trades Review*, 157 (1948), p 647.

30   Craig, Sir John. *Colvilles Annual Report* (1949).

31   Towndrow, R. P. 'Blast Furnace Operation at High Top Pressure', *Journal of the West of Scotland Iron and Steel Institute* (1950–1), p 58

32 Colville's production 1949 (000 tons): coke 309; pig iron 511; ingots 1,855, of which Clydebridge 410, Dalzell 460, Glengarnock 350, Lanarkshire Steel 310, Hallside and Blochairn 325; plates and sheets 646; sections and bars 612; slabs and billets 436. Coal consumed 901, which compared with 1,070, for the lower outputs of 1939

33 *The Economist*, 25 May 1946, p 847

34 Stewart, A. G. *Stewarts & Lloyds Annual Report* (1947)

35 Stirling, A. 'The Production Aspects of Fuel Efficiency at Corby Iron & Steel Works' *Journal of the Institute of Fuel*, 22 (1949), pp 166–74

36 Rimming steel. Low carbon steel deoxidised to a small extent, producing an ingot with a pure skin. Used for deep drawing and pressing.

37 See Andrews and Brunner, op cit, for a full account of this operation and of the costs involved.

38 Elliot, G. D. 'Developments in Ironmaking at Appleby-Frodingham', *Journal of the Iron and Steel Institute*, 181, no 3 (1955), pp 1–16

39 Ibid.

40 'Dorman Long—A Technical Survey', *Iron and Coal Trades Review* special publication, p 28

41 Financial, technical and social arguments were used in defence and attack. See Carr, J. C. and Taplin, W. *A History of the British Steel Industry* (1962), pp 534–7; and D. L. Burn, op cit, pp 461-2

42 'Consett Iron—A Technical Survey', *Iron and Coal Trades Review*, 168 (1954), no 4481A, p 27. The details of this account are taken from this source and from 'Developments at the Consett Works of the Consett Iron Company' *Iron and Steel Institute Special Report no 54* (1955). This was the only Institute publication to be devoted to a single works development, and as such is one testimony to the determination of the company to ignore its critics.

43 There were three spare wagons. The laden weight of these wagons was 85 tons

44 *The Times* leading article, 8 May 1946, D. L. Burn, op cit (1961), p 184

45 I was told that plans were drawn which contained three furnaces. There was enough room to extend the works almost indefinitely without complicating the layout and without producing the difficulties which arose at Port Talbot

46 Talbot, Benjamin. South Durham Steel & Iron Co Ltd, *Annual Report 1945*

47 McCance, Sir Andrew (chairman of Colvilles). 'Production in the Steel Industry. Its Growth, Distribution and Future Course', *Third Harold Wright Lecture to Cleveland Scientific and Technical Institute* (1950)

48 D. L. Burn, op cit (1961), provides information on this pyramidal structure for 1939 and 1953, pp 79, 248–9

49 The Beardmore scheme was developed on a very congested and divided site in Glasgow. The capacity of the works was 0·1 million ingot tons

50 D. L. Burn, op cit (1961), p 89. *The Economist* (May 1946) expressed similar reservations.

51 *BISF Statistical Bulletin*, October 1948

CHAPTER 4

The Prosperous Years pages 76–106

1 Peddie, R. *The United Steel Companies Limited 1918–1968. A History* (1969), pp 55–6. Mr Peddie was Secretary of United Steel from 1946 and became a director in 1967. A further study, *The History of South Durham Steel & Iron Co Ltd* by W. G. Willis (1969), is less incisive than this history of United Steel

2 Iron & Steel Board. *Annual Report 1966*, Table 26

3 Appleby-Frodingham, Cleveland-Lackenby, Corby, Shotton

4 In 1955 the works whose individual output exceeded 100,000 tons came very close to perfect obedience to the rank-size rule. This was not so in 1945, 1960 or later. Perhaps 1955 marked the logical end of an era!

5 Anglo-American Council on Productivity. 'Productivity Team Report', *Iron and Steel* (1952), pp 147

6 Ibid, p 89

7 Ibid, pp 87 and 91

8 *Iron and Coal Trades Review*, 165 (1952), p 1

9 See *Journal of the Iron and Steel Institute*, Vol 183, pp 75 ff

10 Ibid

11 Sara, E. T. 'Progress in the Iron and Steel Industry', *Iron and Coal Trades Review*, 173 (1956), pp 671–7

12 Morton, J. S. 'Continuous Casting of Steel', *Iron and Steel* (1955) 'Steel', *The Structure of British Industry* (1958), p 266, National Institute for Economic and Social Research. Isard, W. (1956). *Location and Space Economy* p 10. *Steel Review* no 40 (October 1965)

13 This view, expressed by this spokesman, is interesting in that Mr Sara was even then an advocate of expansion within both United Steel and the industry at large. United Steel was operating an experimental continuous casting machine at Barrow. Its subsidiary, Distington Engineering, was UK licensee for Concast, Zurich

14 Cartwright, W. F. 'Production Control in an Integrated Iron and Steelworks', *Journal of the Iron and Steel Institute*, 195 (1960), pp 137–44

15 Sharpe, K. C. and Davies, O. G. 'Easing the Burden—A review of burden preparation at the Steel Company of Wales Ltd 1953–1965', *Journal of Metals* (1966), pp 79–86

16 See pages 131–3

17 Robiette, A. G. 'Large Arc Furnace v Basic Open-Hearth Furnace;

Comparison of Economics under British Conditions', *Iron and Coal Trades Review*, 167 (1953), pp 1231–6

18 'Round Oak Electric Melting Shop', *Iron and Coal Trades Review*, 180 (1960), pp 917–24

19 Colclough, T. P. 'Seventh Hatfield Memorial Lecture', *Journal of the Iron and Steel Institute*, 177 (1954), pp 279–304

20 Robiette, A. G. 'Use of Oxygen for Steelmaking', *Iron and Coal Trades Review*, 156 (1948), p 1103

21 *Stahl und Eisen*, 72 (1952), pp 989–1024

22 *Iron and Coal Trades Review*, 167 (1953), pp 93–6

23 Rueckel, W. C. and Irwin, J. W. 'Economic Aspects of the Oxygen Converter', *Iron and Steel Engineer* (March 1955)

24 *Journal of the Iron and Steel Institute*, 184 (1956), p 218; abstract from *Metal Progress* (January 1956)

25 Brandt, D. J. O. 'The use of Oxygen in Iron and Steel Production', *Journal of the West of Scotland Iron and Steel Institute* (1956), pp 211–43

26 Peddie, R. op cit, p 58

27 Jackson, A. 'The Use of Oxygen in a Modified Tilting Furnace', *Journal of the Iron and Steel Institute*, 190 (1958), pp 1–29

28 Jackson, A., Colclough, T. P., Mayorcas, R. et al. 'Iron and Steel Institute Discussion of the Use of Oxygen in Steelmaking, 1959', *Journal of the Iron and Steel Institute*, 194 (1960), pp 63–78

29 Ibid

30 Ibid

31 Kesterton, A. J. 'Alternatives to the Open-Hearth Process', Paper to the Newport and District Metallurgical Society, *Iron and Coal Trades Review*, 182 (1961), pp 1351–60

32 Jackson, A. 'Developments in Steelmaking', *Steel and Coal*, 184 (1962), pp 17–25. See also Jackson, A. *Oxygen Steelmaking for Steelmakers* (1969)

33 Robiette, A. G., op cit (1953), p 1235

34 Iron & Steel Board (1957), para 188

35 Iron & Steel Board (1961), Ch 14 esp para 308

36 *Iron and Coal Trades Review*, 181 (1960), p 987

37 Ibid

38 Talbot, Chetwynd, *Iron and Coal Trades Review* 174 (1957), p 495

39 *Iron and Steel*, August 1954, p 451

40 Warren, K. 'Locational Problems of the Scottish Iron and Steel Industry Since 1760', *Scottish Geographical Magazine*, 81, no 2 (1965), pp 87–103 (p 90)

41 Kilby, J. A. and Gordon, J. C. 'Engineering Aspects for an Open-hearth plant', *Journal of the West of Scotland Iron and Steel Institute 1959–60* (1959), pp 180–210 (p 181)

42 *Iron and Coal Trades Review*, 175 (1957), p 121

43 See Warren, K. *The British Iron and Steel Sheet Industry Since 1840* (1970), pp 260–9

44 Spencer, H. F. managing director. *Iron and Coal Trades Review*, 179, p 752 and 181, p 1074

45 For an examination of the situational aspect see pages 132–4

46 In October 1959, ten days after the election, Stewarts & Lloyds made a rights issue of 7 million £1 shares at 40s each on a basis of seven for twenty. United Steel had made a rights issue in 1957 at 30s and Summers had made a similar issue at par in the same year. Apart from an FCI purchase of £2 million ordinary at par in South Durham in 1959 all increases in capital were via the issue of debentures or through the capitalisation of reserves.

47 Between 1950 and 1960 ingot output increased by 50 per cent. The consumption of scrap and coal increased by 22 per cent and 15 per cent but that of oil and electricity by 180 per cent and 100 per cent

CHAPTER 5

The Prelude to Nationalisation pages 107–44

1 British Steel Corporation, *Annual Report and Accounts 1967–8*, Table 1 (HMSO)

2 *Steel Times*, 188 (1964), p 12

3 British Steel Corporation, op cit

4 Cope, S. G. Chief Technical Officer, Consett Iron Co. 'Oxygen Steelmaking at Consett', *Refractories Journal* (1965), pp 508–17

5 Pearson, S. C. in *The Guardian*, 18 April 1967

6 Allen, J. A. *Studies in Innovation in the Steel and Chemical Industries* (Manchester University Press, 1967), p 202.

7 The practice of supplying pig iron to Shotton had ceased in 1958

8 Wingate, G. N. F., 'Continuous Casting', *Steel Times Annual Review* (1965), p 103

9 Summers, W. H., 'Continuous Casting for Large-Scale Production', *Journal of the Iron and Steel Institute*, 204 (1966), pp 882–6

10 There were three blast furnaces of 17ft, 12ft 6in and 10ft diameter on a site dating from 1858. They were among the few which were not charged by means of inclined skips.

11 Iron and Steel Board. *Development in the Iron and Steel Industry, Special Report, 1961* (20 April 1961), para 310, suggested 1·0 million tons for billet mills and 4·0 million for hot strip mills

12 See Cartwright, W. F. 'The Future of Automation in the Iron & Steel Industry', Fourth Annual Address to the United Kingdom Automation Council, *Iron and Steel* (1964), pp 637–43; Pratten, C.,

o

Dean, R. M. and Silberson, A., *The Economics of Large-scale Production in British Industry. An Introductory Survey*, University of Cambridge, Department of Applied Economics, Occasional Papers No 3 (1965) No 40; *Steel Review*, (1965), British Iron & Steel Federation; Leckie, A. H., 'Technical and Economic Considerations Affecting the Optimum Size of Plant', *Ironmaking Tomorrow*, Iron & Steel Institute Special Publication No 102 (1967), pp 13–20

13 Cartwright, W. F., op cit

14 Iron & Steel Board. *Development in the Iron and Steel Industry, Special Report, 1957* (23 July 1957), paragraph 188

15 Iron & Steel Board. *Development in the Iron and Steel Industry, Special Report, 1961* (20 April 1961), Chapter 14

16 *Steel Times*, 189 (1964), p 91

17 The British Iron & Steel Federation. *The Steel Industry. The Stage I Report of the Development Co-ordinating Committee of the British Iron & Steel Federation* (1966) (Hereafter called the Benson Report)

18 *Iron and Coal Trades Review*, 182 (1961), p 991

19 Iron & Steel Board op cit (1961), para 233

20 BISF, *Annual Statistics*

21 Foreign ore: weighted average according to receipt was 59 per cent fe
Home ore: weighted average according to usage was 27 per cent fe

22 Iron & Steel Board, op cit (1961), para 224

23 Iron & Steel Board, op cit (1957), para 92

24 See Burn, D. op cit (1961), pp 578–81

25 Nijman, D. G. 'Freight Rates of Large Ore Carriers', *Handling and Treatment of Ores*, Iron & Steel Institute Special Report No 65 (1959)

26 Lockerbie, J. (of Consett Iron). 'Materials Handling Arrangements at Consett', *Ore Mining and Materials Handling*, Iron & Steel Institute Special Publication No 82 (1963), pp 62–71
Cartwright, W. F. 'Production Control in an Integrated Iron and Steelworks', *Journal of the Iron and Steel Institute*, 195 (1965), pp 137–44

27 *Steel Review*, April 1965.

28 *Benson Report* (1966), para 124 and Appendix 13

29 Steel Company of Wales, *Annual Report* (1956)

30 *Iron Ore Imports into South Wales*, Cmnd 2706 (July 1965)

31 Meredith, W. G. and Wordsworth, C. 'Size of Ore Carriers for the New Port Talbot Harbour', *Journal of the Iron and Steel Institute*, 201 (1966), pp 1075–8.

32 Manners, G. 'Transport Costs, Freight Rates and the Changing Economic Geography of Iron Ore'. *Geography*, 52 (1967), pp 260–79

33 *Steel Times*, 189 (1964) p 91

34 Peddie, R. *The United Steel Companies 1918–1968. A History* (Manchester, 1969), p 55

35 Ibid, pp 65–7

36 *Steel Times*, 188 and 190 (1964 and 1965), pp 639 and 163

37 *Steel Times*, 192 (1966), pp 237–8

38 In addition the Redcar works had been integrated with Cleveland-Lackenby, and now operated as part of that works.

39 A Kolmogorov-Smirnov Two Sample test indicates that there had been no significant change between 1945 and 1955, nor between 1955 and 1965, but that the accumulation of changes between 1945 and 1965 had produced a significant change at the 5 per cent level.

CHAPTER 6

A Real Steel Industry? pages 145–87

1 Production ranking: 1 USSC, 2 BSC, 3 Bethlehem SC
Sales ranking: 1 USSC, 2 Bethlehem SC, 3 BSC
Assets ranking: 1 USSC, 2 Finsider (Italy), 3 BSC

2 British Steel Corporation, *Annual Report and Accounts 1971–72*

3 Ibid

4 The Iron and Steel Act 1969. This Act also raised the borrowing powers of the Corporation to £500 million, and gave the Minister of Technology the discretion to increase this figure to £650 million

5 British Steel Corporation, *Report on Organisation 1967* (Cmnd 3362)

6 British Steel Corporation, *Annual Report and Accounts 1967–8*

7 British Steel Corporation, *Report on Organisation 1967*, para 64. The same point was made in a *Times* editorial, 8 June 1967.

8 This is a conservative estimate of the number of works. The Corporation admitted to operating '39 crude steel-producing works' but that exaggerates the issue. Ibid para 43.

9 British Steel Corporation (1969)
Second Report on Organisation, HC 163
Third Report on Organisation, HC 60

10 Ibid (HC 163), para 18

11 Ibid (HC 60), para 52

12 For a non-political argument in favour of dividing the Corporation into six multi-product enterprises see Rowley, C. K. *Steel and Public Policy* (New York, 1971)

13 *The Times*, 18 March 1971, Parliamentary Report

14 British Steel Corporation, *Annual Report and Accounts 1970–1*

15 In June 1972 BSC sold its tool steel and tool businesses in Manchester and Sheffield to Edgar Allen & Co Ltd. Elsewhere eleven brick-making plants were sold for more than £2 million

16 *First Report from the Select Committee on Nationalised Industries; Session 1972–73 British Steel Corporation*, HC 141, p 7.

17 Dr B. O'Connor in discussion with Dr K. Warren. 'Recent Changes in the Geographical Location of the British Steel Industry' (1969). *The Geographical Journal*, 135, Part 3, pp 343–64, stated that for each 0·1 per cent reduction in sulphur an increase of 8 per cent in blast furnace productivity could be expected.

18 British Steel Corporation, *Annual Report and Accounts 1971–2*

19 British Steel Corporation, *Annual Report and Accounts 1967–8*

20 The decision to close the blast furnaces, both melting shops, and the primary mill at Irlam before 1973 was announced in April 1971. This involved 4,350 men. A temporary reprieve for the smaller melting shop was declared in the following September.

21 The connection with Scunthorpe was widely reported but the Ravenscraig connection was referred to by Mr T. R. Craig when he announced that BSC had agreed in principle to the Hunterston ore terminal on the Ayr coast. *The Times*, 11 December 1970

22 These would amount to at least 25p per ton on Norwegian ore, 80p per ton on Brazilian ore, and £1·60 per ton on Australian ore.

23 Cartwright, W. F. 'The Future of Automation in the Iron and Steel Industry', *Iron and Steel* (1964), pp 637–43

24 *The Times*, 14 July 1969 and 15 May 1972, and BSC *Annual Report 1971–2*

25 These figures are interpolated from data given by H. M. Finniston, 'Plans for the Future', *Financial Times*, 17 June 1968. The article argues against this very policy of locating ironworks away from the coast.

26 Hargrave, Andrew. 'Hunterston—a symbol of the future', *Financial Times*, 3 February 1972.

27 British Steel Corporation, *Annual Report and Accounts 1971–2*

28 *The App-Frod Record*, 12 October 1967

29 *The App-Frod Record*, 11 April 1968

30 Ibid

31 Ibid

32 *British Steel Corporation: Ten Year Development Strategy* (Cmnd 5226, 8 February 1973)

33 Ibid, para 37

34 *First Report from the Select Committee on Nationalised Industries; Session 1972–73 British Steel Corporation*, HC 141, pp 58–63, 160–2

35 Ibid, p 154.

36 Cmnd 5226, paras 59 and 34

37 Ibid, para 34

38 Ibid, para 44

39 Ibid, para 57

40 Ibid, paras 44, 49 and 55

41 Smith, J. G. 'How Alternative Strategies Were Evaluated' *British Steel* Spring 1973

42 *First Report from the Select Committee on Nationalised Industries;*
    Session 1972–73 British Steel Corporation, HC 141, p 115

43 Cmnd 5226, para 34

44 Gofton, Ken. 'British Steel consults its oracle', *Financial Times,* 16
    January 1973

45 According to Peter Archer, Labour MP for Rowley Regis, Glynwed and
    Cooper Industries were interested in buying the mill for about £1
    million. *Financial Times,* 20 July 1972

46 Gofton, Ken. 'Stainless Steel—what the BSC is taking on', *Financial
    Times,* 4 May 1972

47 *Steel Times,* October 1970, p 726

48 Dunford & Elliott (Sheffield) Ltd. *Report of the directors and statement
    of accounts, 1972*

49 Thos Firth & John Brown Ltd. *Annual Report 1972*

50 *Steel Times,* February and June 1971

51 *Financial Times,* 17 June 1973 and 28 November 1973

52 Cooper Industries Ltd. *Report and Accounts 1972.*
    F. H. Lloyd Holdings Ltd. *Directors' Report and Accounts 1972*

CHAPTER 7

Geographical Perspectives pages 188–200

1 Stafford, H. A. 'The geography of manufacturers', *Progress in Geography*
   No 4, ed C. Board et al (1972).

2 Among the empirical studies are the following: Hamilton, F. E. I. (ed).
   Spatial Perspectives on Industrial Organisation and Decision-Making
   (in press)
   Krumme, G. 'Towards a Geography of Enterprise', *Economic Geography,*
   45 (1969), pp 30–40
   Steed, G. P. F. 'Location implications of corporate organisation of
   industry', *The Canadian Geographer,* 15 (1971), pp 54–7
   Taylor, M. J. 'Location Decisions of Small Firms', *Area,* No 2 (1970),
   pp 51–4
   Townroe, P. M. 'Locational choice and the individual firm', *Regional
   Studies,* 3 (1969), pp 15–24
   Watts, H. D. 'The location of the beet-sugar industry in England and
   Wales', *Transactions of the Institute of British Geographers,* 53 (1971),
   pp 95–116
   Webber, M. J. 'Sub-optimal behaviour and the concept of maximum
   profits in location theory', *Australian Geographical Studies,* 7 (1969),
   pp 1–8

3 Harré, R. and Secord, P. F. *The Explanation of Social Behaviour* (1972)

4 *Iron and Coal Trades Review,* 151 (1945), p 862

5   'Memorandum submitted by the British Steel Corporation', *First Report from the Select Committee on Nationalised Industries; Session 1972–73 British Steel Corporation*, HC 141, p 99

6   Ibid, p 152. Lord Melchett made explicit references to the practices of Hoogovens, a Dutch supplier, and the Ford Motor Company

7   For example, in 1972 the six largest Japanese companies agreed to restrict their sales in Britain and The Six to 1·25 million tonnes. This was a compromise between the original bargaining positions of 1·5 million and 0·65 million tonnes. *Financial Times*, 9 December 1971

8   Mr Charles Baker, Secretary of the International Iron and Steel Institute, stated that the non-communist world industry would need to raise over £83,000 million before 1980 in order to increase output to the necessary level of 900 million tonnes. This could not be met by the combined cash flow, depreciation and retained profits of all the companies. *The Times*, 13 October 1970

9   In 1972 the first international steel company, Estel, was formed out of Hoogovens, Holland, and Hoesch, West Germany

10 The Corporation claimed that continued production at Shotton as opposed to development at Port Talbot would add £8 million annually to its operating costs. In 1972–3 the Strip Mills Division had a surplus of £6·2 million, and the improvement in the results at Port Talbot were given a special mention in the Annual Report.

11 This argument is developed further by Stephen Hymer in 'The Multi-national Corporation and the Law of Uneven Development' in *Economics and World Order*, ed J. N. Bhagwati (1972), pp 113–40

12 There must be doubt that such a works would be profitable. See Busby, J. *The British Steel Industry and its Expansion Plans in Scotland*, North Ayrshire Coastal Development Committee (1971)

13 *Oceanspan 2 A Study of Port and Industrial Development in Western Europe*, Scottish Council (Development and Industry) (October 1971)

Bibliography

Allen, J. A. *Studies in Innovation in the Steel and Chemical Industries* (Manchester University Press, 1967)

Andrews, P. W. S., and Brunner, E. *Capital Development in Steel. A Study of the United Steel Companies* (Basil Blackwell, 1951)

Burn, D. L. *The Economic History of Steelmaking* (Cambridge University Press, 1940)

Burn, D. L. *The Steel Industry 1939–59* (Cambridge University Press, 1961)

Carr, J. C., and Taplin, W. *A History of the British Steel Industry* (Oxford University Press, 1962)

Firey, W. *Man, Mind and Land* (Free Press of Glencoe, New York, 1960)

Isard, W. *Location and Space Economy* (MIT Press, Boston, 1956)

Labasse, J. *L'Organisation de l'espace; Eléments de Géographie Volontaire* (Hermann, Paris, 1966)

Losch, A. *The Economics of Location* (New Haven, Conn, 1954)

Peddie, R. *The United Steel Companies Limited 1918–1968. A History* (C. Nicholls & Co Ltd, Manchester, 1969)

Pratten, C., Dean, R. M., and Silbertson, A. *The Economics of Large-scale Production in British Industry. An Introductory Survey* (University of Cambridge, Department of Applied Economics, Occasional Papers No 3, 1965)

Pratten, C. F. *Economies of Scale in Manufacturing Industry* (University of Cambridge, Department of Applied Economics, Occasional Papers No 28, 1971)

Pred, A. *Behavior and Location. Foundations for a Geographic and Dynamic Location Theory*, Lund Series in Geography, Series B, nos 27 and 28 (Lund, Sweden, 1967 and 1969)

Roepke, H. G. *Movements of the British Iron and Steel Industry 1720–1951*, Illinois Studies in the Social Sciences, Vol 36 (1956)

Ross, G. W. *The Nationalisation of Steel* (MacGibbon & Kee, 1965)

Rowley, C. K. *Steel and Public Policy* (McGraw Hill, 1971)

Smith, D. M. *Industrial Location. An Economic Geographical Analysis* (John Wiley, 1971)

Warren, K. *The British Iron and Steel Sheet Industry since 1840*, Bell's Advanced Economic Geographies (Bell, 1970)

Willis, W. G. *The History of South Durham Steel & Iron Co Ltd* (South Durham, 1969)

The following publications of the Iron and Steel Institute are of especial value:

Basic Open-hearth Practice in Scotland, Special Report No 22 (1938)
Ironmaking at the Appleby-Frodingham Works of The United Steel Companies Limited, Special Report No 30 (1944)
Handling and Treatment of Iron Ores, Special Publication No 65 (1959)
Ore Mining and Materials Handling, Special Publication No 82 (1963)
Ironmaking Tomorrow, Special Publication No 102 (1967)
Energy Management in Iron and Steel Works, Special Publication No 105 (1968)

The following is a select list of papers that have been found of value in compiling this study:

Beaver, S. H. 'Changes in Industrial Land Use, 1930–1967', *Land Use and Resources*, Institute of British Geographers Special Publication No 1 (1968)
Bennington, S. 'Blast Furnace Practice at Ebbw Vale', *Journal of the Iron and Steel Institute*, 208 (1968), pp 572–5
Brandt, D. J. O. 'The Use of Oxygen in Iron and Steel Production', *Journal of the West of Scotland Iron and Steel Institute*, 64 (1956–7), pp 211–43
Brisby, M. D. J. 'Traffic in Iron and Steelworks', *Iron and Coal Trades Review*, 165 (1953), pp 629–35
Cartwright, W. F. 'Production Control in an Integrated Iron and Steelworks', *Journal of the Iron and Steel Institute*, 195 (1960), pp 137–44
Cartwright, W. F. 'New Processes in an Integrated Iron and Steelworks Layout', *Journal of the Iron and Steel Institute*, 196 (1960), pp 249–52
Cartwright, W. F. 'The Future of Automation in the Iron and Steel Industry', *Iron and Steel* (1964), pp 637–43
Clark, C. 'Industrial Location and Economic Potential', *Lloyds Bank Review* (October 1966)
Cope, S. G. 'Oxygen Steelmaking Experience at Consett', *Refractories Journal* (1965), pp 508–17
Craig, P. G. 'Location Factors in the Development of Steel Centres', *Papers and Proceedings of the Regional Science Association*, 3 (1957), pp 249–65
Elliot, G. D. 'Developments in Ironmaking at Appleby-Frodingham', *Journal of the Iron and Steel Institute*, 181 (1955), pp 1–16
Howard, J. C. 'Economics of Melting', *Iron and Steel* (1954), pp 252–5
Howatt, D. D. 'Electric Steel Production', *Iron and Steel* (1954), pp 445–50
Jackson, A. 'The Use of Oxygen in a Modified Tilting Furnace', *Journal of the Iron and Steel Institute*, 190 (1958), pp 1–29
Jackson, A. 'Developments in Steelmaking', *Steel and Coal*, 184 (1962), pp 17–25
Jackson, A. et al. 'Iron and Steel Institute Discussion of the Use of Oxygen in Steelmaking, 1959', *Journal of the Iron and Steel Institute*, 194 (1960), pp 63–78
James, W. L. 'Expansion at Lysaghts', *Journal of the Iron and Steel Institute* (1955), pp 17–25

Kesterton, A. J. 'Alternatives to the Open Hearth Process', *Iron and Coal Trades Review*, 182 (1961), pp 1351–60

Kilby, J. A. 'Production of Steel Plates in Scotland', *Journal of the Iron and Steel Institute*, 166 (1950), pp 29–70

Kilby, J. A., and Gordon, J. C. 'Engineering Aspects of an Open-Hearth Plant', *Journal of the West of Scotland Iron and Steel Institute*, 67 (1959–60), pp 180–210

McCance, Sir Andrew. 'Production in the Steel Industry. Its growth, distribution, and future course', *Iron and Coal Trades Review*, 162 (1951), pp 75–8

Manners, G. 'Transport Costs, Freight Rates and the Changing Economic Geography of Iron Ore', *Geography*, 52 (1967), pp 260–79

Mardon, H. H., and Terrington, J. S. 'The Layout of Integrated Iron and Steelworks', *Journal of the Iron and Steel Institute*, 161 (1949), pp 327–59

Marshall, D. F., and White, H. C. 'The Conversion to Oil-Firing of the Open-Hearth Furnaces at Park Gate Works', *Journal of the Iron and Steel Institute*, 161 (1949), pp 301–7

Meredith, W. G., and Wordsworth, C. 'Size of Ore Carriers for the new Port Talbot Harbour', *Journal of the Iron and Steel Institute*, 201 (1966), pp 1075–8

Robiette, A. G. 'Use of Oxygen for Steelmaking', *Iron and Coal Trades Review*, 156 (1948), p 1103

Robiette, A. G. 'Large Arc Furnace v Basic Open-Hearth Furnace; Comparison of Economics under British conditions', *Iron and Coal Trades Review*, 167 (1953), pp 1231–6

Sara, E. T. 'Progress in the Iron and Steel Industry', *Iron and Coal Trades Review*, 173 (1956), pp 671–7

Sharpe, K. C., and Davies, O. G. 'Easing the Burden—A review of burden preparation at the Steel Company of Wales Limited, 1953–65', *Journal of Metals* (1966), pp 79–86

Shone, Sir Robert. 'The Iron and Steel Development Plan: Some Statistical Considerations', *Journal of the Royal Statistical Society*, 110, Part IV (1947), pp 283–309

Smith, W. *Geography and the Location of Industry*, an inaugural lecture (University of Liverpool, 1952)

Summers, W. H. 'Continuous Casting for Large-Scale Production', *Journal of the Iron and Steel Institute*, 204 (1966), pp 882–6

Towndrow, R. P. 'Blast Furnace Operation at High Top Pressure', *Journal of the West of Scotland Iron and Steel Institute*, 58 (1950–1)

Warren, K. 'The Steel Industry', *South Wales in the Sixties. Studies in Industrial Geography*, ed G. Manners (Pergamon, 1964)

Warren, K. 'Locational Problems of the Scottish Iron and Steel Industry Since 1760. Part 2', *Scottish Geographical Magazine*, 81, No 2 (1965) pp 87–103

Warren, K. 'Recent Changes in the Geographical Location of the British Steel Industry', *Geographical Journal*, 135 (1969), pp 343–64

Warren, K. 'Coastal Steelworks. A Case for Argument', *Three Banks Review* (June 1969)

Index